GW01339150

POPULAR SEA FISHING

Compiled and Edited by
PETER WHEAT

Contributors
DES BRENNAN · LESLIE MONCRIEFF
BRUCE McMILLEN · BRIAN HARRIS
PETER WHEAT · WINSTON HALL
CYRIL PRECIOUS · SID CLOKE
TREVOR HOUSBY · DEREK FLETCHER
KEVIN LINNANE

With line drawings in the text by
BAZ EAST
and sixteen pages of photographs

FREDERICK WARNE
LONDON

First published 1968
New edition 1977

Published by Frederick Warne (Publishers) Ltd, London
This edition © *Frederick Warne & Co Ltd, London 1977*

EDITOR'S ACKNOWLEDGEMENTS

I am grateful for the great help of the contributors and other sea anglers in compiling this work. I should also like to thank the publishing house of J. M. Dent and Sons Ltd, for permission to include an extract from their Everyman's Library edition of *The Voyage of The Beagle* by Charles Darwin.

ISBN 0 7232 2029 8

Text set in 10/11 pt. Photon Imprint, printed by photolithography, and bound in Great Britain at The Pitman Press, Bath

CONTENTS

List of Plates	page	4
Introduction	page	5
Tope Fishing – Bruce McMillen	page	7
Skates and Rays – Trevor Housby	page	23
Fishing for Pollack, Coalfish and Ling – Des Brennan	page	33
Sea Bream – Winston Hall	page	45
Bass Fishing – Brian Harris	page	57
Fishing for Flounder, Sole, Dab Haddock and Pouting – Derek Fletcher	page	71
Cod Fishing – Cyril Precious	page	85
The Wrasse Family – Trevor Housby	page	99
Sharks and Shark Fishing – Kevin Linnane	page	108
The Dogfish – Winston Hall	page	118
Conger Fishing – Bruce McMillan	page	128
Turbot and Brill – Leslie Moncrieff	page	137
Plaice Fishing – Sid Cloke	page	147
Monkfish, Angler Fish and Halibut – Trevor Housby	page	161
Fishing for Mackerel, Garfish, Scad, Whiting and Gurnard – Derek Fletcher	page	170
The Mullet Family – Peter Wheat	page	182

LIST OF PLATES

1 Fishing from a ledge into rocky ground · A beach angler at Holderness, Yorkshire, watches for a bite

2 A club competition on Tynemouth Pier, Northumberland · Trevor Housby's rod bending to the pull of a wrasse in Cornwall

3 Landing a fighting fish off Brodick, Isle of Arran · Feathering for mackerel

4 Evening fishing at Sallyport, Portsmouth

5 A common skate of 114 lb (51·7 kg), caught on mackerel fillet off the Isle of Mull, Scotland · Thornback ray, belly up and beaten, ready for gaffing

6 The toothy jaws of a large angler fish · Ron Barnett weighs in a monkfish at 43 lb (19·5 kg)

7 A hugh monkfish being brought to the surface · A catch of fine tope

8 A boat angler displays a fine cod · A red gurnard, ugly to look at but excellent eating

9 Barnstaple angler, Bob Maunder, with an outstanding conger of 70 lb (31·7 kg) · *Angling* magazine editor, Brian Harris, with a bass which pulled 10 lb 2 oz (4·6 kg)

10 Tony Dolman unhooks a good ballan wrasse from Co. Kerry, Southern Ireland · Small pollack taken on the feathers

11 The late Mr G. Davies displays a 16 lb (7·2 kg) turbot · Plaice of 4 lb 4 oz (1·9 kg) from Poole Harbour, Dorset · Ken Townley displays a wreck-caught ling of 33 lb (14·9 kg)

12 An excellent shore-caught flounder taken by Ernest Merritt · A played-out porbeagle alongside the boat · Clive Gammon fighting a blue shark of Kinsale, Co. Cork

13 Digging for lugworms in Yorkshire · A black lugworm

14 Mussel-baited hook · A sandeel · A hook baited with razorfish

15 Netting shrimps · A shrimp bait correctly mounted on the hook

16 Collecting peeler crabs at low water · Jack Hargreaves baits-up his skate tackle with a mackerel

INTRODUCTION

It is not so very long ago that sea fishing, in comparison with game and coarse fishing in freshwater, was, at the very best, a vastly inferior branch of angling. Tackle, for the most part, varied little and included thick heavy rods, lines like ships' hawsers and huge sea leads attached to 'christmas tree' metal paternosters. It comes as no surprise that, generally speaking, little thought went into the actual fishing! Of course, fish were caught, including many fine specimens, but that was more by sheer luck than sound judgement. Sea fish, it must be admitted, lack the guile of their freshwater cousins; they are, relatively speaking, easier to catch – once they have been located – which is perhaps the most important facet of sea angling.

These days, the old image of a sea angler as an ignorant being capable only of catching fish which hook themselves and can be wound in and beaten to death with the minimum of delay, is fast becoming a vague memory. The number of people going sea fishing increases regularly; due partly to youngsters taking up angling for the first time, and also because anglers from inland waters are turning to the sea for additional variety or even for their total sport. This latter reason is now a common trend. For a very long time freshwater angling has slowly been developing into a strictly organized, costly and commercialized branch of the sport. Lakes and rivers become further restricted, if not completely closed to the average angler, each year as the rich clubs and syndicates buy up every inch of water they can lay their hands on. Other waters are simply polluted and the life within them either ceases to exist or is reduced to such a poor standard that their fishing potential is lost. Many of the better class fisheries, still available on a day ticket, have so many rules and restrictions in order to organize the ever growing crowds, that the pleasure of angling is very often lost.

It is, therefore, only natural that anglers to whom freedom of movement and action are very much essentials will seek their sport elsewhere.

The sea is vast; there is a variety of fish both large and small; rarely do problems of crowding occur, and usually only on piers and the like where it is all part of the atmosphere; and no frantic effort is required to join some exclusive syndicate with an outrageous membership fee. Sea angling can be as cheap or as costly as you like, but there is always the free and easy atmosphere of taking your sport as and where you will.

There have been other changes as well. Fresh thinking has brought about a revolution in sea tackle development and there is now a wide range of rods, reels, lines, hooks and the many other 'essential' items which form the sea angler's kit. Tackle is just as specialized as that which is used for freshwater fishing and it should be chosen to suit the size and fighting ability of the particular species being sought; it should also be as light and sporting as possible – taking into consideration the conditions and the method of angling being employed.

Since the first edition of this book The British Record (rod-caught) Fish Committee have greatly enlarged their sea fish listings; there are now separate records for shore and boat, and in addition a mini-records division for species which have been caught at weights no greater than 1 lb (0·45 kg). Over one hundred sea-fish species are now published by the Committee as record-holders, and clearly the whole subject of record-breaking has become a rather complicated one.

In the first edition some 38 records were given; 25 of them have since been broken at least once, and for this reason, though details of outstanding catches are mentioned, no individual fish has been described as a record-holder in this edition. For anglers interested in record fish, the Committee regularly issue updated lists; details can be obtained by writing to their office at 5 Cowgate, Peterborough, PE1 1LR.

Apart from the overall improvement in knowledge of sea angling and the generally increased interest in record breaking, a further reason for the number of huge fish caught during the past decade has been the upsurge of interest in wreck fishing – particularly the wrecks located far offshore in deep waters. Wreck-marks are often packed tight with many fine fish of many species, but as it has unfortunately been found out the hard way, they can soon be fished out and made barren for many years hence, by overfishing.

Overkill is a menace in any form, and it is as well for every sea angler to understand that wrecks and other popular marks can be ruined completely and utterly through sheer greediness and wanton slaughter. Some species need to be protected more strictly; many sea anglers need to realize that fish do not always have to be killed, and particularly those species which are not good eating. It is high time that the Angling Press exercised a greater degree of responsibility and ceased to publish photographs of groups of sea anglers knee-deep in hundredweights of dead fish.

In this book, eleven anglers, all well known from their books and articles in the Angling Press – but more importantly from their ability to catch fish – have joined forces to write about popular sea fishing as it is practised today. Each writer deals with those species he fully understands and has caught frequently. It is my sincere wish that the expert advice contained in this book will prove of sound value to all anglers who seek to catch fish from the sea, but in particular to the freshwater convert.

PETER WHEAT
Parkstone, Dorset

Note: Fathoms have disappeared from Admiralty charts, depths and heights now being indicated in metres (1 fathom = 1·829 metres). A fathom in nautical measurement is 6 feet.

Approximate metric conversions of weights and measures are given in brackets.

TOPE FISHING   *Bruce McMillen*

The tope is a true shark, and as is the case with many other species, the female attains a greater size than does the male. Of the many large tope taken on rod and line from British waters the 74 lb 11 oz (33·9 kg) female caught by Mr A. B. Harries, off Caldy Island, in 1964, and the 64 lb (29 kg) male which fell to the rod of Lt-Col. R. I. P. Earle, out from Studland, in 1956, are particularly outstanding specimens.

The male tope is easily identified from the female of the species, as it possesses two 'claspers' (channelled apendages of the pelvic fins). When copulation occurs, these 'claspers' are drawn together and inserted into the cloacal aperture of the female. When handling a male tope, great care should be taken to avoid contact with the 'claspers', which are fully capable of inflicting a nasty and very painful wound.

Tope are viviparous. That is to say, they give birth to living young, normally during the period of the year between May and August. The young, which may number as many as 50, are able to fend for themselves, immediately following their birth. Indeed, baby tope as small as 10 oz (283 g) have been caught fairly often by anglers.

A 48 lb (21·7 kg) female which I took while shore fishing from a beach in the Menai Straits contained 34 young. Obviously, therefore, a female in an advanced state of pregnancy will weigh appreciably more than it would otherwise do, and this factor can contribute very largely to the difference in weight between some males and females, particularly in view of the number of young which may be carried and the size they reach inside the mother.

Tope are cartilaginous. In other words, they are entirely boneless apart from their gristly backbone. Their teeth are arranged in several rows; triangular and saw-tooth in shape, and designed for cutting rather than crushing. Consequently they are capable of inflicting severe lacerations – so be warned! I have counted 98 razor-sharp teeth in a 30 lb (13·6 kg) tope. Coloration of this species varies from a dark grey to a brownish grey along the back and flanks; the underside is usually greyish white. *There is no blue shade, despite the claims of some angling writers to this effect.* The texture of the skin resembles fine-grade sandpaper, and its abrasiveness on the angler's line is a major reason why so many tope are lost when hooked on tackle which does not include a wire trace. The eyes are oval-shaped, with emerald green pupils and black centres.

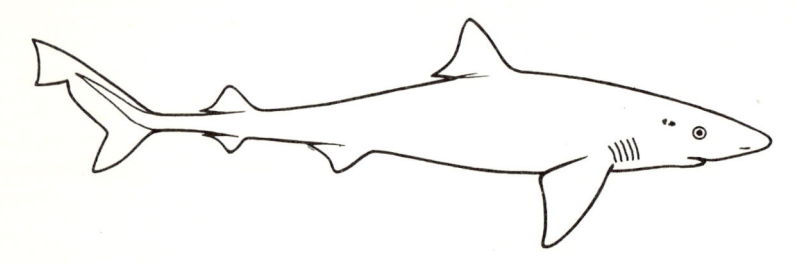

Tope outline: note fin positions and shape

Tope do not possess swim-bladders, and rely upon continuous fin-motion in order to maintain balance. Because of this, when dead, they sink rather than float away on the tide. They are particularly ferocious fish, hunting sometimes individually or in small groups and sometimes in large packs. Sport with pack-tope can often be so fast and furious that the chances of hooking fish of any other species are extremely small.

Tope are widely distributed and are, for instance, found in the waters off Africa, India, southern Arabia, Japan, Australia, California, Europe, and in the Atlantic, the Pacific, the Mediterranean and around the British Isles, etc. In California, they are called 'soupfin sharks', and indeed their fins are eagerly sought by the Chinese for the making of 'shark's fin soup'. The flesh is highly rated in some countries, notably east and west Africa, while a useful oil is extracted from the liver and the skin is used for various rubbing processes. From an eating point of view, tope should be prepared for table as soon after capture as possible – ideally, skinned, cut into inch-thick (2·5 cm) steaks, and fried in deep fat. Some people find the flesh to be excellent eating, others declare it to be an abomination. It is a matter of personal taste.

Water temperature plays a vital part in the distribution of these fish, and the southern and western waters of the British Isles are more prolific with tope than are the cooler, more northerly waters. Swift-moving fish, they are believed to be capable of speeds in the region of 25 mph — a claim which comes as no surprise to anglers who have experienced the exceedingly long and powerful initial run which hooked tope often make. They have been taken in depths of less than two fathoms (3·6 m) to over 200 fathoms (365·7 m).

In common with many other species, tope are inclined to feed more avidly at night, rather than during the hours of daylight, although it is equally true that packs of tope do hunt during daylight and offer first-class sport. Personally, I do not like to fish at night for tope, as in the darkness there is some difficulty in judging whether a hooked tope, while being played, is alongside the boat or some distance away. Similarly, the beach angler in the dark cannot be sure whether his hooked fish has run inwards, close to shore, or whether it is, instead, 100 yards (91·4 m) or more away out to sea. Dawn and dusk are also productive periods, and I have found that, whether it be day or night, the warmer the weather and the water the better is the chance of contacting tope.

At the age of eight I became interested in sea fishing as a sport. That was sixty-five years ago, and many tides have ebbed and flowed since those far-off days, when fish were really plentiful — indeed, far more plentiful than we are ever again likely to experience. Then, even with our comparatively simple greenheart and built-cane rods, centrepin reels, and hemp and linen lines, we could nearly always be certain of quality sport and a variety of fish to provide it. Frankly, I cannot believe such prolific days will ever return, though it is a sad and rather depressing thought to have to admit to.

Anyway, after drifting through a veritable maelström of angling I eventually progressed, during the early 1920s to the fascinating sport of tope fishing — not by the more orthodox boat fishing approach — but instead by way of beach fishing. In those days, the capture of a tope by a beach angler was sufficiently novel to merit mention in the Local and National Press and also on B.B.C. news broadcasts. In fact, relatively few anglers really believed that catching tope from the beach was a feasible proposition, as they tended to associate this branch of sea fishing only with boats.

However, my own embryonic efforts at the game convinced me that tope provide sport of a very high order, both ashore and afloat, so I dubbed it 'poor man's big-game fishing' — a term which seems to have stuck, to this very day!

Many anglers (and non-anglers) have asked what it is which attracts me so greatly to tope fishing: now make no mistake about it, the pursuit of these fish, particularly if relatively light tackle is employed, is a most deeply satisfying experience. I have, for example, taken tope on a 12 oz (340 g) rod and 18 lb (8·1 kg) line — the essential consideration being the vital need to have plenty of line on the reel with which to play hooked fish to a standstill. Modern materials and techniques have made possible rod, reel and line combinations so light and so well matched that even the angler of only a decade ago would never have anticipated that such big fish could be mastered on such apparently 'delicate' tackle.

Tope are one of the rather few species of sea fish which will sometimes leap completely clear of the water when hooked, a characteristic rather more evident in the case of beach fishing, particularly if the water is fairly shallow, although tope will occasionally leap when hooked from a boat over deeper water. This aspect alone endears me to tope angling. Add to this the tremendous initial burst of speed which these fish are capable of, coupled with the knowledge that such a cunning adversary will take advantage of any mistake you make to break free, and you have my main reasons for selecting tope fishing as my first angling love, with the pursuit of bass on light tackle coming a close second. Let me quote just two examples which will serve to typify the thrill of tope hunting.

A vivid demonstration of sheer speed occurred during a Welsh beach trip when I hooked a big tope which immediately, in one breath-taking initial run, tore off 220 yards (201·1 m) from my reel, then drew level with a fast pleasure-steamer which was passing by, and eventually outpaced it – much to the interest of the ship's passengers, who crowded along the rails on one side to watch the fun! The steamer must have been travelling at about 20 knots at the time. Needless to say, the tope, when finally beaten, was beached at a very considerable distance from the spot where it picked up the bait and felt the hook.

On another occasion, while retrieving line, I had the thrill of sighting the dorsal fin of a tope rapidly cutting through the water towards the bait. I paused, momentarily, awaiting the impact. After grabbing my bait the tope turned and went for the open sea at a tremendous pace, the line literally screaming from the reel. I let the run go for about 60 yards (54·8 m) and then struck as hard as I could. Twice the tope leapt clear of the water, and then it changed tactics and came inshore, fast, almost to my feet. Catching sight of me and sensing danger, it turned once more for the open sea, leapt a third time, and gave me many more heart-thumping moments before I could get it high and dry on the beach. These experiences will, I hope, give you some idea of the degree of sport possible from tope. Experience convinces me that these fish possess attributes enough to ensure that any angler using reasonly light tackle may be certain of excitement to satisfy his wildest dreams.

An interesting aspect of tope fishing, at least in my own experience, is that by far the greater proportion of tope taken have been males. This ratio, apparently, applies to many areas, and would seem to suggest that male tope predominate to a surprising extent over the females. I have discussed this matter with a representative cross-section of tope anglers and the consensus of opinion leaves no doubt that the majority of tope taken by anglers, particularly from the beach, are males.

An important factor in tope fishing concerns weather conditions. Warm or hot – even very hot – weather appears to be ideal, with the sea fairly calm and settled. The most prolific fishing in Caernarvon Bay occurs during the period from May to September, though tope are taken from the same area both earlier than May and later than September. In Eire, they are caught from April to

November. The tope season off the south coast of England is similar in duration, but also winter-caught tope are not unknown in this area. Water temperature quite definitely plays a significant role in the distribution of these fish and in their feeding habits.

I have found that bottleneck areas, creating a fast tideway, force large numbers of smaller fish and other food into a comparatively confined space, forming a rich feeding 'larder' for tope, particularly during the relatively 'slack' high and low water periods. On the other hand, of course, tope are often to be found in open bays, on fairly steep, sandy and pebbly beaches, and in deep water alongside rocks. They are also taken in both quite deep water well out to sea and in very shallow water.

I have found that tope respond to all types of fish bait apart from portions of their own species. I say this in the light of my own fruitless efforts to entice tope to eat tope. Other anglers may, however, have had success with tope portions, and tope indeed may even feast on newly-born tope. All I know for sure, however, is that tope-bait has not worked for me.

Tope also take various species of worms and crustacea, such as soft and peeler crabs. The presence of blood and fish oils attracts them greatly, and I would suggest that if the angler obtains a quantity of ox-blood, for example, he will find this substance much to his advantage when used as an attractor.

In selecting appropriate tackle, much will obviously depend on whether you intend to fish from the beach, rocks, pier or boat. The advantage of boat angling is, of course, that you can move about and search for the fish over a wide area. Whereas in beach, rock or pier fishing the fish must essentially be in your immediate vicinity.

Having already expressed the opinion that I prefer to hunt tope from the beach rather than from a boat, believing that it produces a greater degree of sport, I must stress the fact that, for two very simple reasons, lighter tackle may normally be employed from a boat. First, the boat angler is not obliged to cast a relatively heavy sinker and perhaps an equally heavy bait for any real distance. Secondly, he does not have to play out the hooked fish until it is virtually on the beach at his feet. He simply pumps his tope up to the boat and brings it over the side. In this respect, I would point out that, in the interests of conservation, I do not favour the gaff for lifting tope inboard. The gaff kills, and I prefer to return tope alive. Gripping the root of the tail with one hand and a pectoral fin, for additional security, with the other hand, is a secure method of hoisting a tope, which does no harm. Unfortunately, in tope boat-competitions, it is not only somewhat difficult to weigh a big specimen correctly in a tossing vessel, but it is also expecting too much of other competitors to readily accept your statement that you caught 'X' number of tope weighing 'X' number of pounds unless you are prepared to bring ashore the bodies to prove it.

Another reason why the boat angler can fish lighter than the shore angler is that, in the case of a big fish, he can up-anchor and follow the quarry until it tires of pulling the boat along.

In the matter of rods, my own preference has always been for tubular glass rather than solid glass. Tubular glass, as well as being lighter, stronger and more flexible than solid glass, is also more pleasant to handle. Tubular glass rods are, however, more expensive than similar designs in solid glass. And probably for this reason, solid glass rods are more popular. If price is not a main consideration, I strongly suggest choosing tubular glass rods. Built-cane rods have their merits, and there are now graphite rods available, though these are extremely expensive and well beyond the pocket of the majority of anglers.

It is somewhat difficult to lay down any hard and fast rules concerning suitable boat rods for tope fishing. I have seen good fish taken on rods varying from 6 ft (1·8 m) to 12 ft (3·6 m) in length. A comfortable boat rod can be anything from 6 ft (1·8 m) to 8 ft (2·4 m). Above say 9 ft (2·7 m) a rod will prove rather embarrassing if one is fishing from a fairly crowded boat, and even in a boat where there is plenty of room and few anglers, a long rod can still be quite an ungainly weapon, though it must be added that a long rod can increase the sporting enjoyment when a tope is hooked. The rod should be neither too stiff nor too supple, and the ideal is probably achieved when the fighting efforts of a fair tope are sufficient to bend the rod into a satisfying arc. If the rod is too stiff, you risk possible loss of tackle – and fish – for the sudden surge of power from a fighting tope can, if the rod lacks sufficient 'give', cause the line to part. On the other hand, if the rod is too supple, it will result in your taking much longer to tire the fish which, with the extra time it has, may break free.

If you decide to purchase a one piece ferruleless rod then so much the better. The action of a one piece rod is excellent, and of course there is no risk of possible breakage at the ferrule as might happen with a two-piece rod. In fact, my ideal boat rod is a one piece, tubular glass blank, without any form of reel fitting. It weighs only 12 oz (340 g), despite carrying seven Sintox rings, and the reel is fixed in position by means of the clamps on the reel. This type of rod, 7 ft (2·1 m) in length, when matched with an ABU Ambassadeur 12 or 9000C reel, is a delight to use. A commercial design of rod for boat fishing which I like is the ABU 650 Zoom – 7·25 ft (2·2 m) in length, and fitted with roller butt and tip rings.

When choosing a rod, always ensure that the ferrule, if it has a ferrule, is of the reinforced type, and that it carries an adequate number of rings. Normally, the reel, if it is a multiplier, goes on top of the rod, and only correct ringing will then prevent the line from rubbing against the length of the rod when it curves over under strain. The ring lining should preferably be of a strong, smooth, synthetic material such as Sintox or Aqualite, or, alternatively, hard chrome or plain stainless steel. Some boat rods are fitted with hooded rings, for additional protection against accidental damage, but these add to the overall weight of the rod. For a really high quality boat rod, roller rings are ideal and should at least be fitted at tip and butt. Always ensure that the rings are the best quality obtainable, with rollers that revolve freely and have no undue clearance between roller and housing to trap and jam the line. The reel fittings should be of substantial construction and designed to lock the reel firmly in position on the rod — aided by reel clamps.

For rock or pier fishing, a longer rod may be used, while the angler who aspires to catch tope from the beach should choose a surfcaster rod between 10 ft (3 m) and 12 ft (3·6 m) in length. The 11·5 ft (3·5 m) ABU Atlantic 484 is one design I like, another is the low-priced Intrepid Super-Action beachcaster, which has a length of 12 ft (3·6 m).

It should be understood that, while specialized tackle is not essential for tope fishing — many tope are taken by anglers seeking smaller species of fish — the angler with the right tackle for the job is more likely to be consistently successful.

For the more adventurous ultra-light tackle enthusiasts, there is no logical reason why tope should not be tackled with a medium or heavy spinning rod, using an orthodox trace. On such tackle, however, fish take a great deal longer to tire, and it is necessary to have an abundance of line on the reel to prevent a running tope stripping it all off and smashing free.

A great many reels are suitable for tope fishing. Among the models I particularly like is the ABU Ambassadeur 9000C, which features an automatic gear change system — a most helpful aid when it comes to pumping a big fish to the surface. Other reels I can recommend include the Ambassadeur 12 and the Intrepid Fastback.

However, the main essentials of any multiplier intended for tope fishing is that it should incorporate a slipping clutch, an easy-to-operate check which always works, and a spool with a large line capacity — not less than 200 yards (182·8 m). Preferably, the spool should be metal or fibre-glass, rather than plastic. A plastic spool may burst when subjected to the severe crushing effect of tightly-packed line which arises when fighting a heavy fish. A further prevention against crushing is to wind on a few yards (6 m approx.) of soft line to act as a cushioning layer beneath the main-line.

Although for many kinds of fishing fixed-spool reels are entirely adequate, I neither use them or recommend them for tope fishing.

Some anglers favour the centrepin type of reel, mainly for boat work. In this connection some very suitable metal versions designed for heavy boat fishing are available. These reels are, of course, entirely gearless. They allow the angler to be in direct contact with the fish, and they make it easier to pump fish to the surface. They do, however, require a greater degree of skill to be operated successfully against tope — a major disadvantage being that a fish taking line at speed can cause the knuckles to be severely barked against the revolving reel handles, unless, that is, the reel happens to be fitted with a slipping clutch device.

The gear-ratio problem of multipliers has been admirably solved in the ABU Ambassadeur 9000C. This reel is not only extremely lightweight, but it also incorporates a novel and very efficient automatic gear change which normally operates at a retrieve rate of 4·3:1, and drops quite automatically to a ratio of 2·5:1 when a fish turns and starts a powerful run away from the angler. Immediately the run slows up or the fish turns again and runs inwards, slackening the line, the higher, normal gear-ratio comes into operation, enabling the angler to rapidly retrieve slack line. Similarly, when one is obliged to pump a heavy fish, the low gear-ratio automatically engages and considerably lessens the tedium of the pumping process.

It is advisable, when selecting a reel, to buy the absolute best that you can reasonably afford. The reel is a very important and rather vulnerable part of your equipment and one which can, should it suddenly fail you, completely spoil a day's fishing; not to mention the possible loss of a specimen, or even a record fish!

The main types of line used for tope, and indeed for most sea angling, are nylon monofil, braided terylene and braided nylon.

While monofil is inclined to stretch — sometimes to such an extent that, in some sections, the effective breaking strain is reduced to a fraction of the original rating — it does not present such a degree of resistance to wind or water, as does a braided line. Braided nylon is less waterproof than braided terylene, and it is more prone to stretching. Damage, in the form of fraying, is more apparent to the eye in the case of a braided line, whereas damage to monofil can easily pass unnoticed.

The choice of line, therefore, must largely be an individual one, but I should certainly recommend for tope angling, a length of not less than 200 yards (182·8 m). Points which influence the choice of appropriate line breaking strain depend upon such factors as: test curve of the rod; strength of currents likely to be encountered; presence of floating weed; the type of ground over which you intend to fish; the distance you may need to cast in order to reach the fish, and whether you will be fishing from rocks, pier, beach or boat. As general guidance I would suggest a line with a minimum breaking strain of 23 lb (10·4 kg), although it is quite possible, under suitable conditions, to land tope on a considerably lighter line test than this. In a strong current, accompanied by masses of floating weed, I have seen 35 lb (15·8 kg) breaking strain line quite easily broken, due to the combined strain of a fighting tope, weed-festooned line and water pressure. On the other hand, 15 lb (6·8 kg) line fished on a weed-free sandy beach, or from a boat, will successfully handle sizable tope, although the chance of losing fish when employing such relatively light line is always present.

Much controversy in tope fishing concerns the choice of suitable traces. When I first started hunting these fish, I used traces of heavy line, but very soon discovered that they were no match for razor-sharp teeth. The only tope I managed to land were invariably hooked in the lip. Subsequently, I progressed to traces composed of linked sections of wire, and latterly to the stainless steel, nylon covered cable which is now popularly favoured by tope specialists. Generally speaking, the trace should be longer than the fish — 6 ft (1·8 m) being an ideal length. For the purpose of beach angling, the trace should not exceed this length if it is composed entirely of wire, otherwise difficulty will be experienced in casting. Tope often wrap the trace around their bodies, and the tough, rough skin can then fray any kind of trace other than one of wire. A compromise alternative trace consists of 12 in. (30 cm) or 18 in. (45 cm) of wire next to the hook, joined to heavy, 80–120 lb (36·2–54·4 kg) monofil.

It is possible to construct the trace entirely of heavy monofil, and indeed a trace of this type will often take tope when wire traces are not so effective, owing to its greater flexibility. But then again, there is a high risk of breakage and lost fish, and a constant need to check the monofil for the slightest sign of fraying.

Some anglers prefer short sections of single-strand stainless steel, or of phosphor-bronze, or brass piano-wire, linked by swivels, as a trace rig. There are some advantages in this type of trace, as it does not kink or twist up in coils. But nevertheless, my first choice is stainless steel nylon-covered cable.

In any tope trace there should be at least two swivels (size 1/0, 2/0 or 3/0) and the incorporation of a stainless steel screw link fitting for quick attachment and detachment. Hooks should be forged, in size varying from 5/0 to 10/0 according to choice, but always taking into consideration that the larger the bait the larger must be the hook to accommodate it. When whole fish baits (of any size) are used, two hooks may be arranged 'in tandem'. The points of hooks should be kept really sharp by honing them up on a suitable stone. Tope have tough mouths, and a bluntish hook may fail to penetrate far enough to gain a secure hold. Hooks which display any signs of distortion or rust should be discarded completely. Incidentally, it is worth noting that the larger the hook the thicker will be the gauge of wire used in its manufacture. Consequently, more striking force will be required in order to ensure really adequate penetration of the larger sizes.

Angling writers, from time to time, claim that tope are 'hook shy' and that the hook should, in consequence, be completely hidden in the bait. Frankly, I do not believe this to be true – not according to my own experiences or those of other anglers. Here are two examples.

The first concerns an angler who landed the same tope twice, within the space of 15 minutes. He was able to identify the fish the second time from a damaged gill-vent.

The second involved two anglers who, while boat fishing off Anglesey, hooked and boated a tope which already had a set of tackle attached – not only the hook and trace, but also the rod, reel and line! Despite having to tow this outfit about, it was still interested enough in feeding to pick up a further bait. In both cases the tope concerned were obviously anything but hook shy!

In tope fishing gaffs are not really essential, for it is a comparatively simple matter to lift these fish out by grabbing the root of the tail and either the dorsal fin or a pectoral fin. If, however, one is fishing from a large craft and the height of freeboard does not permit this method, it will be necessary to either employ a

POPULAR SEA FISHING

Three suggested tope traces: S = *swivel:* SSL = *stainless steel, screw link fitting*

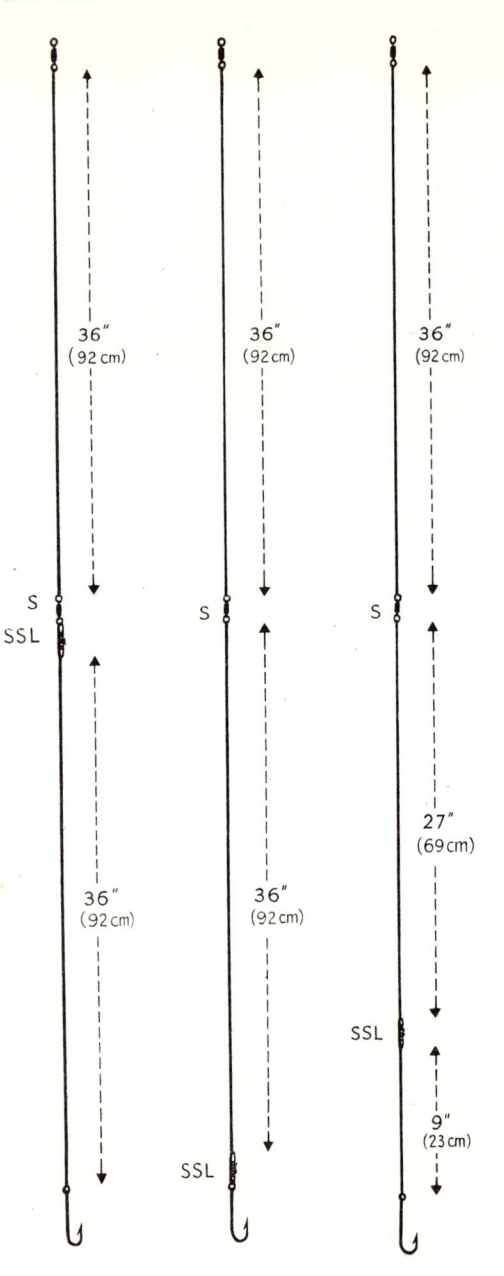

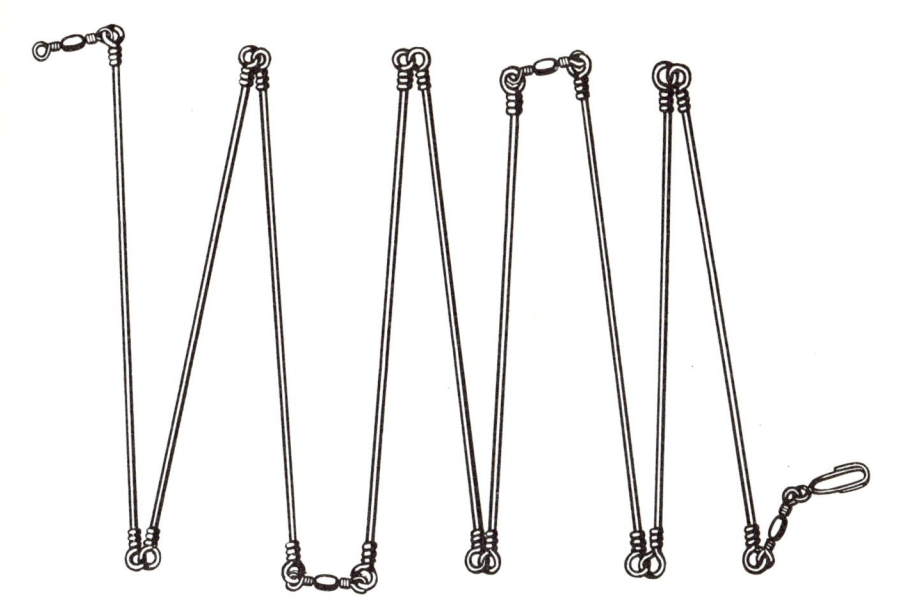

Tope trace formed by linking brass-wire lengths with swivels and eyes

stout, long-handled gaff or, alternatively, to heave the fish aboard by means of the wire trace. Care should always be observed when handling a wire trace to which a struggling fish is attached, otherwise the wire could cause severe laceration of the hand. Strong leather gloves are an obvious help in this matter.

Personally, in the interests of conserving the species, I do not use a gaff, nor do I favour their use. But, if a gaff must be used for some special reason, then let it be a strong one. An adequate instrument can easily be made by purchasing a heavy gaff-hook and binding it tightly to a suitable handle of appropriate length and strength.

The shape and type of sinker used is largely a matter of individual choice. Its actual weight, however, will depend upon such factors as tidal currents, and whether the angler is operating from a boat, the shore or rocks. When distance casting is of primary importance, as in beach angling, I suggest that the shape should preferably be either torpedo or bomb. The sinker is attached to the trace leger-fashion, so that a taking tope will feel as little resistance as possible when picking up the bait. I have found when boat fishing for tope, that it is a distinct advantage to position the sinker as much as 20 ft (6 m) or 30 ft (9·1 m) up the reel line – well away from the trace. This allows complete freedom of movement for both bait and trace, and it seems to attract far fewer skate, which can sometimes prove troublesome when one is exclusively after tope. The sinker can be kept at the correct up-line distance by attaching a match stick just below the

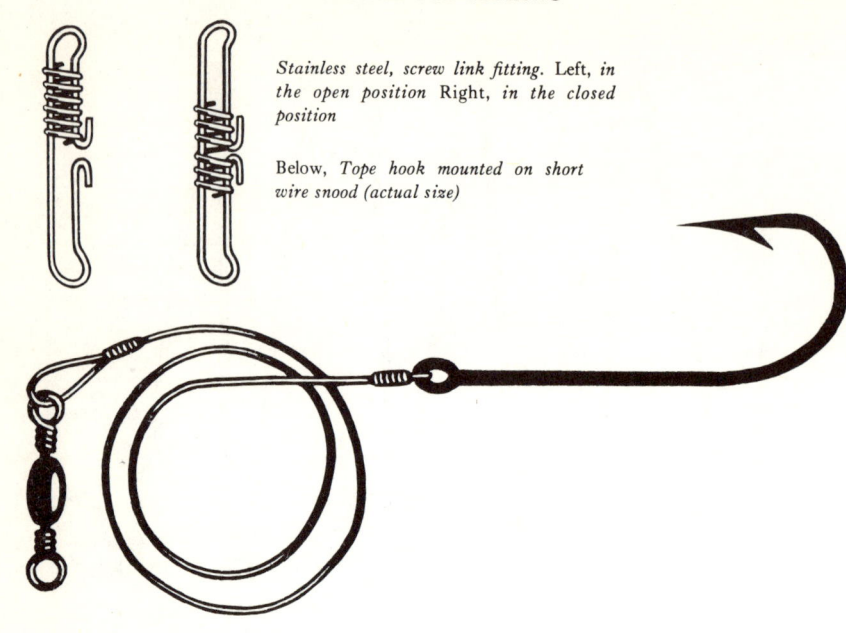

Stainless steel, screw link fitting. Left, *in the open position* Right, *in the closed position*

Below, *Tope hook mounted on short wire snood (actual size)*

sinker. This will act as a stop, but will break when it reaches the tip ring of the rod, and thus permit easy handling of a fish prior to boating it. A similar effect can be achieved by tying an elastic band to the line in place of the match stick.

If desired, a rod-socket, and even a harness too, may be worn by the tope angler, but I cannot say that I have found either item essential – apart from the fact that they do tend to relieve possible tedium.

Attracting the fish to the bait is a vital aspect of tope fishing. It can be achieved by using an onion bag or a container of netting or wire mesh, filled with minced or mashed fish or offal, and lowered over the side of the boat. Morsels are slowly released from the container to form a trail along which tope are attracted uptide to the baited hooks. Another attractor method involves attaching a handmincer to the gunwhale of the boat so that its outlet overhangs the water. Fish and offal are placed in the mincer, to drop as fragments into the water whenever the handle is turned. This is a simple and very effective method of creating the necessary trail which can often make all the difference between a productive day and a complete blank.

As with all forms of fishing, I believe that for consistent success attractive presentation of the bait to the fish is vital. It is also essential that the bait should be attached to the hook in such a manner as to minimize the possibility of the fish taking a portion of the bait, or even the whole of the bait, without getting hooked in the process. Tope seem to be particularly adept at this trick, and many are lost by anglers who failed to correctly secure the bait to the hook. No loose ends should be left dangling and the hook point and barb should be exposed.

Tope baits need to be fresh. The more oil and blood in the composition of the bait, the more fish-enticing it will be. Whole fish baits, unless they are very small, prove somewhat difficult to cast from the shore, but they present less difficulty from rocks or piers, and of course none from a boat. I have found that mackerel, pilchard and herring, are the most effective, although in areas where whiting or pouting are plentiful, tope sometimes show a distinct preference for these species. Fillets from freshly caught flounders, plaice and bass are all excellent baits for casting from the shore, as they are relatively tough and remain firmly in position on the hook. However, I do not suggest that the slow-growing and highly sporting bass should ever be used as a regular tope bait. Its flesh attracts tope well enough, it is true, but what a waste of a good fish!

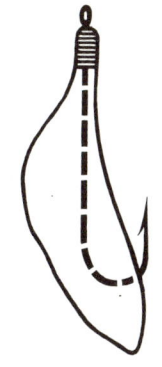

In the absence of fresh fish, deep frozen fillets offer a good substitute. Left indicates the correct way to mount the fillet: bind the the thin end of the fillet to the hook with thread and secure in position through the hook-eye. Right indicates the wrong way: this enables the fish to take either end of the bait and pull it from the hook without coming into contact with the hook point

In the absence of fresh fish, deep-freeze fish are the best substitute. In this respect, mackerel, herring and sprat are all productive. Other tope baits include: soft and peeler crabs, and bunches of lugworm and ragworm.

The technique of baiting a whole fish on a double-hook assembly is best achieved by using two snoods of trace wire; one approximately 6 in. (15 cm) and the other 9 in. (22 cm) in length. A tope-hook, say 7/0 to 9/0, is attached to each snood. At the other end of each snood a loop is formed. The bait-fish must be attached with its head pointing downwards; the loop of the longer snood being inserted through the mouth or the eye of the fish, and that of the shorter snood at about its middle. A baiting needle is employed for this purpose. Both of the loops are then drawn through the fish, coming out at the tail and leaving one hook

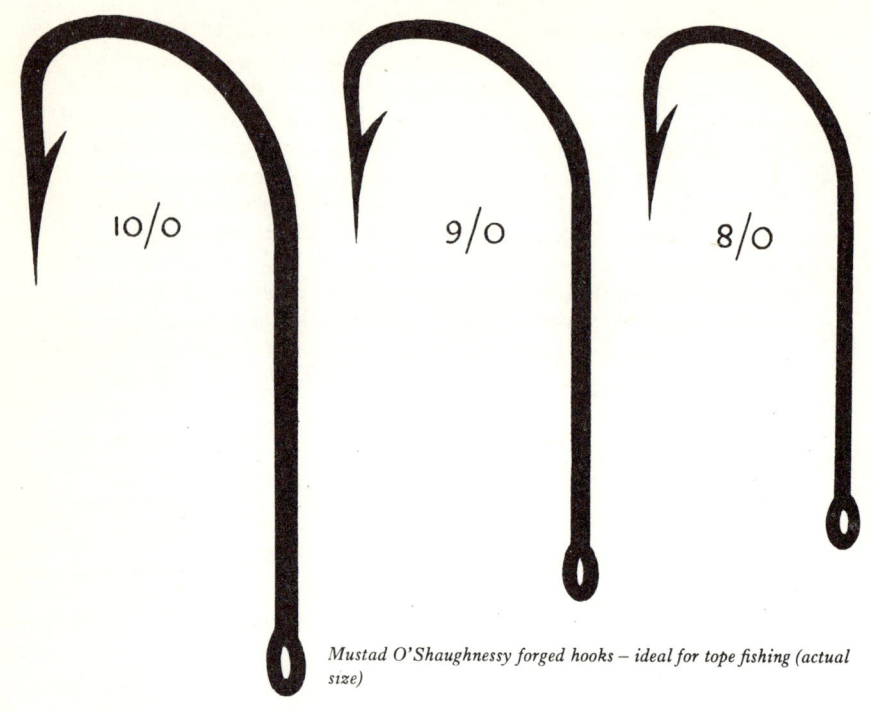

Mustad O'Shaughnessy forged hooks – ideal for tope fishing (actual size)

projecting from the mouth or eye, and the other from its middle. The two loops are then drawn together and secured to the trace by means of a stainless steel screw link.

Tope fishing from the beach involves a technique somewhat different from that of boat angling. The ability to cast – sometimes quite an appreciable distance – is a decided advantage. Beach angling for tope also differs from beach angling for other species, in that the weight of the bait may, if a large whole fish is used, exceed that of the casting weight. I have, for example, occasionally cast a whole mackerel from the beach, and the resulting 'pendulum' effect caused by what is virtually a rig with two sinkers has to be experienced to be fully appreciated. I recall that when I first introduced Eric Horsfall-Turner (himself an expert caster and co-author of *The Angler's Cast*) to this technique, he could not initially make head or tail of it. However, with his excellent casting abilities he very soon mastered this unorthodox style.

Once mastered, it becomes a relatively simple means of putting a bait out, although the pendulum action of the casting weight in the centre of the trace and the fish-bait at the end of it, is always present. If you do find it too awkward for comfort, then I suggest that you limit your bait selection to small fish, portions and fillets, when tope fishing from the shore.

TOPE FISHING

It must be appreciated that spots where tope can be taken from the shore are the exception rather than the rule. Sandy or pebbly steep-shelving beaches, especially where there is likely to be a concentration of food-fish forced shorewards by strong tidal currents passing through 'bottlenecks', are often, but not essentially, productive marks. Before commencing to fish, it is advisable to seek local information concerning the known presence or otherwise of tope. Such facts can be gleaned from tackle dealers and from local boatmen or anglers. Unfortunately, such sources are not always available, in which case one has to learn the hard way, by 'trial and error' effort, which beaches produce tope.

I continue to be convinced that there are numerous places along the coastline where tope can be caught from the shore, but where no angler has so far seriously tried for them. Many of my favourite hotspots have been discovered by pure accident, when I have been fishing for other species and instead have contacted 'bonus' tope.

When beach angling for tope, cast out as far as possible, disengage the reel clutch and engage the check. The initial bite of a tope varies from quite a gentle taking of line to a sudden and decided grab.

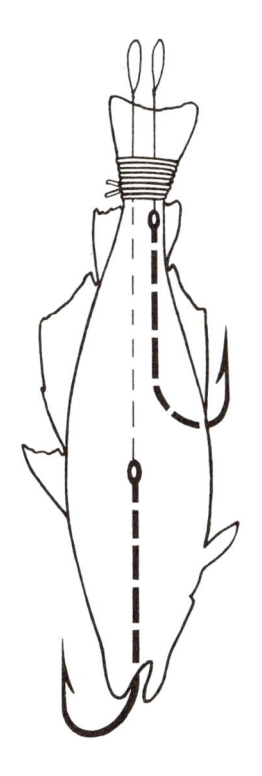

Whole fish mounted 'tandem' fashion. The loops are secured together with a stainless steel screw link fitting

It is essential that the tope should feel a minimum of resistance during its initial run. Let it move off for 50 or 60 yards (45·7–54·8 m), then engage the reel clutch and strike – really hard, to drive the hook point firmly home. If the fish continues to run outwards, let it do so, but gradually bring pressure to bear, either by finger control on the side of the reel drum, or by tightening the reel drag.

Should the run be inwards, recover line as rapidly as possible and try to maintain a 'braking' strain on the fish, in an effort to tire it quickly. It is when the line is allowed to fall slack that many fish are lost.

In the event of the fish running parallel with the beach, it is advisable to try to keep level with it, by running in the same direction as the fish, always maintaining a tight line and a steady strain on the fish.

When you have beached your fish, lose no time in baiting up and casting out again. Sport will often be fast and furious for only a short time, particularly when tope are hunting in pack formation and moving rapidly from one area to the next.

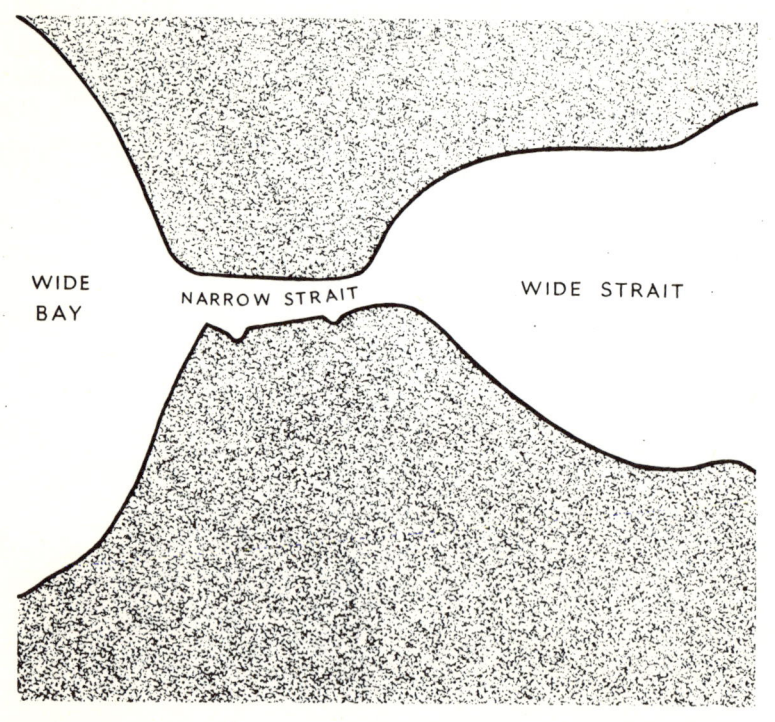

A typical tope area. Tope frequenting the wide bay follow fish shoals forced by strong tideways through the narrow strait. It is in the strait that the greatest concentration of tope will normally be found

SKATES AND RAYS *Trevor Housby*

Despite the fact that numerous good books are available on fish identification, the majority of anglers still find it difficult to distinguish one species of skate or ray from another. This situation results in mass confusion, and on more than one occasion possible record fish have been cut up and eaten before positive identification had been made. I find this strange, for in these days of competitive angling most sea anglers are, to some extent, record conscious. Yet when it comes to the skate and ray tribe, we seem to suffer from a national blind spot.

Probably the most common species of them all is the thornback ray, a fish with a wide selection of local names including, 'roller', 'ray maid' and 'fair maid'. It gets the name thornback from the large number of thorn-like spines situated along its back. Only the rarely caught starry ray has more of these spines than the thornback. Thornback rays reach weights exceeding 35 lb (15.8 kg), but the average rod-caught specimen will tip the scales at between 7 lb (3.1 kg) and 12 lb (5.4 kg). They live in fairly shallow water, and prefer a mud, sand or gravel bottom. In many areas they come within easy casting range of the shore, and are therefore a popular target of beach fishermen.

Another fairly common member of the group is the blonde ray, a less angular shaped fish than the thornback, and without the large back-spines. The blonde ray has an attractive sandy-coloured back, well spotted with small black dots. It is further distinguished by white blotches on the wings – each blotch set in a surround of black. The underside of the fish is white. Blonde rays are strong, active fish, which prefer to live in hard tide areas. On average they are larger than

Thornback Ray – male

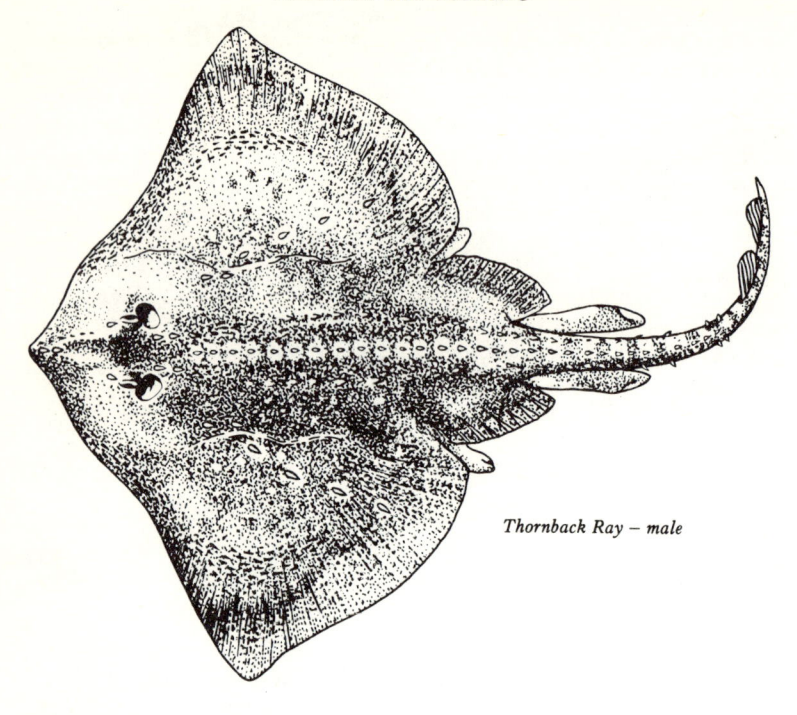

thornbacks, and a 20 lb (9 kg) specimen is regarded as a fair but not outstanding catch.

A fish which is often confused with the blonde ray is the homelyn or spotted ray. Put the two species together, however, and the exterior differences are quickly apparent. The spotted ray, for example, has a more prominent snout, and a darker coloured back, marked with fewer and larger spots than the blonde ray. The pale wing blotches are also less pronounced. Spotted rays rarely exceed a weight of 5 lb (2.2 kg).

The cuckoo ray is, in my opinion, a most attractive creature with its neat heart-shaped body and coloration of yellowish brown above and white below. Each wing carries a single distinctive 'eye' spot, marked with yellow dots and lines. Basically a small-growing species, the cuckoo ray rarely exceeds a weight of more than 2 lb (0.9 kg).

A fish once thought to be a colour variant of the cuckoo ray is the sandy ray, now generally regarded as a separate species. The sandy ray is light brown with yellow or cream spots.

The rays so far described are rather short-snouted in comparison with the larger, long-snouted 'true' skate. The common skate is, as its native name implies, a quite prolific species in our waters, although in some areas where it was once common, over-fishing and over-killing by anglers has ruined what were once top-class big skate grounds. I think it would be wise to learn a lesson from this result. To reach great weights, skate have to live a long life – a life which can be snuffed out in 30 to 60 short minutes by an angler who just simply wants a trophy carcase to hang up for photographs. Catch big skate by all means, but afterwards photograph them in the boat, and then slide them back alive to grow larger still and fight again another day.

On a recent trip to the Isle of Mull, I had a skate of 150 lb (68 kg) and a friend had a smaller one of 114 lb (51·7 kg), both of which were weighed alive and returned in good health. Frankly, I found it most satisfying to watch these big fish swim slowly down and away out of sight. So much a better end to the day than finishing up with a brace of monstrous, evil-smelling corpses to dispose of.

In colour, the common skate is greyish brown above and streaky grey beneath. The back may be marked with light coloured spots and tiny dots, although many big fish are completely devoid of these markings. Common skate are known to reach weights of over 400 lb (181·4 kg), but the average rod-caught specimen is between 80 lb (36·2 kg) and 150 lb (68 kg).

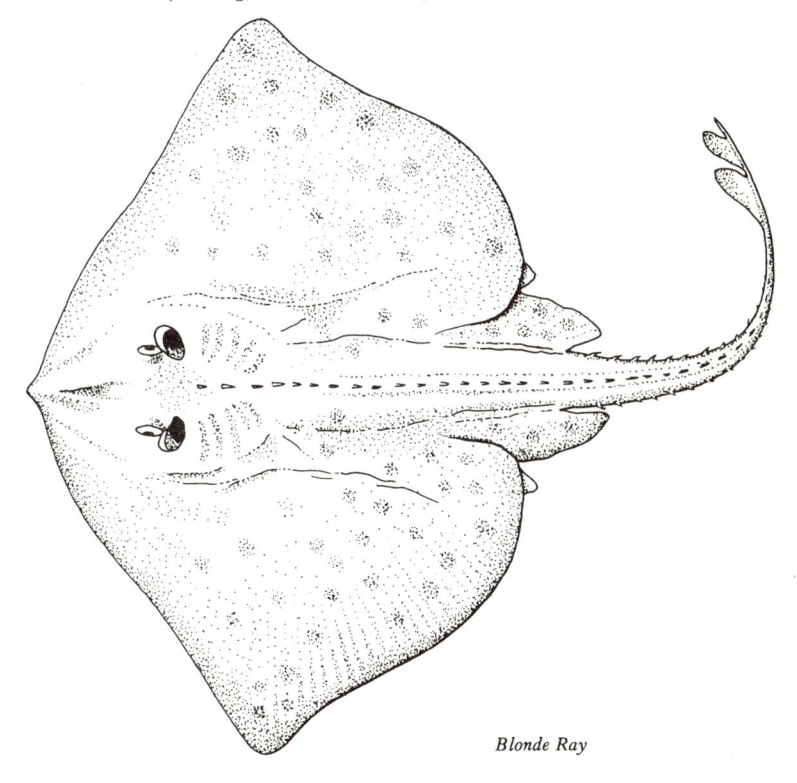

Blonde Ray

Common Skate – female

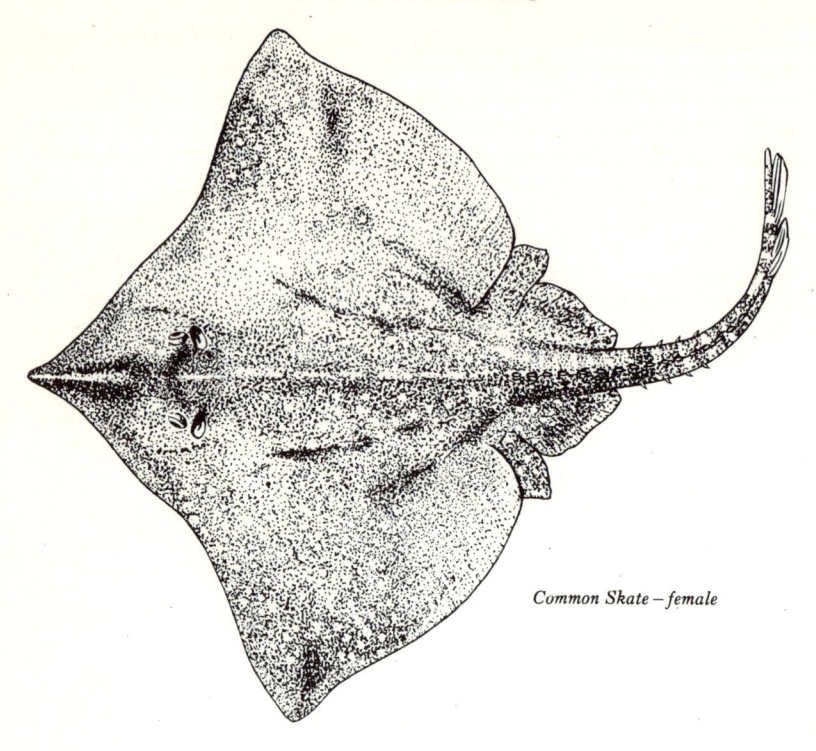

The white skate or 'bottle-nosed' ray is also rather common, but is inclined to a more southerly distribution than the common skate. This species has, however, been recorded in northern waters. A very large specimen was caught in Strangford Lough, Northern Ireland. This is the farthest north this species has so far been taken. The name white skate stems from the pure white underside of the fish; the back is bluish grey. Immature specimens, sometimes wrongly called 'bordered rays', occasionally have dark borders along the line of the wing tips.

The long-nosed skate is easily identified by its extra long snout and short, stubby wings. The back of this fish is normally greyish brown with pale spots and darker markings. Its underside is grey and also marked with streaks and dots.

Probably the easiest of all the ray species to identify is the sting ray or 'fire tail', which gets its name from the barbed spear set into its whip-like tail. Sting rays are both dangerous and messy to handle. The wicked tail barb can cut deeply, and the body is covered in thick, evil-looking slime. Sting rays are generally brownish in colour on the top side and white beneath. The barbed and grooved tail-spear is coated with a poisonous substance which is capable of causing temporary paralysis. Anybody who gets badly cut or ripped by this spear can expect to experience a period of acute discomfort before the wound is properly healed. Knowing this, many anglers habitually cut off the tail before attempting to remove the hook. This is fair enough if the intention is to keep the fish, but if it is to be returned it is a cruel practice. True enough, plenty of tailless sting rays have been caught, proving that they can survive without this, their only means of defence, but that is hardly an excuse for needless cruelty.

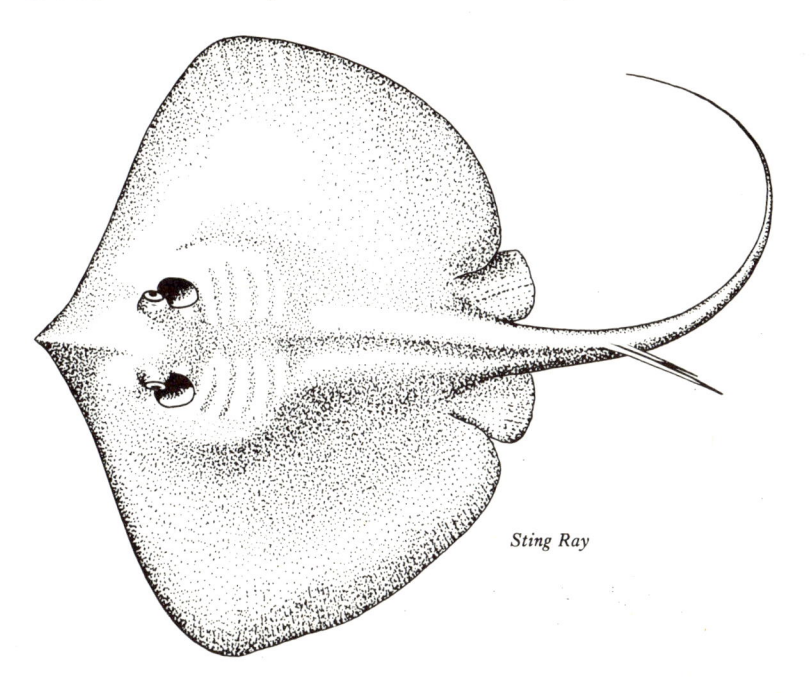

Sting Ray

An extremely interesting but rather rare fish is the torpedo ray, sometimes called the electric ray, of which two kinds occur in home waters. The ancient Greeks referred to these creatures as 'numb fish', because the electrical discharge from a mature specimen is powerful enough to numb any portion of unprotected anatomy with which it comes into contact. Rather lethargic in habit, the torpedo ray catches its prey by stunning them with a discharge from its powerful 'battery-cells', located in the pectoral fins. These 'batteries' are honeycombed structures of prism-shaped jelly-filled cells. The underside of the fish is the negative electrode, while the upper part forms the positive electrode. Sea water is the conductor through which the current passes. Any small fish which receives a shock is immediately stunned and falls an easy victim to the hunting ray. Fresh from the sea, a torpedo ray should be handled with extra care for, although the shock it can produce is comparatively small, it is still sufficient in strength to give a nasty jolt. Fortunately for the angler, this species is rarely taken on rod and line, and all the species I have seen were taken in nets trawled over soft muddy ground. In each instance, the ray disgorged the remains of small flatfish, indicating that immature plaice and sole, etc., form a major part of the staple diet of these ugly, unusual fish.

In recent seasons, a growing interest in the skate and ray tribe has led to specialized fishing for two of the lesser known species. The small-eyed ray and the beautifully marked undulate ray, or 'pop-art' ray as it is sometimes called.

Both of these rays are rather localized in distribution. Isolated pockets of small-eyed rays occur right along the Channel, but undulate rays are only truly common around the Channel Islands and one or two places off Southern Ireland, such as the sheltered waters of lovely Tralee Bay where they are notably prolific. I was fishing this area in recent years with a party of nine other anglers, and in a week's fishing we boated no less than 209 undulate rays between us. Many of them were large enough to be accepted for the Irish specimen-fish lists, and all were returned alive to the water.

The undulate ray is a truly impressive creature. Its sandy grey back and vivid dark markings giving it the distinctive look of a modern painting – hence its nickname. The small-eyed ray, although less boldly marked, is also a pretty-to-look-at fish.

Close to where I live in Hampshire, there is an area of sea (off the Isle of Wight), that is alive with large small-eyed ray, which can be relied upon to give sport on most occasions. This stock have sandy coloured backs, with distinctive lines of bluey white over-marking the basic shade. Both small-eyed rays and undulate rays give a good account of themselves when hooked, and both make excellent eating. Off the north coast of Cornwall, local beach anglers specialize in catching small-eyed rays; the bait invariably being fresh-caught sandeels.

Many anglers who have caught a big skate never wish to repeat the performance. On the other hand, there are anglers who get the 'big-skate bug' so badly that they dream constantly of hooking one 'barn door' after another, and when awake they continue to think of nothing else.

In recent seasons, most of the big skate taken on rod and line have come from Orkney, Shetland, or the Sound of Mull on the west coast of Scotland. The Sound of Mull is, in fact, one of the newly discovered big-skate grounds which has the potential to yield specimens of record-breaking proportions.

Big skate can hardly be classed as great fighters, but their sheer weight and huge wing span are still enough of a problem to make them formidable opponents, particularly for anglers who have never tackled such a large quarry before. Long fights with big skate are rare, but one epic battle I am not likely to forget took place in 1967. I was boat fishing in deepish water off the Isle of Wight in the company of Lymington angler, Dave Fawcett, when he hooked a large skate which fought hard for nearly five hours. Hooked on reasonably strong tackle, it made no less than 11 unstoppable runs before steady pumping brought it to the surface. In superb condition, it weighed 110 lb (49·8 kg), exactly 10 lb (4·5 kg) heavier than the previous local record for the species. Why it fought so hard and so long continues to remain a mystery. Although I have been involved in a number of battles with big skate, I have never come across one which put up anything like the kind of epic resistance which Fawcett's fish did.

If you intend to concentrate on catching large skate it pays to think really big. Specimens of 100 lb (4·3 kg) class are regarded as average fish in many areas, and in Irish and Scottish waters a common skate must better 150 lb (68 kg) before it can be considered notable. To relieve the strain of playing fish in this weight range, strong tackle is absolutely essential, and nowadays most skate specialists use heavy-duty hollow or solid fibre glass rods, large capacity centre-pin or multiplying reels, and 60 lb (27·2 kg) to 80 lb (36·2 kg) breaking strain lines linked to size 6/0 or 8/0 hooks by stout wire traces – which are essential for big skate, because of their razor-sharp lip plates which can cut easily through ordinary monofil traces.

This is typical gear for big-skate hunting, but it may seem too heavy for a species with a poor fighting record. It should be understood, however, that skate tackle has to work very much like a crane in order to lift such massive fish from the sea bed to the surface. Lighter tackle than this would not have the strength to take such strain, and consequently it is essential to fish with a really heavy outfit in order to stand a chance of boating the majority of big skate you hook.

Obviously, not everyone has the opportunity to specialize in big-skate fishing, but fortunately there are plenty of medium size fish about to compensate for this, and by scaling down tackle strength to suit local conditions it is simple enough to match an adequate outfit to your own requirements. My own tackle consists of a hollow glass boat rod, a Penn Super Mariner reel, and 50 lb (22·6 kg) breaking strain line. Using this gear, I have taken a number of very good skate from marks along the south and south-west coasts, and for general, all-round skate fishing it has served me very well indeed.

Skate are scavengers. They wander over the sea bed, acting rather like animated vacuum cleaners, gobbling up anything and everything edible they come across. At the same time, however, skate display a distinct liking for fresh food, and the wise angler will therefore present recently caught bait as often as possible. Many of the skate I have captured have disgorged whole pouting, flatfish, and, in the case of one large specimen, a small dogfish, proving that despite an awkward shape, skate are perfectly able to catch small fish when they want to.

One of the deadliest of all skate baits is a small pouting, a bait which often enough catches fish when all other offerings fail. Half a fresh mackerel also makes a first-class bait, and I have found that the head section, cut carefully so that the guts of the fish remain intact, works best of all. Messy and revolting perhaps, but a genuine fish attractor. The 110 lb (49·8 kg skate mentioned earlier fell to just such a lure.

Skate are obviously bottom feeders, and leger tackle is the only practical rig to use. They can be caught at almost any time of the year, but the top months, both for beach and boat fishing, are those from May to September. Probably the best time of all to go afloat in search of a really big skate is between late August and early September – the period of the year when larger fish move into waters close inshore to indulge in a wild feeding spree, to build up a store of body fat on which to survive the winter months when food is more difficult to find.

Thornback rays often move around in small groups, which usually consist of one female and two or three attendant males. Should the female be caught, the males usually remain for long enough to find the bait and get themselves hooked, too. Due to this pattern, it is often possible to take a nice bag of prime thornbacks in a very short space of time. Once a few fish have been caught, it is advisable to move on and try a new mark in the hope of finding a further pack in feeding mood.

Small and medium size skates and rays make splendid eating. Large skate, on the other hand, are tough fleshed, with a distinct smell of ammonia, and not really suitable for the table.

Skates and Rays from the Shore

In areas where skates and rays are abundant, shore fishing can be a most rewarding method of angling during periods of calm, settled weather, when these fish swarm close inshore to feed on the worm and mussel beds in the shallows. All British species of skate and ray have been caught by anglers fishing from the shore, but as a general rule thornback rays are by far the most common.

Almost any bait can be used from the shore, though in certain areas the local anglers have a preference for one type of bait only. This preference varies considerably from one stretch of coastline to the next: East Anglian and northern beach experts choose bunches of black lugworm before all other baits, whereas Hampshire fishermen swear by fish baits. Further west, peeler crab is the favourite, and in Scotland I have discovered that mackerel strip is very highly rated. It just goes to show what a wide variety of baits you can use.

During the past few seasons I have experimented with small livebaits angled on short-link leger rigs for the skate along my local beaches. They have worked well enough, but I cannot honestly say that they have proved superior to freshly caught, dead fish.

Shore Fishing for Sting Ray

Throughout the summer months, sting rays are very common along parts of the Essex and Hampshire coastlines – though outside these areas they appear to be rather rare. Sting rays seem to prefer a muddy bottom in shallow water, which is probably why they are so common in the Solent – that interesting and prolific stretch of water dividing the Isle of Wight from the mainland.

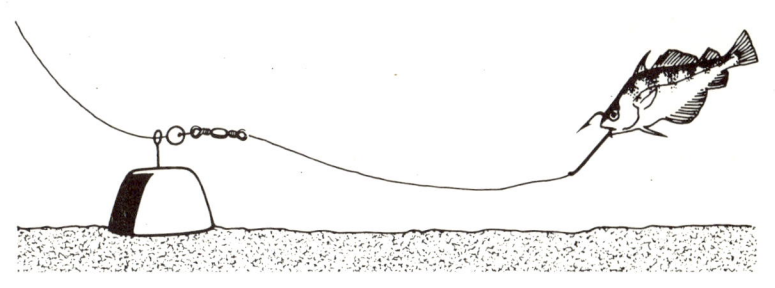

Live fish used with a short-link leger rig for skate

The first sting rays arrive in Solent waters during mid-May. They remain until early autumn when, presumably, they move offshore into deeper water. I say presumably, for although I have trawled extensively in the deepish water off the Isle of Wight, I have never yet taken a sting ray in the nets. This fact leads me to believe that sting rays may hibernate during cold weather, especially as most of them appear to be covered with thick layers of muddy slime which could easily accumulate if they passed the winter months buried in the bottom silt.

Ideal conditions for sting ray fishing occur during periods of hot, settled weather, when the sun has thoroughly warmed the mud of the shallows. Then it is that the rays come right into shore in a search for food. Indeed, many a lunker specimen has been taken in water less than 3 ft (0.91 m) deep by shore fishermen. Although not truly a shoal species, sting rays seem to have a herd instinct and tend to collect together. Where one fish is caught, there are usually quite a number, and under the right conditions it is quite common for as many as a dozen to fall to one rod during a single tide.

I have no real experience of sting ray fishing along the Essex coast, for just about all my expeditions have been made in Solent waters near my home – particularly at Park Shore and Sowley beaches, both of which can only be approached by long walks along the foreshore.

Sting rays feed mainly on marine worms, and most specimens fall for either lugworm or ragworm bait. Some have been taken on mackerel and herring strips, but this, at least in my experience, is a rather rare event, and the angler who desires to specialize in sting ray fishing is well advised to use worm baits exclusively.

There is very little finesse in such angling, and the usual tackle consists of a 10 ft (3 m) or 11 ft (3.3 m) heavy duty beachcaster rod, a fairly large multiplying reel, and 35 lb (15.8 kg) breaking strain line. Fixed-spool reels are not recommended for sting ray fishing, where the brute force required to play these fish will quickly distort the bale-arm mechanism. The 4 oz (113 g) to 6 oz (170 g) lead is attached to the line by a single or double sliding boom, and the 2 ft (0.61 m) trace is made up from monofil, fitted with a swivel at one end and a size 4/0 stainless steel hook at the other end. Some anglers prefer to use a wire trace, as this gives them a chance with a tope or conger, but strictly for sting ray a wire trace is unnecessary, as these fish are equipped with little in the way of teeth.

Having tackled up, the hook should be baited and cast out 40 yards (36·5 m) to 60 yards (48·7 m) from the shore. Afterwards, the angler can either hold the rod or place it in a beach-rest while waiting for a bite. Sting rays are far from cautious, and most 'stinger' experts leave the rod in the rest and stand back until the nodding rod tip and screaming ratchet indicates that a ray has swallowed the bait and is making a run.

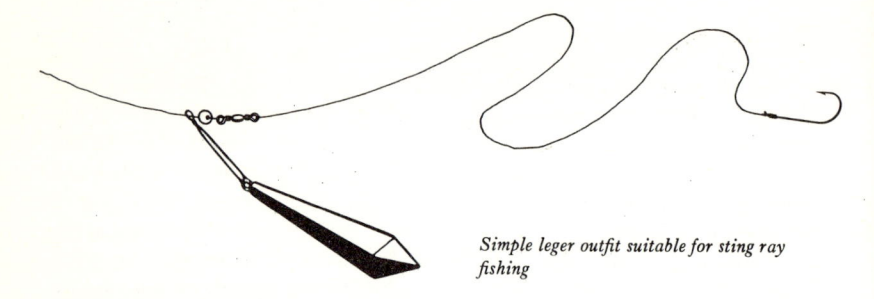

Simple leger outfit suitable for sting ray fishing

Some anglers use a two-hook rig for sting ray, but this, to my way of thinking, is rather dangerous, for it is quite common to hook two rays at once, and this may easily lead to a broken line. And even if both fish are successfully played out, there is still the problem of how best to land the catch. This would be a simple enough matter, but for the ever-present danger of the barbed tail-spears. Take my warning, and only fish a one-hook rig when sting ray are the target. The spears are lethal, and two big fish thrashing about together on a short length of line is more activity than most anglers can cope with.

A final point: sting rays make poor eating, so weigh them carefully and return them unharmed to the water. There is never any sense in killing for killing's sake.

FISHING FOR POLLACK, COALFISH AND LING *Des Brennan*

Pollack

In recent years, the discovery of populations of very big pollack, coalfish and ling on deep-water wrecks has, to my mind, created a division in fishing for these three species. Pollack weighing 10 lb (4·5 kg) to 12 kg (5·4 kg) would be classed as good fish if taken in the normal course of boat fishing, and yet on wrecks fish of 20 lb (9 kg) and over are often commonplace. As only a minority of anglers in these Islands can enjoy wreck fishing, I feel that the frequent reports of enormous catches of really big fish is creating a false set of standards in the minds of many anglers. For this and other reasons, I would prefer to deal with normal fishing and wreck fishing separately, and to leave the latter until the conclusion of my chapter.

Clive Gammon, writing in the first edition of this book, considered pollack, in his estimation, as second only to bass in our hierarchy of saltwater game fish: 'They are big, handsome and tough. They can be fished for on light tackle and by a variety of methods. Where they occur at all, they occur in big numbers and nearly always are obliging enough to fit into a feeding pattern which hardly varies from Land's End to Cape Wrath. I could not imagine sea fishing without them.'

The pollack, *Pollachius Pollachius*, is an eastern North Atlantic species

Pollack

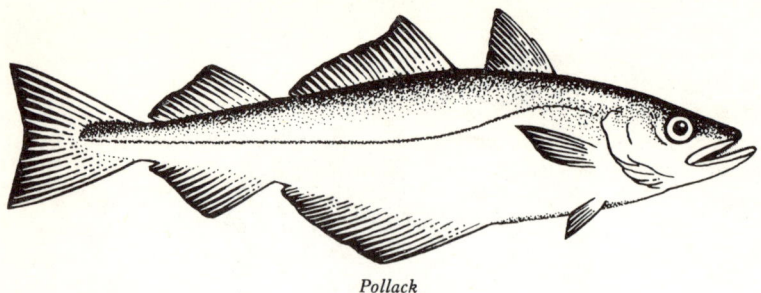

ranging from the Mediterranean to Norway. It is found all around our coasts, but the best quality fishing, both for size and for quantity, is found in the rich Atlantic waters off the south and west coasts of Ireland, off Devon and Cornwall, and off west Wales. They are fairly abundant in Scottish waters, but towards the north they are outnumbered by their close relative the coalfish, *Pollachius virens*.

To the inexperienced eye, both species look similar. They are streamlined 'round' fish with prominent lateral lines, and are frequently taken on the same grounds. The following are the more obvious points of difference to check if you are in any doubt.

The lateral line in the coalfish is a nearly straight, narrow white 'seam' on a darker background, while that of the pollack is a dark line on a lighter background — noticeably curved over the shoulder of the fish. In pollack the lower jaw is decidedly longer and protrudes beyond the upper jaw, while in the coalfish the lower jaw is only fractionally longer in the larger fish and may actually be shorter than the upper jaw in the smaller, immature fish. Coalfish have markedly forked tails, while the tail in pollack is only slightly forked.

In summer, pollack are found chiefly on rough and rocky bottoms, in depths ranging from a fathom or two (1·8–3·6 m) to over 20 fathoms (36·5 m). They arrive in our inshore waters during April, and in normal seasons are usually quite plentiful by the end of the month. At this time of the year most of the fish are 'spent', and in the month of May, they are at their most numerous on reefs and over rough ground. They are hungry after spawning and consequently take suitable baits readily. The month of May often sees the best of the season's pollack fishing. Big pollack are solitary fish, although large numbers of them will be found on the one reef or over an area of rough ground or rocky headland.

During July and August, however, when fry are plentiful, pollack may combine to harry the shoals of sprat and sandeel, and may at such times be found quite some distance from the nearest rocky or rough ground. Normally, pollack swim deep during daylight, particularly in bright sunshine, and a bait or lure has to be fished deep, right on the rock, to interest them. At times, however, I have found them right at the surface in brilliant sunshine, chasing the shoals of fry in the company of bass and other species.

FISHING FOR POLLACK, COALFISH AND LING

In early morning and late evening, at dusk and dawn, pollack rise up through the water to feed and may be found right at the surface. Indeed, sometimes, they can be observed breaking the water or dimpling it as they feed freely, and it is during such periods that the greatest sport may be had with them. After the September storms, pollack begin to leave the shallow reefs and to move out to deeper water for the winter. However, during October, on the west coast of Ireland, I have found a very definite inshore migration of really large pollack for a period before they too move offshore into winter quarters. I suspect that pollack winter in shoals over clean ground in deep water of 40 fathoms (73·1 m) to 50 fathoms (91·4 m), as I have frequently seen large catches of big fish ranging in weight up to 30 lb (13·6 kg) taken by trawlers fishing such ground during the months of November and December.

Pollack are taken in the course of general boat fishing, usually on fish baits or feather jigs, either bottom fishing to an anchor or when drifting over rough ground. The tackle used is normally too heavy for the fish to show its true worth, and personally, I prefer to fish specially for pollack with the type of gear that gives me pleasure and the fish a chance to give a good account.

My choice is a single handed salmon spinning rod and a small multiplying reel filled with 10 lb (4·5 kg) to 12 lb (5·4 kg) breaking strain monofil. I find this a perfectly adequate outfit, even for handling heavy fish in deep water. The light line enables me to fish a variety of lures or fish bait, using the least possible amount of lead to reach the bottom. On deep water marks – 10 fathoms (18·2 m) to 15 fathoms (27·4 m) or more, there is little danger of a hooked fish snagging you on the sea bed, as there is no significant weed growth at these depths. However, when fishing over shallow reefs with a heavy kelp growth, one must fish with care and attention in order to avoid loss of tackle.

The classical method of catching pollack is the Cornish style, with live sandeel as bait. Apart from a ready supply of live sandeels, this type of fishing requires an accurate knowledge of the fishing marks, so that when the due allowance is made for tide and wind conditions the bait will drift onto the rock when the boat is anchored. The sandeels are kept alive in a 'courge', and should be mounted on a 2/0 hook linked to as long a trace as your rod can manage – 9 ft (2·7 m) being ideal. The trace is joined to the main line by a swivel, below which you should fasten a spiral lead of sufficient weight to take your bait down to the rock. Remember to bend the lead 'banana-shape' so that it will remain firmly in position. When drifting, the spiral lead thus mounted will also act as an anti-kink aid and prevent line twist.

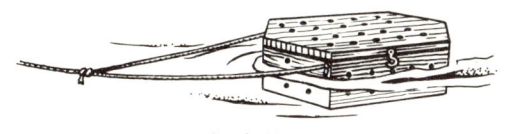

Sandeel 'courge'

The sandeel should be mounted carefully on the hook to avoid damaging it, as it will work best if it remains lively. Slip the point of the hook in through the mouth and out through the gill cover. Then draw it down the side of the bait and nick it lightly through the belly skin. The sandeel is then lowered over the side, and the line carefully paid out so that the bait drifts downtide far enough for the spiral lead to tap on the rock. When the knock is felt, the rod is quickly raised to clear the lead and the bait off the bottom, and the slow retrieve begins.

Sandeel correctly mounted for pollack fishing

This is the fascinating part of pollack fishing. Some anglers bring up the eel at normal spinning rate, but this I find is far too fast. The sandeel should be wound in slowly, and in deep water this may seem to take an eternity. The slow retrieve is maintained all the way to the boat, as pollack take at any and every level. Normally, the brighter the light the deeper the pollack will be, but they do tend to follow the bait up a long way before deciding to take it. I have actually seen pollack finally take the sandeel only just a few feet below the surface. Of course, in dull conditions pollack may be feeding well up off the bottom, and at dawn and dusk they may be right at the surface.

The first sign that a pollack has taken interest in the bait will be a tight tap or pluck on the sandeel. When this is felt, you will need all your self-control to resist striking and to continue retrieving at the same pace. It is not easy to reel slowly on as if nothing is happening, but to strike at this stage, or at any subsequent taps, is to miss the fish. Instead, wait until you feel a heavy take or feel the fish 'latch on' to the sandeel before striking – and then be ready for the first explosive dive as the fish responds to the unnatural resistance.

Your rod will bend over – the rod tip frequently being pulled hard under the water – as the fish rockets down towards the bottom at amazing speed from a standing start. Indeed, if your brake has not been pre-set correctly you could very likely be broken before you have time to react. In deep water let the fish run as there is little danger of being snagged. In shallow water with heavy weed growth a good fish may take you into the kelp – but there will be little you can do about it anyway! The pollack will make several diving runs before it begins to weaken and give ground. Then each run will be shorter and less explosive, and the fish easier to off-balance and bring back.

On light tackle, pollack, even when taken deep, will fight all the way to the boat. Be prepared for that last minute crash dive when the fish sees the net or the boat. Many a beaten fish has been lost at this juncture. Pollack have an unjustified reputation for giving up easily after the first few powerful dives. This is because on heavy tackle the fish can be fought up through the water too quickly for its swim bladder to adjust to the varying pressures, and at a certain stage the distended bladder simply floats it up to the surface despite the efforts of the fish to prevent this happening. When taken on light tackle the fish does have time to adjust and therefore does not suffer this disability.

In most areas, sandeels are not so readily available as to allow for this style of fishing regularly, but a long thin lask of mackerel cut to resemble a sandeel may be substituted – or artificial lures may be used. The technique employed is exactly the same and is very effective. The old fashioned rubber eel is familiar to most anglers and is still a successful lure, but I must confess a preference for the more natural-looking Red Gill and Eddystone eels, which in recent years have proved most effective.

Spoon baits such as the Toby are also good, but here I have a preference for heavier types such as the ABU Krill and Shiner, which have sufficient built-in weight to reach the bottom without the need for an uptrace weight. Uptrace weights, even on long traces, present little difficulty when the bait is just drifted down to the rock with the tide, but if you wish to *cast* the lure there are obvious problems. I find it an advantage to be able to cast when fishing to an anchor over a pollack reef. While large numbers of pollack will be found on the one reef or area of rough ground, they tend to be solitary in nature rather than shoal minded, and I find that by casting I am able to cover a greater area of ground and so present my lure to a greater number of fish.

Reefs can also be fished by drifting over them, but of course, unless one is fishing very alertly and carefully, there is a greater danger of snagging the sea bed. Fishing on the drift is the most productive method for searching a large area of low, rough ground. Most anglers seem to prefer to tackle up to catch a variety of species when fishing over this type of bottom. This means multiple hooks and baits or a string of feathers, and, consequently, heavier gear and leads. This, for me at any rate, takes away much of the pleasure of pollack fishing, and I prefer to fish specially for them with the type of equipment already described.

Fishing successfully and safely while drifting requires all your attention and skill. The lighter tackle permits you to feel what is happening below more sensitively than is possible with heavy equipment, and so helps you avoid getting caught up on the bottom. You can either drop down to the bottom and then start a slow retrieve, as in the Cornish style, or else touch bottom and then come up a few turns of the reel to clear it. If you use the latter method, you will need to test for the bottom occasionally as you drift along – in case the depth has increased and you are fishing too far off the bottom. Of course, should you touch the bottom as you drift, you will need to come up quickly in case the water is shallowing or you are crossing a reef, otherwise you will snag-up.

When fishing just off the bottom on the drift, I prefer to use a sandeel or long lask of mackerel as bait, or, if using an artificial, a Red Gill eel. Pollack feathers are also proven killers, but on light tackle never use more than three feathers at a time. Baiting the feathers with a strip of mackerel can increase sport considerably at times, as indeed it will with most other lures providing it does not interfere with the action of the lure.

Trolling over shallow reefs is also an effective method for taking pollack. The speed of the troll should be slow, and again use as long a trace as possible. During the daytime it may be necessary to get right down to the weed on shallow reefs in order to interest pollack, and on bright sunny days you may not be able to move them at all. At dawn and dusk, however, they will be right at the surface and provide exhilarating sport. Nevertheless, in these conditions, I prefer to let the boat drift, and to spin rather than troll. In fact, during the daytime I would prefer where possible to drift over a reef and bait fish or jig, for to be honest I find trolling a rather boring form of fishing.

Now we come to shore fishing for pollack. Wherever a rocky coast drops off sheer into deep water over a rough bottom there is a chance of good pollack fishing. Shore-caught pollack are, of course, on the whole much smaller than boat-caught fish, and most will not exceed 2 lb (0·9 kg) in weight. However, on light spinning tackle they are excellent fighters – a 2 lb (0·9 kg) pollack will test any angler. At places along the wild Atlantic coast of Ireland, shore pollack weighing 5 lb (2·2 kg)–7 lb (3·1 kg) are not uncommon, though it must be added that such exciting fishing is quite exceptional.

Depending on the size of fish expected, light to medium spinning tackle and 8 lb (3·6 kg)–12 lb (5·4 kg) breaking strain line is the order of the day. I find a fixed-spool reel more suitable than a multiplier, mainly because one can cast a variety of the lighter lures without adding an uptrace weight but also because of the cramped situations in which one frequently finds oneself on good rock marks. Indeed, good rock fishing for pollack often seems to be located in the most difficult and inaccessible places. Rock fishing can be dangerous. One can easily slip and damage or break a limb, so never go fishing alone and always let someone know where you will be and when you expect to be back. The sea can be treacherous, too, and an unexpectedly large wave has washed many an angler off a rock to his death. Never let your excitement dull your senses to the dangers of rock fishing. Be sensible and always take care. Remember that some places are easy enough to get down to but very difficult to get back up out of – particularly when weighed down with tackle and fish. Always leave before total darkness sets in, while you can still see what you are doing and where you are going.

Pollack will take a large variety of artificial lures, and I tend to go for those with built-in casting weight for fishing from rocks. These make it easier to cover the ground and contact more fish. Rubber eels – Red Gills, etc. – are also excellent, but they require an uptrace lead to give them casting weight and are difficult to control in strong winds and confined spaces. Some anglers recommend fast-spinning for pollack but, with one exception, I find that a slow spin (but fast enough to keep the lure from sinking too deep and fouling the weed) takes more fish.

The best of the sport is to be had in the evening after the sun has gone down. As dusk falls and the detail of distant objects begin to blur and become indistinct, the pollack rise up to the surface to feed. On calm, warm evenings they can be seen breaking and dimpling the water or splashing noisily in pursuit of fry. They will take lures readily under these conditions, and it is often possible to cast to individual fish. Indeed, in suitable places where there is space to cast, one can fly fish for them with streamer flies. A 2 lb (0·9 kg) pollack on a trout rod is something to remember. As dark approaches it often pays to retrieve the lure or feathers as fast as possible, whipping them across the surface so that they leave a wake of disturbed water behind them. This can drive pollack into a frenzy, and it is then most exciting to see fish leap clear of the water in their efforts to catch the speeding lure.

Float fishing can also be effective. A variety of baits may be used – live prawns, sandeels, slips of mackerel, ragworm and lugworm will all take fish – though the latter bait is also much favoured by wrasse, which inhabit the same locations. A sliding float is a must for this type of fishing. It may be necessary to fish deep, depending on the time and type of day, and a fixed float can present major casting problems in these circumstances, even with a long rod. It is essential to watch the float carefully, lest you be taken unknowingly into the heavy kelp by a fish. Too often the only way out is to pull for a break, leaving the hook in the fish.

Coalfish

The coalfish is a more northerly species than the pollack, and also attains a much larger size. The bigger coalfish prefer deeper water, but the smaller of the species – as large as 3 lb (1·3 kg) and known in many areas as 'billet' – have a distinct preference for shallow water. They are found all around our coasts, in depths ranging from a few feet (0·91 m approx.) to several fathoms (5·4 m approx.) but mostly in less than 10 fathoms (18·2 m). They are very numerous on the coasts of the North Sea and parts of the Irish Sea, where they are present for

Coalfish

most of the year. Larger coalfish are most plentiful on the coasts of Scotland, the Orkneys and Shetlands, where they outnumber pollack.

Billet favour the same type of ground as pollack, being found on reefs and over rock, but they range much more widely and are as likely to be encountered over clean ground as elsewhere – in the vicinity of headlands, off islands, in sounds and tideways, and where there are tide rips and tidal eddies. They are gregarious and are frequently found in very large shoals. They can be taken by the same methods used for pollack. They feed voraciously, and once located are easily caught. Indeed, I can recall occasions when I have seen a small party of anglers clean out a whole shoal. Using multiple lures and baits they just kept on catching small coalfish until none were left to catch.

There is little real pleasure in catching small fish which give themselves up so readily unless one's tackle is scaled down to match their strength and ability and to catch them one at a time rather than in two's and three's. Perhaps the most rewarding method is fly fishing at dusk from the rocks, when the fish rise to the surface of the water to feed. The fly – called a cuddy-fly in the north of Britain – is a crude concoction of white wool with a tinsel ribbing and a wing, traditionally from the pin feather of a swan.

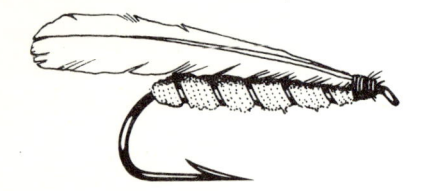

Cuddy-fly used for catching coalfish at dusk from the rocks

Larger coalfish, averaging between 3 lb (1·3 kg) and 7 lb (3·1 kg) are strong, tough fighters. They are more migratory-minded than the smaller fish, and they tend to prefer deeper water. They may be met over any type of ground and at any level from the bottom to the surface. I have contacted immense shoals of coalfish which have literally filled acres of water off the north of Scotland; distributed in depths of 40 fathoms (73·1) from midwater right to the surface, where they were breaking through in pursuit of fry. Little skill was required to catch these fish (they took as readily as do mackerel) and to have hunted them in any other way but singly would have been sheer slaughter.

Big coalfish are a different matter altogether. To be quite frank, apart from deep-water wrecks (of which more will be said later) I know of no area or type of ground around these islands where one would fish specially for, and be reasonably sure of meeting, lunker-size coalfish. They are very much deep-water fish, seldom to be taken in less than 15 fathoms (27·4 m). They are both demersal and pelagic, and may be encountered anywhere from the bottom to the surface over any type of ground. They have a preference for rock, rocky-reefs and rock holes, but may be met anywhere and at any level when in pursuit of herring, sandeels, or any other shoal fish.

Big coalfish are taken by anglers around the British Isles every season. However, such captures are, I feel, more luck than judgement, and made by anglers engaged in general fishing. The fact that most anglers in the British Isles tend to fish on or near the bottom reduces their chances of encountering big coalfish. In some areas, particularly those where tide-rips channel and concentrate bait-fish species, they may be present for a time, but usually their migratory tendencies urge them to seek pastures new before very long.

Ling

The ling is a fish of the north-east Atlantic, and is found all around our coasts. Although it is sometimes taken over clean ground, it is essentially a rough and rocky ground species, haunting the reefs, rock ledges and low, rough ground in deep water. A bottom dweller and fish eater, the ling, like the pollack, is a solitary fish, but also like the pollack, fair numbers will be found on the same reef or over an area of ground. If you catch one ling it is worth fishing specially for them as there is an excellent chance of contacting others on the same mark. Mostly they are taken in the course of general fishing on rough ground, but in some areas there are recognized ling hotspots where it is worthwhile seeking them out and fishing for them specifically.

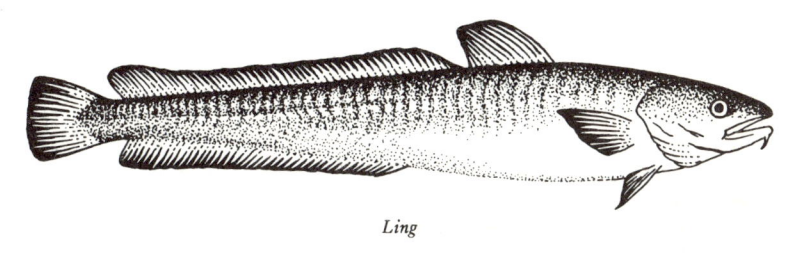

Ling

Baby ling are taken in shallow water, even from the shore sometimes, but are not a serious angling proposition. Adult ling are deep water fish, and must be sought in depths of 15 fathoms (27.4 m) or more. They have been caught commercially in depths of up to 150 fathoms (274.3 m), but are most plentiful in the 20 fathom (36.5 m)–50 fathom (91.4 m) range. They attain a large size: fish in excess of 100 lb (45.3 kg) have been reported. The average weight, however, runs from 10 lb (4.5 kg) to 30 lb (13.6 kg), and on good ground a 15 lb (6.8 kg) fish would be considered a satisfactory average.

The ling is a strong and powerful fish, in appearance rather like a cross between a cod and a conger eel. Built more for strength than speed, it pulls every ounce of its weight. When hooked, it does not run, but tends to resist hard and with considerable stubbornness not to yield ground. If taken on heavy tackle and fought up quickly, like the pollack, its swim bladder becomes distended and after a while it comes easily to the surface. On light tackle, ling do not suffer this problem and will fight every inch of the way to the boat.

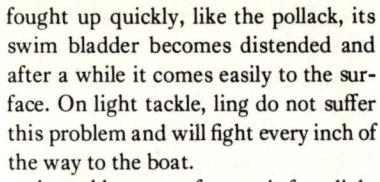

As tackle, my preference is for a light boat rod such as, for example, the Hardy No. 1 Sidewinder, combined with 27 lb (12.2 kg) breaking strain braided line and a 2/0 Policansky multiplier. The ling has a mouth full of formidable teeth, so it is advisable to use a short wire link – and to take care when removing the hook! When fishing for ling to an anchor my favourite rig is a partial leger to a 6/0 hook. Many anglers prefer a straight one or two hook paternoster, and certainly I would agree that the paternoster is a more suitable rig for fishing on the drift.

Ling are fish eaters, so there is no point in offering them anything other than fish or squid. I like to use a big bait, such as the whole side of a mackerel or, if obtainable, a whole herring. The latter is an excellent bait for ling. I also like my baits to be as fresh as possible, so I change them frequently when bites are few and far between to avoid fishing baits which have had all their oil and blood washed out.

Paternoster rig for drifting over rock. Bottom hook is wire-linked to the three-way swivel. Top hook is optional and looped on a blood-loop tied in monofil. The monofil link between weight and three-way swivel is of a lighter breaking strain

The bite from a ling is positive enough, and if you pause for just a few seconds to make certain the fish has hold of the bait you will rarely miss on the strike. If you do miss, however, drop the bait back immediately. Ling will nearly always have been aroused enough to come a second time. When fishing to an anchor, I find that it pays to search the ground with the help of tidal movement. This can be done by selecting different weights and trotting the bait gradually downtide. This way the bait is presented to as many fish as possible. When drifting, fish close to the bottom – within 4 ft (1·2 m) – dropping down and feeling for the bottom from time to time to allow for changes in depth as the boat moves along.

Wreck Fishing

Wreck fishing has become well established in recent years, and most anglers are now well aware of the class of catch this kind of activity produces from the frequent reports in the Angling Press – not only of huge bags which may exceed a ton (1·0160 tonnes) in weight, but also of exeptionally large individual specimens. Indeed, the breaking of records for certain species occurs so frequently as to have become almost commonplace.

Wrecking can be a rather arduous form of fishing, as many wrecks are situated a very long way offshore and weather can be a serious limiting factor. At first it was mainly a summer approach, but then it was found that some of the best fishing and the biggest fish were found on the wrecks during the winter months.

Pollack are found in their greatest number over the wrecks during the summer months. They average 9 lb (4 kg) – 10 lb (4·5 kg), with some larger fish also present. But the winter pollack, which seem to be a different population, are much bigger than this on average. Pollack of 18 lb (8:1 kg) and over being common captures. This may well tie in with the migration of big pollack from inshore waters which I mentioned earlier in the chapter.

Coalfish are absent or fairly rare on the wrecks during the summer, but they are found there with the pollack in the winter. These are huge, powerful fish, running up to 30 lb (13·6 kg) or more in weight, and are a star attraction of wreck fishing for most specialists.

Ling are present throughout the summer and winter, until late January when they migrate to spawn.

While pollack and coalfish may be considered transient (each season bringing a new contingent), ling, like conger eels, seem to be residents of wrecks and as such are very vulnerable to over-fishing. Indeed, many wrecks have been fished out for both ling and conger, and stocks have not be replenished, sad to say. This has led to a search for new wrecks with virgin fish populations, to satisfy the wants of anglers who have come to expect large catches of big fish and who are not satisfied with less. Newly found wrecks have been raped in their turn, and so the process of find, fish and fish out, is constantly being repeated.

Apart from the obvious need for some form of conservation where vulnerable species are concerned, anglers need to keep things in clear perspective. Wrecking is a highly specialized form of fishing, and because of its very nature there are limitations on the amount of fishing it can provide. Its standards should not be accepted as general, otherwise the majority of boat anglers will tend to undervalue what they already have and so diminish their enjoyment of the sport.

In summer, pollack can be fished for with the tackle and methods already described. Light tackle and single lures, such as Red Gill eels and fluttering or wobbling spoons, give the most sport. It may not be possible to fish as light as you wish, as in many areas the catch goes to the boat. This can be very valuable, and is the reason why skippers may frown on tackle which will not land fish fast enough to make the catch as large as possible.

In winter, however, the angler has little choice but to fish with heavy tackle. A paternoster rig of three Red Gills fished on short snoods is a popular terminal lay-out. Dropped down to the massed ranks of coalfish and pollack, the angler may fill every hook, and with a leash of very heavy fish pulling frantically in opposite directions on short lengths of monofil even 50 lb (22·6 kg) to 60 lb (27·2 kg) line will not hold.

Single lures are not the answer (although when the fish are feeding ravenously they will take anything) because if they are at all finicky three lures are far more attractive and therefore effective. A single pirk is a very good alternative, and it helps to bait the treble with natural bait – particularly if one is trying for ling.

Ling are down on the bottom with the conger and, especially in winter, the problem is to get down to them through the pollack and coalfish without having one's bait taken. Wrecks are fished either on the drift or to an anchor, depending on weather and tide conditions as well as the species of fish being hunted. The wreck is marked on arrival with buoys to define its exact location and the angle at which it is lying. When drifting, the echo-sounder assists in deciding what depth to fish for pollack and coalfish as their tracings usually show up on the graph quite clearly. If fishing deep with a baited pirk or baited feathers for ling (I prefer to make up my own feathers in sets of three mounted on 9/0 hooks) it is essential to keep an ear open for the skipper's warning that the boat is drifting over the wreck. When this is happening, it is necessary to raise the tackle smartly, high enough to clear the wreck, otherwise a lot of tackle will be lost. At the price of pirks today, such losses can prove expensive to replace.

When fishing to an anchor for ling, there is the added complication that one may encounter very big conger. Because of this possibility, and the fact that big ling are well endowed with teeth, I recommend using a short wire link to the hook. A size 9/0 hook is about the right calibre for a good sized fish bait, and I would stress that the hook-point should be kept needle sharp at all times. Some wrecks lie in very deep water, and the sharper the hook the easier it is to drive it home at 40 fathoms (73·1 m).

SEA BREAM *Winston Hall*

Sea bream, which number around a dozen species, are found in waters ranging from the tropical to the Arctic. Only three species are of interest to British anglers: the black bream; the red or common bream; and the ray's bream. And of these, only the first two are worthy of serious consideration or of specialized angling.

Both black and red breams appear to be strongly conservative in their choice of hunting grounds. The 'black' confines itself almost exclusively to the Channel coast between Folkestone in the east and Dorset in the west, and even within these narrow limits it tends to concentrate mainly off the Sussex shores, where it can be expected to arrive any time during April. The Manacles, Portland Bill, and the waters off Littlehampton, are noted 'hotspots'.

Once they have arrived, sport with black bream improves rapidly, and if you can hit the right combination of circumstances and feeding fish, you can enjoy hectic fishing activity which is second to none for sheer excitement. Later, towards the end of July, the shoals disperse and the fish are not so easily to be taken in any quantity. Bream fishing, however, remains profitable until the September migration gets underway.

The black bream grounds off Littlehampton are generally accepted to be among the best in this country. Whether this is due to a prolification of fish, or to an abundance of facilities for the sport is a moot point, for Littlehampton Harbour is particularly well suited to the needs of angling.

The black bream, sometimes known as 'old-wife', is a deep bodied handsome fish, clothed in a uniform of hard shiny scales. The back varies in colour between the deep blue of flame-soiled steel and purplish black. The underparts and lower flanks are usually silver, but may also be tinged with muddy pink. Like all bream, its high rounded shoulders give it a hump-backed appearance.

The fish is muscular and knows exactly how to use its flattened body to advantage when fighting against the hook. Weight for weight it is stronger in the water than the average sea species, and taken on light tackle has a habit of boring down deep just when you think it is ready for the net.

During spring and early summer the shoals prefer rocky ground. However, any obstruction along the sea bed is an attraction to them, and the weed covered timbers of old wrecks are particularly promising marks.

As with most active species, black bream prefer to feed in a tideway but when this becomes too fierce they tend to seek shelter behind anything that offers a tidal lee. From this hide they will make short forays into the current whenever any morsel which appeals to their taste is carried past on the tide.

The shoals break up as the year advances, with individual fish scattering widely, though still keeping within chosen territorial limits. Finding them then is largely a matter of chance.

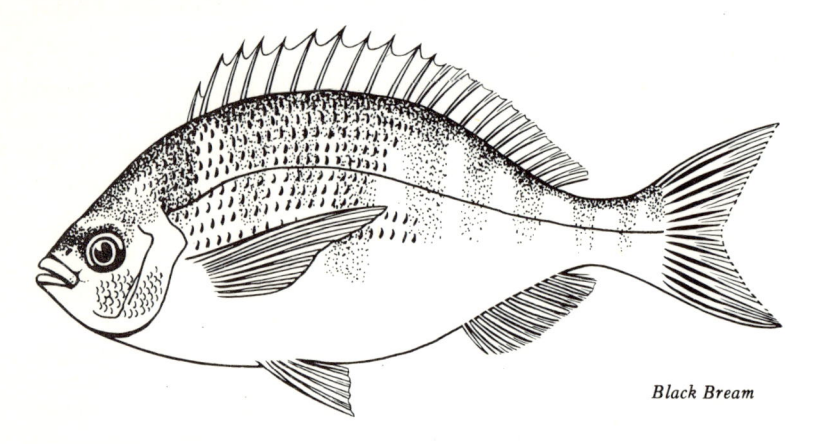

Black Bream

It cannot be too highly stressed that, for taking black bream, a boat is an essential to reach the hotspots. It must, however, be added that there are odd places in the West Country where bream can be taken from deep water rock marks located along the shore.

The boat-angler intent on catching black bream is fortunate since he needs little in the way of heavy gear and encumbrances. Only the super-optimist would consider taking a gaff to such a small and lively species, and all that is needed to bring the fish inboard is a reasonably large landing net.

Although spring and early summer breaming may call for trips as far as 6 miles (9·6 km) offshore, the choice of craft is largely a matter for the individual.

Power is naturally desirable, and providing care and common sense are exercised a modern outboard will prove adequate.

Nevertheless, only the foolhardy and complete novices in matters afloat, are likely to venture far from a safe landing or harbour in a tiny car-top type dingy. Go for the biggest craft your pocket and circumstances allow. My choice is for a stout, high-sided hull with plenty of freeboard and beam. I have little time for those 'lean' hulls designed mainly for speed. As far as I am concerned, power in the engine is a far greater safety factor than high revs.

I believe too, that boat equipment should comply with standard safety regulations. It should include distress flares (kept in their original waterproof pack), some form of life jacket for each member of the party, spare engine fuel, lubricating oil, a first-aid kit, and a second anchor complete with cable. A waterproof torch, an oilskin, and a bottle of drinking water are invaluable accessories for emergencies.

The majority of anglers, however, book aboard one of the charter boats working their chosen stretch of coast. In the nature of things some of these are better than others, as are their skippers. Nowadays though, competition has bred a generally good, all-round service, and with stringent safety regulations governing passenger craft, the stranger need not be over concerned with his choice.

As regards bait selection, close attention should be paid to the area to be fished. This is a matter to which few anglers give sufficient thought — whatever the species they are after. My feelings are that fish, generally speaking, are inclined to become preoccupied with any single item that happens to be around in quantity. In my experience, it pays to use a bait indigenous to the mark fished.

Fish clearly visit lugworm beds in the expectation of finding lugworms, as, at inshore rock and weed grounds, they expect small crustaceans. It is the task of the angler to present the same choice of diet on the hook, and providing one has a knowledge of what lies beneath the boat this should be obvious — if not always available in the bait-box!

When fishing an unfamiliar coast, without first hand experience or guidance, the charts published by the admiralty will be found extremely helpful. The larger scale charts — mainly covering harbours and their surrounding sea — are excellent guides for the serious angler. On them is indicated, in abbreviated form, the nature of the sea bed at given points. For example, S. St. Sp. Ks. Sh. etc. A full index of these abbreviations and their meanings is given on chart No. 5011 which should be in the possession of every keen boat angler.

This information should be combined with soundings — figures which show the depth of water — (watch this point, as it may be indicated in feet or fathoms), the locations of submerged wrecks, and the sitings of conspicuous buildings ashore, and the value of charts is plainly revealed.

But even without a chart, plenty of information can be found out about the sea bed, with the help of a simple sounding lead. This can easily be made at home for very little cost or effort. Necessary materials consist of a few pounds of lead, a wide but shallow watertight tin, a length of copper or brass wire, tallow, 15 fathoms (27·4 m) of cod line, and some strips of different coloured rag.

Invert the tin, and drill or punch two small holes in the bottom. Pass the wire through the holes and twist the ends together inside the tin. This forms a loop on the outside to which the line will eventually be attached.

Bury the tin right way up in a metal box filled with sand and, remembering how dangerous molten lead is when handled carelessly, pour the lead into the tin. Leave at least a 2-in. (5 cm) margin between the lead and the lip, and do not forget that lead retains its heat for a very long time after it has set. When it is finally cold melt the tallow and fill the remaining space in the tin until it is level with the edge. If tallow is not available, heavy waterproof grease will serve the same purpose but will need replacing more frequently.

Before bending the line to the wire loop, mark it off in 1 fathom (1·8 m) lengths by tying-in different coloured strips of rag at appropriate intervals.

In order to use a sounding lead, the boat is slowed until the engine is just ticking over and the lead tossed well ahead of the bows. The moment the boat overtakes the lead, the line will be straight 'up and down'. As this point is reached simply note the colour of the nearest cloth marker and you will have the depth reading.

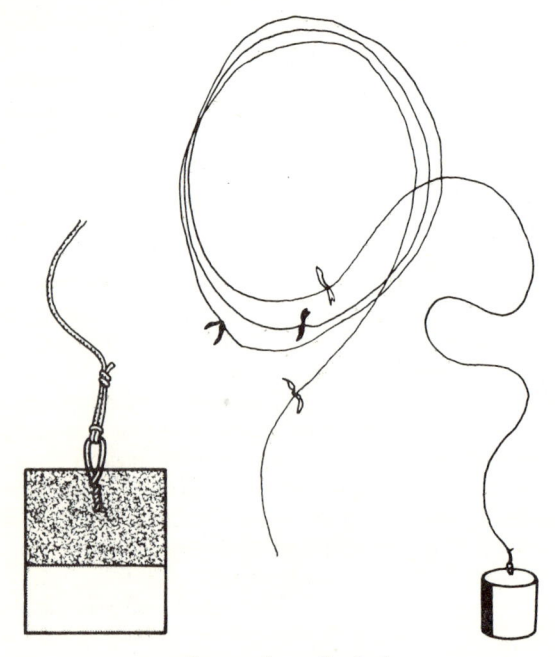

Home-made sounding lead

To determine the nature of the bottom, haul up the sounding lead and examine the tallow. Scraps of sand, mud, shell, weed or stone adhering to it are the clues to look for. If the tallow comes up perfectly clean (particularly on a second try) you can be reasonably certain that you are over clean, hard rock – 'flat-scar' as it is known in the north. This is quite good bream ground, particularly after the shoals have broken up.

Bream are catholic in their taste for baits. Almost all recognized lures, and some unusual ones too, will tempt them to the hook, but a glance at their powerful jaws and strong teeth so obviously designed for crushing shellfish, offers a clue too significant to be ignored.

Mussel, a bait that has unaccountably lost favour in the south, is to my mind one of the best of all bream baits. But any shellfish is worth trying. Shrimp, prawn, cockle and limpet are all effective, and in times of emergency I have even boated bream caught on the despised winkle.

Soft baits will not, of course, remain in place during casting, and since they are so easily torn from the hook, their use may appeal more to the sportsman who chooses to make things difficult for himself by giving the fish every chance! Nevertheless, it is possible to increase a soft bait's holding power by binding it to the shank with weak cotton. I have applied this idea to crab meat, a first-class lure. The job requires a certain knack, but this comes with practice. It is very necessary to scrape all turns of cotton free from the hook before mounting a fresh bait – otherwise the penetration of the hook will be greatly impeded.

Tail of hermit crab is a fine all-round bait that bream often find irresistible. You will find these tiny creatures living in empty whelk shells in the rock pools of undercliff beaches. Larger specimens can often be scrounged from lobster and crab fishermen. Sometimes civility and kind words are all that is required to raise a supply, but the bait is so valuable to the angler that almost any reasonable price will represent a profitable investment.

Controversy exists among experienced bream anglers as to whether or not the species feeds on certain strains of sea anemone. Personally, I am a fence sitter as far as this theory goes – though inclined to the belief that the fish seek not to eat the anemone itself, but rather the minute food particles collected on its tentacles. Clearly there is room for experiment here.

Lugworm, ragworm, cuttlefish and strips of pilchard, herring and mackerel are further suitable bream baits. Normal methods of baiting-up are satisfactory. When the fish are choosy it is often advantageous to trim fish strips into smallish pieces which are similar in shape to tiny fish. The use of mackerel skin slivers is a useful dodge – particularly in a tideway, where movement imparted by the current makes such a lure behave attractively lifelike.

Tackle and methods

It was one of those glorious June afternoons that somehow seem to have been far more frequent before the war than now. A jewel of a day, with everything sparkling in wind and sunlight. Nothing vicious about the breeze, though – just enough of a blow to set the yawl dancing in time to the lapping of waves against the clinker-built hull.

Conditions were perfect for catching bream from mid-water, but even in those days we knew that fish paid little regard to omens, or to anglers' wishes. So, lying some half-mile (0·804 km) off Brighton's Paston Place, with several shifts of mark behind us, we were all resigned to a blank day.

Then Freddie, who was fishing with a hand-line and single hook flowing trace set at midwater, hooked and landed a small black bream.

Such was my introduction to the species. Copying his hook mounting I took only three insignificant 8-oz (226 g) specimens that afternoon, but small as they were they taught me how a black bream can use its muscle and slab-sided body to take advantage of tide and wave. Although more experienced older friends advised me to adopt tackle and methods specifically designed to catch bream, impatience, plus a lacing of green, prevented me making such changes. Childlike, I wanted both jam and cake – bottom fish and bream – and all during the same session. Fortunately, I soon evolved a method which allowed me the best of both worlds. A method, with modifications, which proves a successful compromise to this day.

Basically, the rig is built around a rubber band fixed on the main-line at the required fishing depth. Simply fold the band over the line, pass it through its own bight, and draw tight.

A fine trace of 7 lb (3·1 kg) approximately breaking strain monofil – length dictated by existing tidal strength – is tied direct to a small, fine gauge hook of size 4, 6 or 8. The free end of the trace is then bent to the ring of a small, quick release swivel.

In practice, you lower the bottom tackle, wait until it has settled on the sea bed, then clip the swivel to the main-line. Providing there is sufficient tide to carry the line away at an obtuse angle, it will also carry the trace as far as, but not beyond, the rubber stop.

If a bream is captured it is necessary to retrieve only as far as the rubber stop. Should a fish be taken on the bottom tackle, unclip the swivel as it comes inboard and the rubber band will pass without hindrance through the rod rings until a normal retrieve is completed.

The method is hardly the acme of efficiency, but nevertheless it does add interest during those long hours when bites are few and far between – bites which are as likely to come from the bottom as from midwater. And the impatient, non-specialist type of angler should remember that his chances in midway are not necessarily limited to bream.

Like all compromises it has drawbacks. My chief objection to it lies in the comparatively heavy sinker weights required, which do not allow a very sporting species to display its fighting qualities to the full. In slackish water, where mini-

SEA BREAM

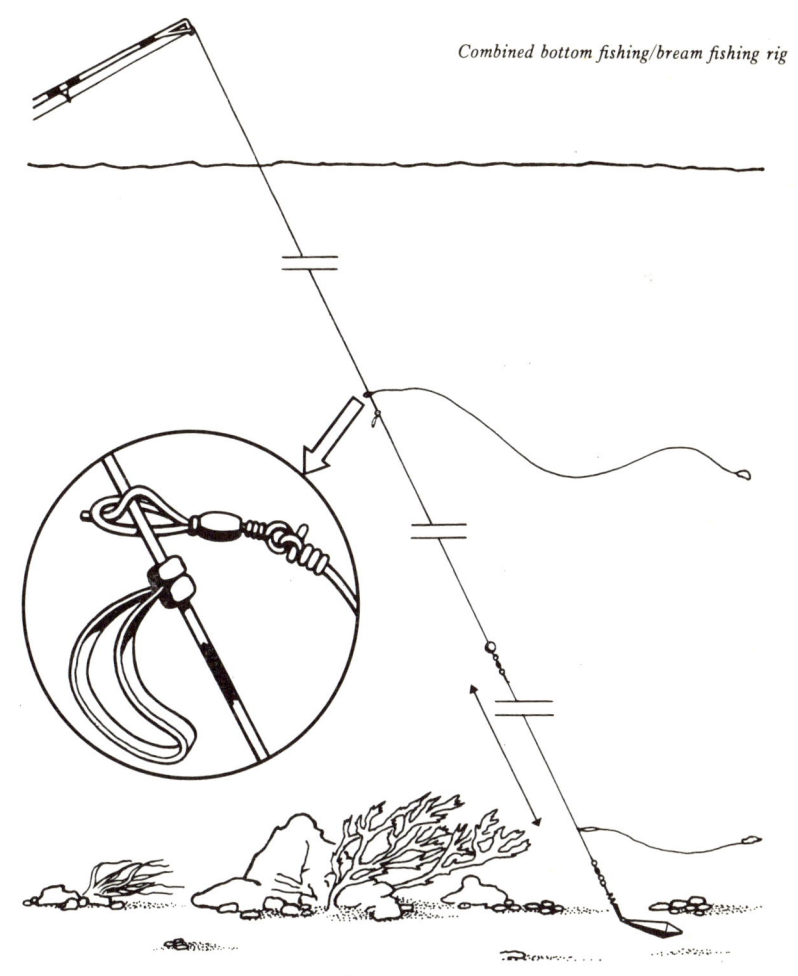

Combined bottom fishing/bream fishing rig

sinkers are sufficient to take a low breaking strain line to the bottom, this problem is not so bad, although I should point out that I have rarely experienced good black bream sport during very slow running tides.

Before dealing with specialized bream tackle, I must mention that next to mullet and flounder fishing, breaming is the nearest approach to coarse angling found in salt water.

A rod between 6 ft (1·8 m) and 8 ft (2·4 m), light, supple, and capable of casting a $1\frac{1}{2}$ oz (42 g) lead is ideal. Hollow glass is marginally better than solid glass. The reel is relatively unimportant, but it must match the rod. For boat fishing a small multiplier or centrepin leaves little to be desired. Shore fishing

Above, *trace fitting to prevent snarling* Top, *plastic anti-kink vane* Centre, *anti-kink drilled lead* Bottom, *drilled barrel lead*

10 - 15 LB.
(4·5 - 6·8 kg)
MAIN LINE

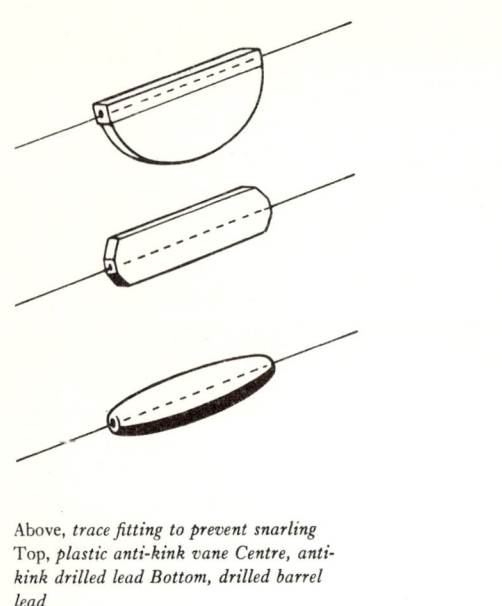

7 LB.
(3·2 kg)
TRACE

7 OR 10 LB.
(3·2 OR 4·5 kg)
LEAD LINK

BOMB LEAD

Right, *weak lead-link rig for fishing over snaggy bottoms. The strength of both the mainline and the lead link can be increased to suit the conditions*

demands a longer rod, and many anglers will probably be happier to use reels of fixed-spool design, though such a reel should not be too small.

Sea water contains an abundance of minute gritty particles held in suspension, and these, plus the salt, play havoc with both ultra light lines and the working parts of reels. I cannot honestly recommend a main-line of under 7 lb (3·1 kg) test, and 10 lb (4·5 kg) to 11 lb (4·9 kg) will give far better service. Both reel and line should be held under a running freshwater tap as soon after use as possible.

The secret, if it can be called that, of successful bream fishing is to present an apparently live bait. In essence this limits the terminal rig to a flowing trace with a single hook attached to the end. The use of swivels, anti-kink vanes and lightweight barrel trace leads, is incidental to, and governed by, prevailing conditions.

Nylon of 7 lb (3·1 kg) or even 5 lb (2·2 kg) breaking strain is ample for the trace. But although I like my reel lines to be soft and supple, I definitely prefer these light traces to be tied from a more springy brand, which has less tendency to twist back on itself and snarl-up during fishing.

To rig the trace to the main-line, I connect a three-way swivel as a link-up. A freely revolving boom is equally efficient, but my maxim is always to keep things as simple as possible. The sinker can be attached to the swivel by a short length of main-line strength monofil for fishing a sandy, snagless bottom, but when fishing a rocky-ground mark it is a better plan to select a link of lower breaking strain so that if the tackle gets snagged – as frequently it will – it can be broken free again with only the loss of the sinker.

The trace follows the pattern of that previously described, and can vary in length between 6 ft (1·8 m) and 3 ft (0·91 m).

Only experience of different combinations of fishing conditions can guide the angler to select the right match of trace length, line strength and terminal fittings.

Early season bream are usually located at any level between the bottom and a fathom or so above it. So lower the sinker until it touches bottom, retrieve approximately 3 yards (2·7 m) of line, and then let the reel revolve slowly until the bottom is again felt. Not only does this pattern of fishing effectively fish through a fathom's depth but, since the tide is continually working against the lead and line, more and more line is demanded and therefore a correspondingly greater area of the sea bed is covered. Ringing the changes with sinker weights of different sizes also aids the searching of a wide area.

Later in the year, when the shoals have broken up, it is necessary to fish through higher levels as well as near to the bottom. Do this by slowly retrieving line from the bottom until the first bite is registered. As with mackerel, bream are inclined to feed at a settled depth, so it is most important to count the revolutions of the reel during the retrieve. By allowing the same number of revolutions to turn out on the drop, the same depth can be reached again.

Two points to keep in mind here. Firstly, be sure to make allowance for the rise or fall of the tide. Secondly, when dropping the tackle overboard, lower the trace to the water and let it stream away before allowing the sinker to follow. Check the reel from revolving quickly to prevent the trace from snarling back around the main-line.

During slack water, or when the current is negligible, it is possible to use a float for bream. Unfortunately, the liking of these fish for deep water severely limits the use of this method. It is, however, always worth trying when circumstances are favourable.

Bream have a distinctive bite. When taking freely, they register a positive sharp tug followed by a fluttering knock, reminiscent of a dab bite. Generally speaking, the strike should be made not on the initial knock, but on the flutter. Here the angler experienced in freshwater fishing has a distinct advantage, since his instinctively gentle reaction is more likely to score than the stronger strike of the sea-only angler.

Bream bites can, nevertheless, be misleading. They may register as only the feeblest of nibbles, too weak to 'telegraph' through a stout rod – perhaps this is when bream are preoccupied with feeding on weed and the tiny creatures the weed contains. However, whatever the reason, it calls for a change in the normal strike routine. Sometimes nothing but a sharp reaction will hook a fish or, alternatively, a delayed response. Trial and error is the only way of finding out exactly what is required.

As with all 'at-anchor' fishing, groundbait is a considerable asset. Anything will suffice – mashed green crab, minced fish, discarded worm-bait or shellfish. Simply put the mixture into an onion sack and tie it to the anchor cable – either close to the bottom or at mid-water according to the feeding level of the fish, or the level at which the fish are thought to be feeding.

Black bream, though excellent fighters, do not run large. Specimens of 3 lb (1·3 kg) or 4 lb (1·8 kg) weight are rated good fish. Among outstanding black bream, the 6 lb 7 oz 12 drm (2·9 kg) fish caught by Mr J. L. D. Atkins from the Blackstone Rocks, Devon, and the 6 lb 5 oz (2·8 kg) fish caught by Mr M. Brown from the Menai Straits, are exceptional specimens. The larger of the pair was taken in 1973, and the smaller in 1935.

Red Bream

Virtually all the foregoing applies to red bream, with the exception that the shore angler stands a much better chance of catching this species than he does black bream.

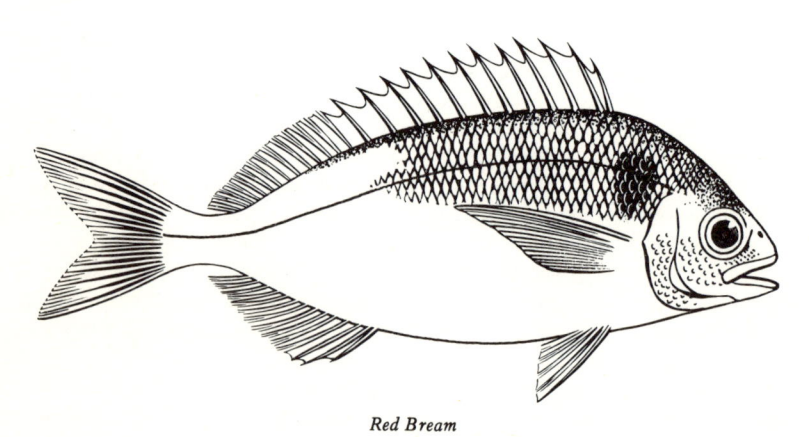

Red Bream

Red bream rarely venture far from rocky bottoms, and from early July onwards they can be taken in numbers anywhere along the Cornish coast. They are also reasonably plentiful off the rocky south and west shores of Ireland.

The greatest problem lies in locating a shoal, but once found the shore angler using float tackle can expect first-rate sport. Calm evenings on the neap tides offer the best of this fishing, both boat and shore. Peak feeding periods seem to run from half an hour before sunset to the sinking of the sun below the horizon. I have enjoyed marvellous sport at such times, with bream taking from the bottom so fast that it has been a continuous sequence of casting, striking and hauling up gleaming, fighting fish one after another.

Sport of this sort soon palls, however, and it is as well that the fish stop feeding with the suddenness of a thrown switch immediately the sun drops out of sight.

This is Cornish fishing, but in Ireland, though red bream can be taken easily enough during daytime, they definitely feed better still at night. Suitable venues are the rocky outcrops so familiar to visitors to the south and west coasts. Needless to add, these places are dangerous and the angler needs to take every precaution to prevent accidents. A really powerful torch is an essential item of equipment.

Baits, tackle and methods are as for black bream. Irish anglers also find mackerel feathers successful, and one day I intend to take feathering a stage further by trying for red bream with a pukka fly fishing outfit. I am convinced that if I can persuade my lure deep enough the rewards will be well worth the effort. Incidentally, for rock fishing with the float, I have never found any bait so successful as those wood-louse-like creatures called sea slaters, found in the crevices of sun-warmed rocks.

Red bream weighing over 9 lb (4 kg) have been captured in both British and Irish waters. A superb specimen weighing 9 lb 8 oz 12 drm (4·3 kg) fell to the rod of Mr B. H. Reynolds while boat fishing off Mevagissey, Cornwall, in 1974.

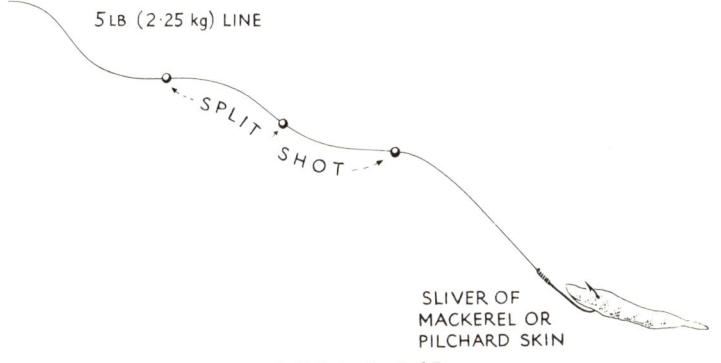

Drift-lining for Red Bream

It is interesting to note that red bream disappeared from the Irish coast just before the last war and only began to return during the mid-fifties. Since then they have been taken in increasing numbers and weights right round the south and west coasts, from Rosslare, in Co. Wexford, to Bunbeg in Donegal, and now they are almost as well-distributed as before the war. Popular red bream venues include Kinsale, Achill, Ballycotton, Valentia Island, Kilmore Quay, Belmullet and Dungarvan.

At times of flat calm and tidal slack, red bream may occasionally be taken from the rocks by drift-lining a single hook weighted with split-shot and baited with a sliver of mackerel or pilchard skin.

Ray's Bream

The ray's bream is of little interest to anglers and far too infrequently taken on rod and line to warrant specialized fishing. Most shore captures have come from very shallow water, where these fish have a curious habit of giving themselves up – not to hook and bait, but literally to the hands of anglers otherwise engaged in general fishing. Ray's bream taken fairly on rod and line are caught mainly from

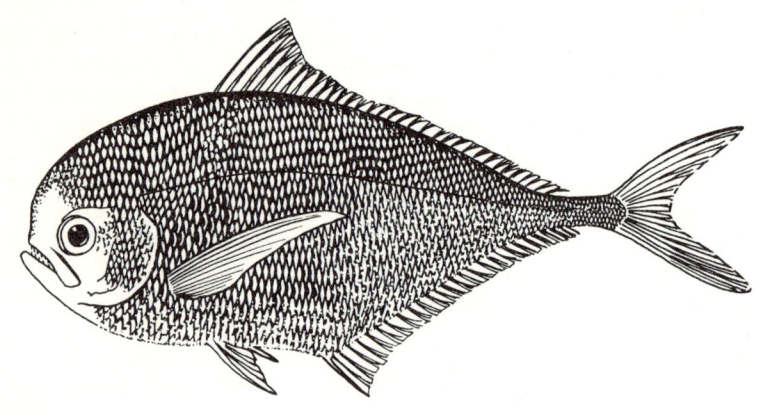

Ray's Bream

very deep water. A particularly large one fell to the rod of Mr G. Walker in 1967. Weighing 7 lb 15 oz 12 drm (3·6 kg), it came from Crimdon Beach, Hartlepool. The successful bait was mussel.

Red bream averaging only a few ounces are taken in their thousands from the western harbours of Cornwall during the summer months. Since these tiny creatures are rarely returned to the water, and call for no skill in the catching, I have ignored this aspect of breaming, and sincerely hope that all serious anglers will do the same.

BASS FISHING   *Brian Harris*

The Quarry – Its Range and Seasons

Shy, big and beautiful, a rugged opponent on the hook, the bass commands the same sort of admiration and respect from discerning saltwater anglers as barbel, carp and reservoir trout get from the freshwater men. Because I fish the year round for coarse, game and saltwater fish I am able to make comparisons, and I rate the bass as one of the most game and interesting fish the sporting angler can tackle – in fresh water or in the sea.

I am not a competition angler, nor am I a pot hunter – I prefer to fish in the quiet places, alone or with one or two companions, for fish that fight – yet few things would give me more pleasure than to catch the first properly ratified British specimen of 20 lb (9 kg) or more.

No sea fish – apart from the grey mullet perhaps – demands from a man the application of so many skills, the careful use of knowledge, hard-won at different times and in many places, for its regular capture. The bass attracts only those who are prepared to learn the lessons in the difficult schools of splendid surf beaches, estuaries and rocky shores.

Bass fishing is essentially a sport of the warmer months, late April to the end of October, perhaps, though in the West Country, western Wales and south-western Ireland the fish may be taken in winter, too. Most of my bass fishing has been done on the shores of Kent and Sussex, but I have had wonderful sport, even in November, January and February, in Kerry, where the Atlantic surf beaches can produce bass the year round.

Winter bass, wherever you fish them, are usually a smaller run of fish than those of the spring, summer and autumn, but a week in Kerry with the big white surfs running resplendent up the hard sands, from storms sired way out in the ocean between Dingle and the Americas, can make up for the smaller size of the bass.

The range of the main bass shoals in British waters seems to be between Anglesey and a point north of the Thames Estuary, although during some years a surprising number of fish are taken farther north of those points. Cumberland coasts have produced good bass fishing, the Whitehaven area in particular. Bass, mainly small shoal fish, are also regularly caught on parts of the west coast of southern Scotland, notably in Luce Bay between Drummore and Port William in Wigtown. Both these areas flank the Solway Firth which no doubt forms a catchment for the warm water of the North Atlantic Drift.

Although bass are most prolific on the south and south-west coasts of Ireland, south-west England and west Wales, the fringe areas seem to produce the bigger fish. Hence the 18 lb 2 oz (8·2 kg) specimen taken in 1943 from the beach at Felixstowe by Mr F. C. Borley, and the big fish regularly taken in the Menai Straits on the other side of the country.

In recent years, however, the south-east coastline of England has become far more prominent as a successful hunting ground for the man seeking big bass – much to my delight – and so has the Hampshire coast, particularly Highcliffe Beach and Hengistbury Head. Indeed, it has been my experience fishing Kent and Sussex coasts in the past few years to find plenty of bass in occupation and to rarely catch fish below 4 lb (1·8 kg). The average fish to my rod over the seasons of 1965, '66 and '67 scaled around 4 lb 8 oz (2 kg), including a good proportion of specimens over 7 lb (3·1 kg) with a top weight in 1969 of 11 lb (4·9 kg). My next biggest went 10 lb 2 oz (4·5 kg) and was caught in 1967. In the '74 and '75 seasons, the bassing was often exceptional, and average weights were well maintained at the areas of rocky shores where predatory commercials cannot easily pillage the stocks.

Another pattern has emerged, too: most good fish have fallen to ground fishing with big baits. More of this later.

Bass then, move inshore, into those areas they quit in the autumn, during April, give or taken a week or so. I believe they do so – in the south-east anyway – to spawn, for fish I catch at that time have often been in a ripe condition. The old theory that bass spawn in deep water does not impress me; I have caught little ones between 4 in. (10 cm) and 6 in. (15 cm) long in high summer while mullet fishing with harbour ragworm, three miles (4·8 km) upstream of the estuary in the Rother, east Sussex.

I believe bass establish communities along specific areas of coastline, moving into deeper water offshore perhaps with a westerly inclination, for the winter and returning in the spring. This is one reason for militant action by sea anglers against commercial fishing for bass – an efficient fishing team can probably come close to clearing a bass population from an area of water.

I also believe bass have two types of feeding pattern. One pattern which seems prevalent in clear water conditions – like those of the West Country, west Wales and the Atlantic coast of Ireland – involves chasing fish like mackerel, brit, small flatfish, sandeels and other small fry. The other, found particularly in the south-east where the water inshore is mainly turbid due to river washings from clay country, involves bottom feeding, particularly among rocks, and on the more exposed shingle beaches and in estuaries, probably carried out mainly by scent.

I have also detected a difference in the appearance of western, clear-water feeding fish, and those which grub around in the murk of the south-east. The former, smaller on average, seem to me to be slimmer, more silvery fish with pointed noses and smallish mouths; the bottom feeders seem to be bigger and more portly on average, darker in colouring with bronze overtones and large mouths. Slim, fast fish for chasing quick-moving prey; portly rugged fish with vast mouths for browsing the bottom for crabs, squid and cuttlefish, offal and the like. Of course, there is an overlap of feeding patterns but the variation is sufficient to permit a division.

All bass are extremely slow growing. The 10 lb 2 oz (4·5 kg) fish I caught in 1967 was a little over 15 years old; the 11 lb (4·5 kg) fish I caught two years later was the same age. While it is true to say the females attain far greater weights than males, there is a new awareness that big male bass do occur; again this has shown up to a greater extent in Kent and Sussex than elsewhere – another pointer in favour of the local community theory – although some big Irish males turned up in 1967 during the survey conducted by The Inland Fisheries Trust led by Dr Michael Kennedy.

It was once a popular belief that male bass seldom exceeded about 4 lb (1·8 kg). In the past few years I have taken south-east males to around 8 lb (3·6 kg) – not just odd fish either. One day in May 1967, while fishing the rocks at Fairlight, Sussex, I landed three males between nearly 6 lb (2·7 kg) and 7 lb 12 oz (3·5 kg)! Big males seem to turn up in rocky, shallow-water areas in spring.

The south-east also produces fish which appear to have a quicker growth rate than those farther west.

Fishing Techniques and Tackle

Please remember when you come to bass fishing – if you are not already an enthusiast – that you are pitting yourself against what the *afficionado* believes to be the finest fish that inhabits our inshore waters. Not only is he a good fighter, but he is also one of the most difficult saltwater fish to catch consistently through a season.

Sporting considerations apart, this means you must use the lightest tackle to take the bigger fish in calm conditions, although from time to time big bass do fall to the guileless, heavy-handed brigade, armed with their long-distance casting 'poles', metal spreaders and other ironmongery – but these catches mostly occur in thick rough water following an onshore blow. Most bass, especially big fish, are caught by ground fishing – and this is true even of those clear-water areas I have already mentioned. My personal opinion is that there is more skill involved in legering effectively for bass from the shore, in varying conditions, than there is in most other bass fishing techniques.

Bass are predators, and they are caught by spinning from shore vantage points, or from boats, using long, silver wobbling spoons like Toby and Condor, rubber and plastic eels or dead sandeels on flights, or strips of mackerel, squid or cuttlefish. Other methods include float fishing with sandeel, peeler or soft crab or prawns or small fish like pouting, wrasse and blennies (especially in rocky gullies) and drifting lightly loaded tackle down a tideway from a boat or shore vantage point. Trolling is also extremely rewarding. An 18 lb 6 oz (8·3 kg) bass has been taken by this method off the Eddystone Reef, Plymouth. The captor was Mr R. Slater.

All these methods – apart from the use of float-fished crab baits among the rocks – are only consistently effective in clear seas and are mainly used to catch the smaller, shoaling fish.

Let us face it, there is not that much skill in spinning in the sea – witness the heavy catches once regularly made over the Splaugh Reef in Ireland – unless you are fishing in rocky gullies where spot-on accuracy in casting is called for. Neither is drift-lining or trolling that demanding of personal skill, although good boat handling enters into it. Yet the fighting qualities of a bass do show best on the type of light tackle used in spinning, trolling, drift-lining and float fishing, although, as we shall see later, there is often no need to use heavier gear for some ground fishing from the shore.

The same gear may be used for spinning, drift-lining, trolling and float fishing – and some lighter aspects of ground fishing. The most versatile outfit consists of a hollow glass carp-, pike- or medium salmon-spinning rod of the normal 10 ft (3 m), two-piece construction, and with salt-water-proof fittings, with a small multiplier – like the Ambassadeur 5000 or 6000 and the cheaper ABU 3000 – loaded with 8 lb (3·6 kg) to 10 lb (4·5 kg) monofil. Use a fixed-spool reel if you must, but I dislike them for any purpose other than throwing ultra-light baits and in the outlined bass fishing techniques you are seldom likely to be casting a rig weighing in total much under 1 oz (28 g).

Multipliers give a more direct contact with the terminal tackle, and with a fighting fish, and they cast better and more accurately, too. The only fishing where you will need something different from the 8 lb (8·1 kg) to 10 lb (4·5 kg) monofil is drift-lining, where you want a line to possess a section thick enough to be held by the water and taken out on a tidal current without too much lead; the requirement is adequately met by braided terylene of about 12 lb (5·4 kg) breaking strain. One point here: make sure you ask for a solid braid line. Lines braided over a core are not to be trusted, I find.

The glass salmon/pike/carp rod, the little multiplier and 8 lb (8·1 kg) to 10 lb

(4·5 kg) monofil will be found a beautiful combination for a great deal of estuary legering where lead bombs of no more than 1½ oz (42 g) are used. But for ground fishing from real whitewater surf beaches — like those in the West Country, west Wales and the south and south-west of Ireland — and for a first-line outfit for ground fishing from quieter shingle beaches, and for legering among rocks, you will need an outfit a little more substantial.

In the first edition of this book I had to say there was no factory-made rod suitable for light tackle ground fishing for bass from the shore, but since then there has been a great increase in the number of anglers pursuing this aspect of saltwater angling and the rod makers have just had to produce the goods.

The rod needs to be of good hollow-glass construction, 10 ft 6 in. (3·2 m) to 11 ft (3·3 m) long, and weighing no more than about 16 oz (453 g). That means no heavy reel fittings, no metal ferrules, no cumbersome rings. It does mean hollow-glass spigot joint. Fuji reel clip or the use of simple hose-clip type clamps, and nothing more than a slim skeleton cork handle or a length of rubber or plastic tube or a wrapped handle of tape of the same materials for something comfortable to hold. Rings should be centre-supported hard-chromed, from about 1 in. (2·5 cm) inside diameter for the butt ring to about 3/16 in. (4·7 mm) for the tip ring. I used to be a fan of the hard tungsten carbide tip ring, but having had so many of them crack or break when the rod bangs a rock, shingle or whatever, I have now, like many other bass anglers, abandoned them.

A rod like this is so easy to make — it takes in all about three hours — that I am amazed so many commercially made rods are sold. You can make a rod to suit yourself perfectly, and for roughly half the price of a good rod from a shop. Suitable blanks are produced by Fibatube, Sportex, Carroll-McManus, North-Western, Lerc.

Companies producing completed bass rods for the job include Milbro Sport, Hardy Brothers, Bruce and Walker, Modern Arms, Going Brothers, Essex Angling Centre, Don's of Edmonton.

There are a number of reels that make good companions for a light bass rod, and the need is for something with a light but strong spool to hold about 200 yards (182·8 m) of 12 lb (5·4 kg) to 15 lb (6·8 kg) monofil and which will run fast and smoothly when casting leads of 2 oz (56 g)–3 oz (85 g). Seldom does even a double-figures bass run much more than 50 yards (45·7 m) in one burst, even in a strong tideway or shallow water, but you will need a reserve of line if, as often happens, a tope, sting ray or smooth hound picks up your bass bait.

Suitable reels include Penn Baymaster and Surfmaster 100, both with plastic spools, not metal, the ABU Ambassadeur range, and the very similar Daiwa Millionnaire. The Ambassadeurs are excellent but very expensive: the very best of the range for bass fishing is the 6500C which has a rapid recovery rate which is useful when retrieving the gear over rocky ground or when a bass in the surf decides to dash towards you and can throw the hook if slack line is gained.

For those who need to use a fixed-spool reel or who prefer them, the Mitchell

Intermediate, ABU Cardinals 66 and 77 and the DAM Quick Finessa light saltwater models are hard to better.

From this point on I shall be discussing the ground fishing techniques which have worked best for me. I have caught bass by spinning and float fishing, but I do not do enough of either to be able to offer very much useful advice. Too many writers on angling deal with species of fish and techniques of fishing by plagiarism because although they have little or no personal experience, they feel obliged to pretend they have.

My personal experience – and the results of many other anglers whose exploits are reported – prove that (as I have said before) ground fishing from the shore in one form or another results in the capture of most big bass; this trend includes those areas in which clear water conditions predominate and in which spinning, float fishing, etc., are also carried out more than ground fishing.

The best way to deal with ground fishing techniques as I practice them is to divide the fishing into four kinds: surfcasting, which includes fishing into the more gentle waves found on beaches other than the pure surf beaches washed by the Atlantic; fishing into rocky ground; fishing from piers and similar projections; and fishing estuaries.

Surfcasting

First let us examine surfcasting. You are to fish a sandy strand in the south-west of Ireland or west Wales where, even during calm weather, there will be four or five lines of white-crested breakers rolling in with wide tables of water between them. This surf comes from the Atlantic swell and is sometimes increased by onshore wind or ocean storms.

Bass love this aerated habitat and roam its mostly clear water in great shoals. They are likely to average about 2 lb 8 oz (1·1 kg) with the occasional big ones. There seldom appears to be much food in the real Atlantic-bred surf – but the fish will mostly take lugworm widely. Other good baits are razorfish or clam and strips of squid or cuttlefish.

You need the 16 oz (453 g) rod and 15 lb (6·8 kg) line with a 3 oz (85 g) bomb for this fishing. If the surf is heavy and the bomb rolls too quickly into the shallows you can use the same size bomb equipped with 2 in. (5 cm) stainless steel anchor wires. 'Breakaway' leads are best.

Sometimes a cast upwards of 100 yards (91·4 m) will be needed; at other times, especially when the surf is wild and the day dull, or after dark, a 40 yard (36·5 m) lob will put the bait among the fish.

For long casting and to avoid tangling in the turbulent water, I suggest you make up a simple nylon paternoster. Tie a No. 8 barrel swivel to the reel line, using the tucked half-blood knot, then tie an 18 in. (45 cm) length of the same line to the free eye of the swivel. Take another piece of nylon about 1 yard (0·91 m) long and join it to the piece you have tied to the swivel, using the blood knot

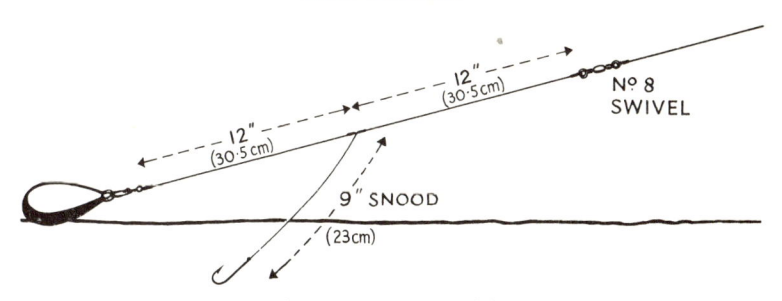

Nylon paternoster for surf fishing

and leaving one end coming out at right angles about 1 ft (0·3 m) long. To this you tie, with the tucked half-blood knot, a fine wire bronzed hook; I recommend the Mustad Round No. 79510. About a 3/0 size is right. The remaining end of nylon takes a small simple lead link and the 3 oz (85 g) bomb. Measurements from the swivel are: to blood knot − 1 ft (0·3 m); blood knot to lead link − 1 ft (0·3 m); blood knot to hook − 9 in. (22 cm). Load the well-sharpened hook with lugworm, one large one or several small ones, making sure they lie tail first straight up the shank (the tail is firmer than the head end) to cut down wind resistence and increase casting distance.

Try a long cast first, wading into the surf knee-deep (if you wear thigh boots) or deeper if you have chest-high waders. Take up the slack and stand comfortably with the rod held ready for an instant strike. Some hold the tip high − this is necessary to keep the tackle out there in a big surf which holds floating weed − but in a moderate surf I like to cradle the rod with the tip low and almost parallel with the shore, both for comfort and quick striking and also to receive every movement 'telegraphed' up the line from the terminal tackle.

If bites do not come within (say) 20 minutes, reel in about 20 yards (18·2 m) of

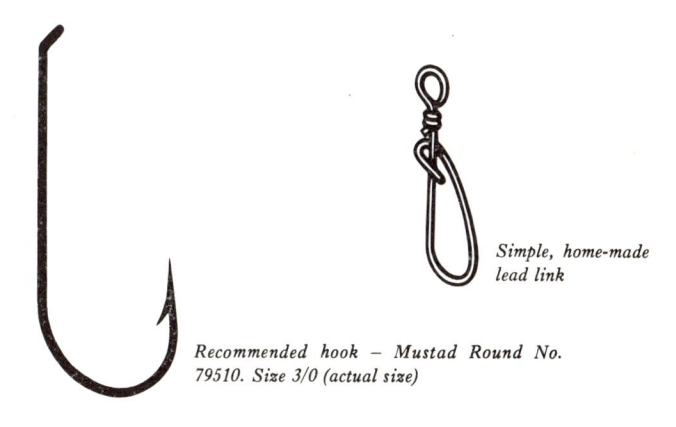

Simple, home-made lead link

Recommended hook − Mustad Round No. 79510. Size 3/0 (actual size)

line, slowly, and repeat the operation at intervals until either fish are located or the tackle is too close to the shallows to be effective.

Once bites come you must remember the distance and cast accurately each timem Bass shoals on surf beaches tend to run laterally along the surf between two lines of breakers.

Bites can be of several types. The most common seems to be a rapid slackening of the line as the fish shifts the lead, and the others are a hard pull, jagging lunge or a sharp double knock. All these should be hit hard and instantly; the slack line bite results in most fish hooked if you strike correctly, and this means moving smartly away from the water, running even, to take up the slack before banging the hook home. Monofil stretches.

Some people still hold the view that only the flood tide is worth fishing, and many surf beaches do fish best at this time, but many also fish best on the ebb. It is advisable, therefore, to get local knowledge before you fish.

Bass inhabit very shallow water, especially when the water is turbulent, and bites will often come when the tackle lies at a depth of less than 1 ft (0·3 m). You will sometimes wade out to cast and have bass flurry away from your feet, or see them swirling *behind* you. Surf beaches are shallows in the main, and even casts of 100 yards (91·4 m) may put the bait into only about 5 ft (1·5 m) of water. One comes to learn that depth is not the point to consider where bass fishing is concerned. Surf beaches often have streams of fresh water running across them and these nearly always attract bass.

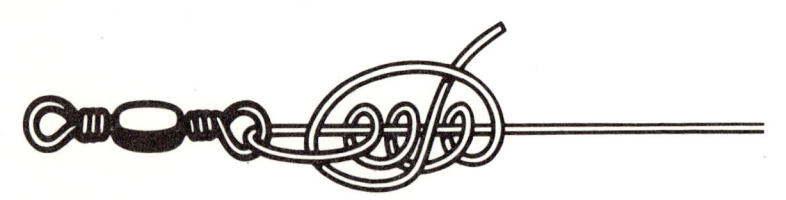

Tucked half-blood knot for attaching hooks and swivels. The nylon is passed through the eye, and twisted at least three times round its own part, before being taken through the space next to the swivel eye; then finally through the large loop

Other Open Beaches

Fishing the steeper, open beaches, on the south and south-east coast of England, and other shingle or sand beaches which are not true surf beaches, imposes some different problems, and requires a variation in tactics.

The same outfit is used, although lateral currents may be more powerful, demanding the more frequent use of the wired bomb to hold out. The water is likely to be more coloured and, when there is a strong onshore wind, or after a gale, the rollers are likely to be high, but the extent of the breaking water covers a short distance from the beach. When the water is rough the nylon paternoster

PLATE 1

Fishing into rocky ground from a ledge at the base of sheer cliffs. For this type of fishing it is necessary to know the exact height of the tide, and to take into consideration weather conditions which might make such a narrow perch dangerous at high water

Photo:
A. Nevison

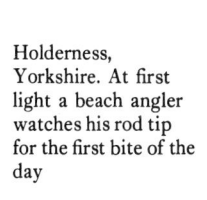

Holderness, Yorkshire. At first light a beach angler watches his rod tip for the first bite of the day

Photo:
Ernest Merritt

PLATE 2

A club competition in progress on Tynemouth Pier, Northumberland. Conditions are breezy, but in the warmth of suitable clothing, adverse elements mean little to the hardy sea angler

*Photo:
John Hanney*

A rock gully 'somewhere' in Cornwall, and Trevor Housby's rod bends to the pull of a good wrasse

*Photo:
Trevor Housby*

PLATE 3

Off Brodick, Isle of Arran, a fighting fish is brought struggling to the surface and lifted inboard with the aid of a landing net

Photo:
Ernest Merritt

Feathering for mackerel to be used as bait. Light tackle methods should be employed to get any sport from this species

Photo:
Winston Hall

PLATE 4 Evening fishing at Sallyport, Portsmouth. The high tide washes over the pier, to which fish are attracted by the warm water discharge from a nearby electricity station

Photo: S. Woodriffe

PLATE 5

A superb common skate of 114 lb (51·7 kg). Caught off the Isle of Mull, Scotland, it fell for a double fillet of mackerel bait fished on a wire line, and took 1 hour 20 minutes to beat

Photo:
Trevor Housby

Thornback ray, belly up and beaten, ready for gaffing

Photo:
Ernest Merritt

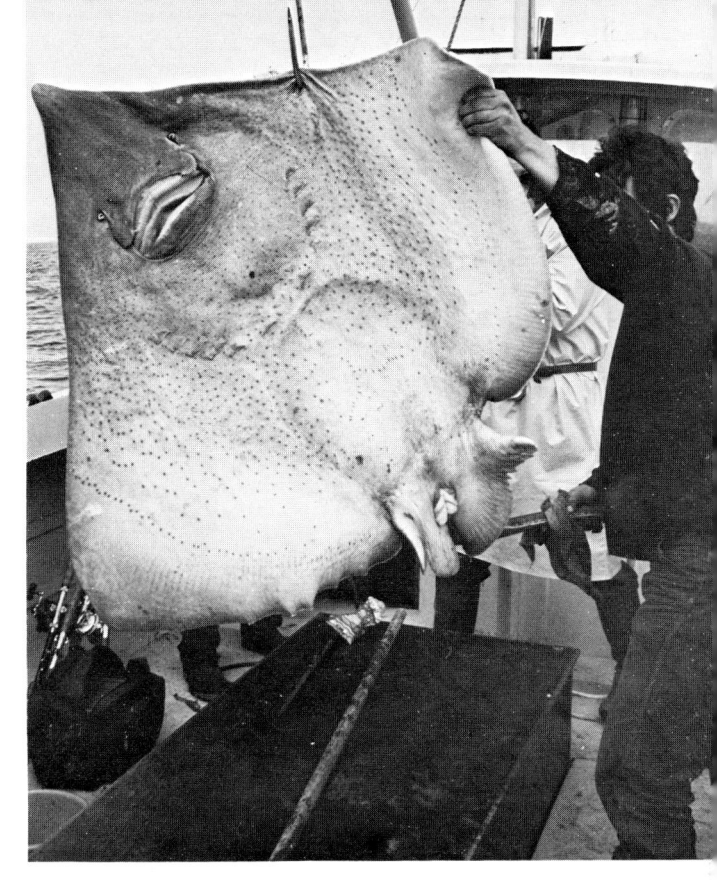

PLATE 6

Without doubt the angler fish is one of the ugliest of the saltwater species in British waters. This large-mouthed, toothy specimen caught at Milford Beach, Hampshire, is typical of its kind

Photo: Trevor Housby

Well-known all-rounder, Ron Barnett, weighs in a monkfish at 43 lb (19·5 kg)

Photo: Trevor Housby

PLATE 7

Almost to the surface, a huge monkfish – the mackerel bait can still be seen protruding from its jaws
Photo: Trevor Housby

A catch of fine tope. In the interests of conservation it would have been better if they had been returned alive to the sea
Photo: John Lawson Reay

PLATE 8
Looking well pleased with himself, a boat angler displays a fine cod
Photo: Trevor Housby

A red gurnard, ugly to look at but excellent eating. The 'feelers', three on each side near the pectorals, assist in finding food and in locomotion

Photo: Edward Hincliffe

BASS FISHING

used for the true surf beach will suffice, for in these conditions bass will take savagely. But in conditions of relative calm a running paternoster will give better results, for then the fish may sample the bait tentively before engulfiing it in that vast mouth. Failure to give line freely at the sampling stage will often cause the fish to drop the bait.

Make up the paternoster by threading a No. 8 swivel on the reel line, then sliding on 1 in. (2·5 cm) of hard plastic tubing or a bead as a stop before tying another swivel to the end of the line. To the free eye of this swivel tie about 1 ft (0·3 m) of monofil and your hook. To the swivel running on the main line tie 2 ft (0·61 m) of monofil which takes the lead.

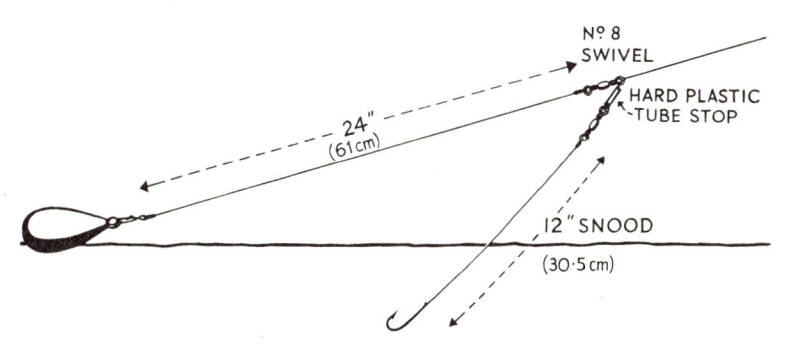

Running paternoster for open beaches. The bomb weight may be from 2 to 4 oz (50 – 100 g), and the link between weight and swivel, for rough ground fishing, reduced to 9 lb B.S. (4 kg) to enable breaks without the loss of the hook

My experiences have led me to have little faith in lugworm on these beaches, and not much more in razorfish. Lugworm attracts small bass and flatfish and other 'unwanted' species, so I give the bass a big bait, such as a whole side fillet of a fresh mackerel, a complete head from a fair-sized squid or cuttlefish, or a strip, or a large crab. I have caught fish on a herring head with the entrails attached and on large pieces of kipper, especially in dirty rough water. Some baits go well in some areas, others in different places – so again seek local knowledge.

Bass have vast mouths and a 6 lb (2·7 kg) specimen, for example, will swallow a 12 oz (340 g) mackerel in one gulp, so fish your big baits on big hooks. The Mustad pattern mentioned, in size 5/0 – the biggest I have been able to buy – works well. Also remember that a big hook carrying a big bait takes a lot of pull to sink it past the barb in the boney maw of a big bass; so use fine wire hooks – always, and keep them sharp! Personally, I do not favour stainless steel or nickel-coated hooks for bass fishing; I like hooks of bronzed steel, which blend with most baits and have no 'flash' which may arouse suspicion.

These big baits I recommend may at first look ridiculous but if you want to sort the wheat from the chaff, persevere with them. Of course casting presents a problem and you have to learn how to lob a big bait and a 2 oz (56 g) or 3 oz (85 g) lead some 50 yards (45·7 m) with a slow-motion swing of your flexible rod.

Bites in these circumstances can also vary, from a nerve-shattering smash take, which can pull the rod from your hand – or from a rod rest for that matter – to a series of very gentle plucks which may lead to a smooth strikable run away from you, or a sensation that the lead is being bounced on the sea bed, line slackening at the same time. Both the run and the bouncing slack line should be hit firmly.

When fishing these steeper southeast type shingle/sand beaches with big baits during or after a blow, it is possible to catch bass by fishing the rod in the rest. You really need a monopod to keep the rod nearly vertical so that line is kept clear of surf. Fish a slack line with the running paternoster and have the check on the reel – light clutch as well if the pull of water repeatedly takes line against the check – when the reel is in free spool.

You must watch the rod closely, of course, and pick it up gently when a pluck registers. Sometimes you will get a screaming check-run which you hit, if the line is still peeling off the reel when you grab the rod.

Again my personal experience on these beaches have been that, although the flood may normally be fished with optimism, there are times when it is fruitless and the fish feed on the ebb. I and my bass fishing friends have taken good fish at all stages of the tide.

A worthwhile point to always remember, I feel, in these days of so-called 'scientific angling' is that it is the bait in the water which catches the fish. In other words, fish hard at all stages of the tide; there is no such thing as a bad time – some stages of tide are better than others – on some days!

When using your light surf outfit for these types of fishing you will – if you have fished alongside any of the heavy-handed brigade – have appreciated how your tackle has held position with only the 3 oz (85 g) lead while they have trouble holding with the 6 oz (170 g) lead. Your fine line is the answer, cutting the water cleanly – that and your anchor wires when you use them.

Many shore anglers have only one solution to the problems of drifting gear – a heavier lead. If they used finer lines and lighter leads with stainless steel wires they would see the light! Anyway, slowly drifting gear is sometimes an advantage.

Rocky Ground

Now let us look at rocky ground. It is this type of fishing that requires most skill and results in the capture of most big bass.

The best ground is where low, loosely bedded rocks and stones, with sand or shingle patches between them, are revealed at low water. The depth over the fishable area (from the last high-water mark) need not be more than 4 ft (1·2 m) or 5 ft (1·5 m), but try to avoid fishing inshore of unbroken reefs or high banks of sand or stones as these tend to make bass quit the area soon after the ebb begins.

Ideal spots are where big rocks reach out to sea in long fingers with ledges up which you may retreat before the incoming tide. If there are cliffs behind, make sure you are not trapped at their base by the high water. In fact, the ideal rock fishing situation proves to be the exception rather than the rule and you have to make the best of the ground.

Naturally the first thing to do is to examine the ground at low water. If you arrive towards the end of the ebb you can do your survey and collect crabs for bait at the same time. I like to find boulders – about football size – and flat slabs of rocks with pools of water between, when I make a low-water survey. I like to see some weed on the rocks and I like larger scaurs of rock to be close by but I make sure never to fish on the downtide flank of any seaward projection of rock. This has proved to be a barren area; it is better to fish on the side on to which the current flows so that it forms a food trap.

Most learners at bass fishing over rocky ground make the mistake of looking for snag-free areas. Certainly you should try to find spots where you can drop your bait into gullies or on patches between the rocks and boulders. But do not look for wide open sand patches for the fish will be looking for crabs and small fish in the rocks – and there is where your bait must be. In fact, some of my best fishing, and some of the best fishing I have seen others do, has been when throwing caution to the winds and casting bang into the rocks. Of course you will lose tackle but you can often get it back as the tide recedes – and you will get the good fish!

Use the surf rod and small multiplier with 15 lb (6·8 kg) line and make up a running paternoster, as for fishing the big bait in relatively calm conditions from an open beach. Use a length of nylon of about 9 lb (4 kg) breaking strain to attach the lead to the running swivel so that if the lead – it can be any old piece of metal if you do not fancy risking a lead sinker – snags, you lose only that and retrieve the hook, together with the bass you might have hooked! My advice when fishing the rocks is to use the Mustad bronzed hook I have mentioned, in size 5/0, nothing less. And keep the hook link short – I often have it less than 1 ft (0·3 m) – to prevent the bait from washing under the rocks (or being pulled there by crabs), to aid casting, and most important, to enable you to feel more quickly the first, often subtle, plucking of a big bass.

This is the crux of the matter when fishing for rock-feeding bass; although the odd fish may take the bait with a lunging run, most bites, especially from big fish, will be initially 'telegraphed' up the line to your thumb (which should be resting on it lightly) so gently you may think a little fish or a crab is messing about.

In very calm weather, when the water has barely the impetus to break against the rocks and the water is clear, so that you can see the dark patches of weed waving beneath the surface, you may get only a twitch at which to strike – or a slight slackening of the line. Yet, in the same conditions, the first gentle indication may be only the start of the bite; yield slack line to avoid giving the bass any inkling that something is wrong and you may get a firm run of several yards at which to strike.

This is the main problem with rock-feeding bass, especially when using crab baits. They are adept at taking a crab without registering more than a tickle on the line. I do not believe in this oft-quoted sixth-sense business, but the fact remains that I have often found myself with a fish on, having struck unconsciously at *something*. This has occurred with sufficient regularity when I have been fishing close to friends with identical tackle and bait, who have gone fishless, to convince me that a person may, after many years of bass hunting, become very sensitive to tiny movements of the line, or get on the bass wavelength, so to speak.

You have to learn to distinguish between strikable twitches or slack line bites and those twitches which will develop into firm runs of several yards. You have a split second to make the decision: hit it or leave it. You also have to learn that rock-feeding bass only deal with soft and peeler crabs in this pernickety fashion. These big, solitary fish will take a squid head, a lead, a large strip or a whole side of fresh mackerel with the sort of rush that a taking tope makes – sometimes, that is!

All the time you are fishing you must retain in your mind the picture of the ground as you saw it at low water. You can cast into that interesting gully, or that one, and perhaps try another cast into a cluster of weed-covered stones where you found so many crabs earlier on.

A few words about baits are appropriate here. Soft crabs may be simply mounted on the big hook and secured with green elasticated thread (only a few pence a reel at haberdashers') so that the point stands well clear. It should be put in under the V-shaped part of the belly at the back of the crab's body, out and through again. Tie some of the rear legs above the shank of the hook to support it when casting. Some people use treble hooks for mounting crabs, but I do not like them because often two hooks meet the jaw and neither goes properly home.

Peelers must be peeled completely – and that means the panel-like belly shell as well as the carapace. Many anglers remove only the carapace and then wonder why they miss fish. The answer is that bass can bite off the soft body, leaving the belly shell and legs. The shell can also smother the hook point, so peel the whole crab carefully and remove all the legs except one at each side at the back end. Tie these above the hook as with the 'softie'.

After experimenting with various methods of hooking a squid head, I now simply put the hook in through the severed side and out about 3/4 in. (19 mm) back. With a large strip – say 6 in. (15 cm) by 2 in. (5 cm) – I put the hook in near one end and thread it through about three times so that the point finally emerges approximately half-way along with some of the strip pulled on to the nylon above the eye.

I hook sides of mackerel in the same way, through the tail end first, but tied above the hook eye with elasticated thread.

Piers and Jetties

Few types of fishing appeal to me less than fishing from the heights of piers, jetties and harbour walls. My pet aversion to them, I think, is that they are normally crowded and to my mind pier anglers, on the whole, lack the expertise possessed by many who fish from beaches and rocks.

Most piers are badly placed for bass fishing. On most, fishing is restricted to the pier head while the bass are further inshore hunting the surf line, yet some piers and harbour walls do yield good bass at times. Main points to have in mind are that bass are more likely to be found browsing around the pier supports or among the rubble along the bottom of the wall, so fish close to piles and walls instead of casting out a long way to open sand.

You can float fish with ragworm, prawn, crab or fish strip, using the carp-type rod and 10 lb (4·5 kg) breaking-strain line, or leger with a running lead. One good legering bait for piers, etc., is a small, live pouting, fished on a trace between 4 ft (1·2 m) and 6 ft (1·8 m) long. Some piers and walls have a tide race off one corner and bass, being lovers of turbulence, will be found there. A bait can be worked down a tide race and cover a lot of ground if the right amount of lead is found to drift and hold, drift and hold, when the rod tip is raised and lowered.

Estuaries

Next to rock fishing I enjoy fishing estuaries. The bass are a mixed crowd usually, with shoal fish running alongside the big, solitary specimens. With a few exceptions you will be able to use the lightest of the three outfits and a 1 oz (28 g) bomb rigged running leger or running paternoster style. Baits as for rock fishing.

Estuaries have great character and each one is a law unto itself. It may be stony or of sand or mud, or a mixture of all three. There may be no weed, or masses of it. The fish may feed best on the flood or on the ebb – or at differing times on different occasions. My favourites are small estuaries that almost dry out at low water, leaving a narrow channel to the sea and being perhaps less than 10 yards (91·4 m) wide at the junction with the sea.

One such estuary kept its secret for three years while I fished it with my bass-hunting friends. We caught good fish during that time but we never really discovered the complete pattern of movement of the fish. We knew they ran in with the flood alongside a low rock-strewn and weed-covered wall affair, and that was where we laid ambush for them. There were numbers of fine fish to 8 lb 8 oz (3·8 kg) taken, and one evening when I fished there alone in September, I hooked a monster bass – all of 15 lb (6·8 kg), I guessed – which when hooked made a long, surface run, showing me his great dorsal and broad back before rolling over the line and coming adrift. That happened after I had landed a fish of 8 lb 8 oz (3·8 kg)!

However, one day the tide was getting well down and we prepared to pack up. We always reckoned that by then the fish which had been up the river had come back past us and had moved out to sea. We used to get them halfway down the ebb, often in a hectic half-hour spell before the ebb run of water moved away from our vantage point, leaving just a wild race of water between 2 ft (0·61 m) and 3 ft (0·91 m) deep close to a low wall.

I had a nice crab on, however, as the others began to pack, so I went down, waded through a shallow of fast water running over the wall and lobbed the little bomb downtide and across. The current swept it down and towards the sunken wall. The lead held momentarily, rolled, held again. It came to rest not 2 ft (0·61 m) away from the wall and some 40 yards (36·5 m) downtide of me, when the rod was slammed round and I was fighting a good bass. That day I took two more nice fish from that shallow racing water and we had at last found where the bass went after we had lost track of them during those previous three years.

Few would have guessed they would wait those extra minutes in that sort of water before dropping back over the sand bar. Since that day of discovery we have had many fine bass from that little spot, the best just over 10 lb (4·5 kg) to my rod. Since that day we have discovered the shallow race is best fished with the carp/salmon/pike rod, 10 lb (4·5 kg) breaking strain line, Ambassadeur reel and 1 oz (28 g) bomb. Several fish have made powerful runs of 50 yards (45·7 m) or so, and on that light gear provide exhilarating sport.

This is another example of shallow water holding bass. A rocky and stony estuary we fish on occasions has yielded bass that have had barely 1 ft (0·3 m) of water over their backs. This one, too, fishes well on the ebb. It also yields fish at other stages of the tide, and the hotspot is where the overfall of the water coming downriver meets the incoming breakers, creating a maelström of white water. Turbulence equals bass. Remember? And the depth at that state of the tide? About 2 ft (0·61 m)!

So there it is. This has been my view of bass fishing for sport.

I love all my fishing – trout, salmon, carp, barbel, pike, cod and tope – but each spring, when the rocks begin to show their covering of fresh green weed and the crabs begin to move inshore again, I get that old tingling feeling and take up my bass tackle once more.

It is bass fever. One sickness from which I wish never to recover.

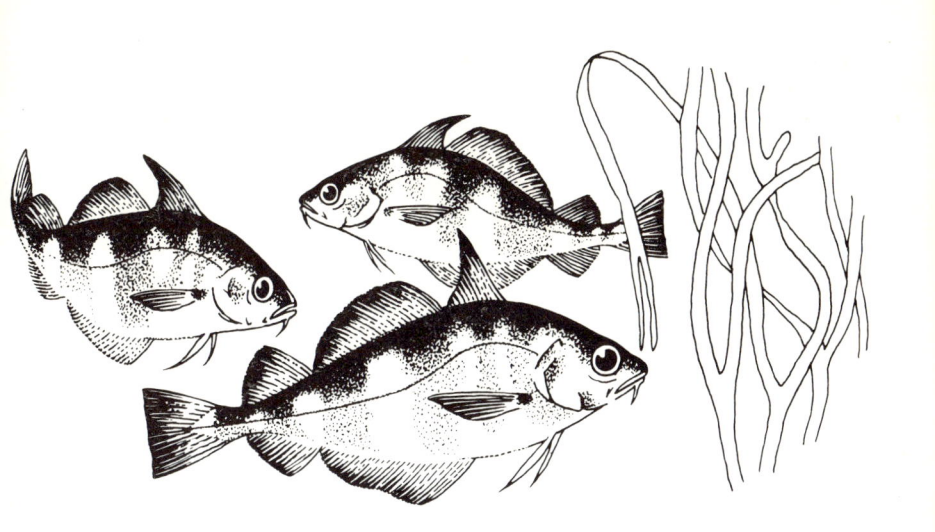

FISHING FOR FLOUNDER, SOLE, DAB, HADDOCK AND POUTING
Derek Fletcher

Flounder

The commonest of the flatfish species found in British waters is the flounder, or fluke as it is known in some areas. They are caught in good numbers by anglers from the beach, and from piers, groynes and inshore boats, although the best bags come from muddy creeks and harbours. Occasional useful sized specimens are caught from tidal rivers, for this is a species possessed of a strong liking for fresh water. Average size fish weigh around the 1 lb (·45 kg) mark, but they do grow very much larger than this. A 5 lb 11 oz 8 drm (2·6 kg) specimen was taken at Fowey, in 1956, by Mr A. G. L. Cobbledick.

Flounders are often variable in colour, according to the locality in which they are caught and the type of sea bed they most frequent. Nature has given them the ability to change their colouring to suit their surroundings, and this, with the aid of sand which they flap over themselves, is a good protection from their enemies, as well as a camouflage when they seek food.

Generally the upper side is dark brown and the underside white, but mottled-coloured specimens are likely from grounds which are strewn with various coloured shells, such as razorfish, mussels and slipper limpets; from the thick, dark harbour mud one may take black coloured flounders; and occasionally you might come across one that has a slight reddish or orange hue because it has frequented seaweed of similar colouring for a period of time.

This variation sometimes causes identity mistakes when weighing-in at fishing festivals, a problem easily avoided by a simple stroke-test. Run your finger lightly over the back of the fish from head to tail. The flounder will feel smooth except for the occasional rough patch near the shoulder. In comparison the dab will feel rough overall. Another identification aid is that a flounder's lateral line is slightly curved at the shoulder, and there are also tiny tubercles at the base of the fins. The head is fairly large, with a matching mouth, and the body quite plump.

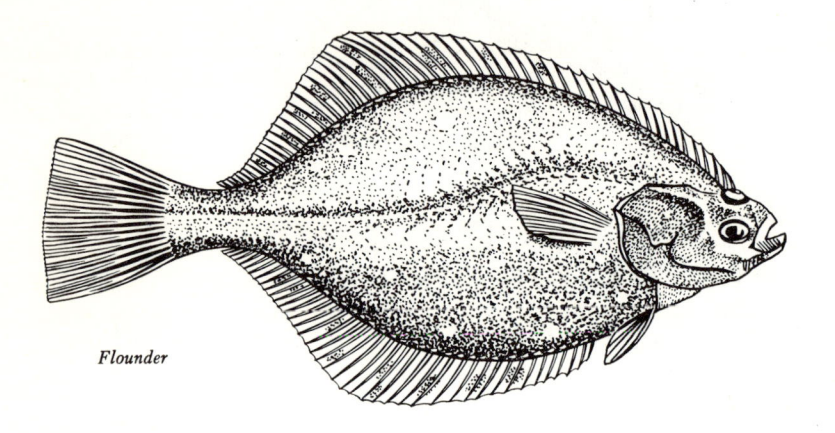

Flounder

The flounder has an interesting life history. When the fish is young its eyes will be found in the normal position, one on each side of the head. Later, as it makes growth, it tends to swim on its side, and then the 'under' eye moves over to set beside the other. At this stage it is ready to start its 'second life', flapping about on the bottom, although it can rise quite quickly when it desires to do so.

Flounders are caught on many baits, but quite often there is a preference shown for regional ones. Along a coast where there is plenty of slipper limpet washed up on the shore, a taste may be acquired for this offering. In another area razorfish might be the best bait, or alternatively ragworm or lugworm. If you are fishing in a new area it is essential to find out this local bait information in advance. They will also take sandeels, peeled shrimps, peeler crabs, cockles, mussels, and sometimes even garden worms when normal baits are in short supply.

When fishing for them it should be remembered that they are inquisitive fish. Any disturbance on the bottom which might cause alarm to other fish will help to draw flounders to the area. Many a time, when fishing has been poor, especially in estuaries, I have scraped the bottom with a rod-rest or net handle; this has been sufficient to create an attraction.

Although the old-style brass paternoster with three hooks is still used, even in these enlightened days, the trend is towards lighter tackle, and the modern angler will have better results using tackle which is not associated with ironmongery! 'Wander tackle' is a sporting way of taking flounders, and many large catches are made by this method which was originated by Percy Wadham. As the name suggests, the tackle works by being kept on the move, or wandering. It has many advantages over paternostering and can be worked from many stations. The best conditions for using the tackle occur during reasonably calm weather when a gentle surf is slowly moving in.

Wander, or roving tackle, as it is sometimes known, is not difficult to set up. At one end of a 6 ft (1·8 m) trace attach a small swivel for line attachment. Then, 1 ft (0·3 m) away from this fix a plastic boom with a short trace to a No. 4 hook. Add a spiral lead, about $\frac{1}{4}$ oz (7 g), 6 in. (15 cm) along the main trace. Between this and the final hook, arrange a small ball-type lead stopped by a split shot.

In practice, the lead stirring up the bottom as the tackle is slowly reeled in creates an interest to the flounder. More ground is covered, and the movement will also prevent hungry crabs taking the bait. Recovery speed should not be too fast; slow down if no bites are felt after a trial cast or two. This tackle can be used from the shore, from boats, and from low breakwaters, but it is not much use from high spots such as piers. The disadvantage of the last is that the upward line recovery will pull the gear off the bottom and away from the fish.

Another method is with a roving float, very useful around piers, over gullies, and in estuaries where there are known mud holes. All that is required is a 4 ft (1·2 m) light nylon trace, a spiral weight and a float. The state of the tide and sea conditions will govern the size of the latter two. The bait should be arranged to trail the bottom, and allowed to roam at will with the current. Often this proves best on an early morning tide, and is ideal if you can pin-point a gully at low water. In either of the methods, do not be in too much of a hurry to strike, for flounders often mouth the bait before taking it. If a strike is too hurried, especially with worm bait, it might well be pulled from the fish's mouth without the hook getting a hold.

More sea anglers are realizing the advantages of the baited spoon method of taking flounders, and it is certainly a way of interesting them when they seem reluctant to go for ordinary baits. Very often I have caught fish during boat matches when other competitors have been fishless – providing enough room was available for smooth operation. Some anglers, if they are unsuccessful, give up after only a day's trial, which is a mistake for this method definitely needs plenty of experiment in order to master it. Often the angler is at fault through presenting the tackle wrongly – usually because he allows the hook to spin round with the spoon. Flounders are suspicious if this happens because there is insufficient chance of examining and mouthing the bait.

Ragworm is mainly used to bait the spoon, although other offerings can be successful. I have caught them with lugworm and sandeels, and sometimes a red

Flounder spoon

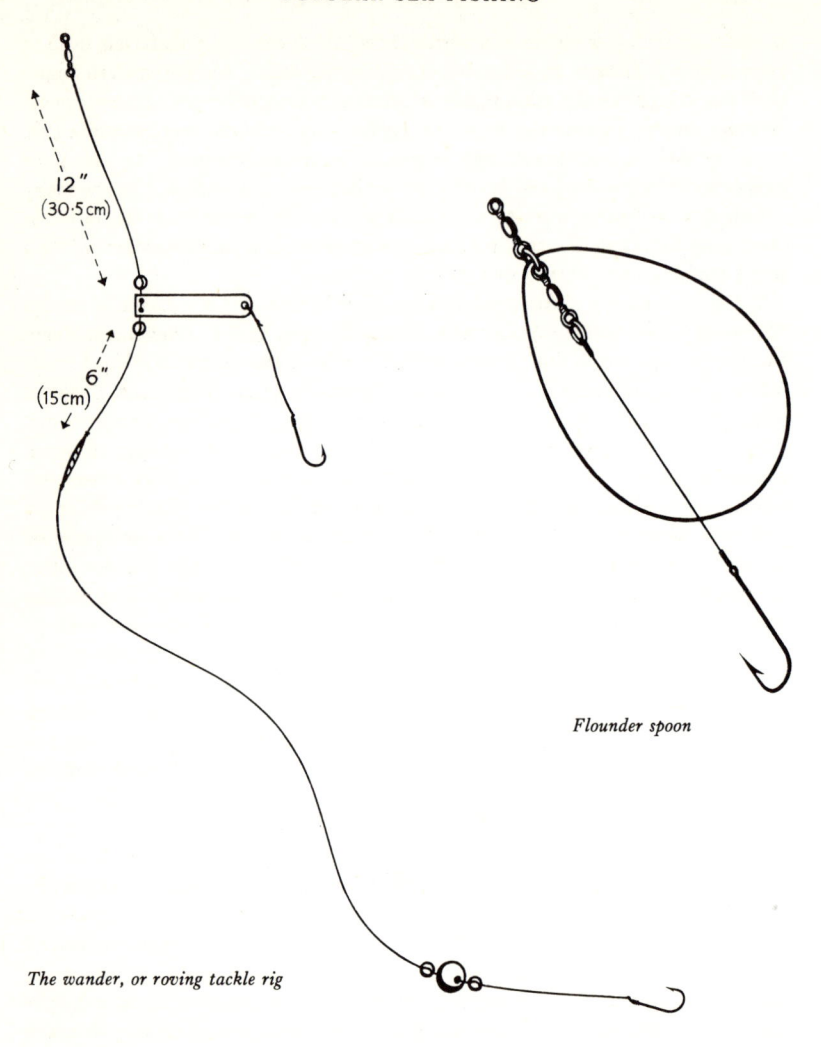

The wander, or roving tackle rig

rubber band on the hook is sufficient lure. Other anglers have reported success with strips of bacon rind or herring, and also lobworms. Even thin strips of squid will take in some localities. The reason why a flatfish moves after a fluttering spoon is that it believes it to be another flounder chasing food. Anxious not to be left out, the flounder swims up to investigate, and eventually takes the bait.

Spooning is at its best practised from a boat, but there is no reason why it cannot be employed from certain shore marks, in favourable conditions. The ideal way is worked by two anglers in a boat taking turns at rowing and fishing. Have your light rod resting on the stern, constantly watching it. As the boat slowly moves along, the rod tip will beat in rhythm with the revolving spoon, only changing in pattern when a fish shows interest. As the flounder mouths the lure, the tip of the rod will start twitching. Finally, as the satisfied fish dives with the bait, hooking itself, the line quickly tightens up.

Spoon fishing sometimes becomes difficult when there is a lot of weed on the move, especially the thin wispy strands. Once this snags the spoon, as it quickly does, the smooth rhythm is hampered.

There are several spoons marketed, but generally a white one is best, although I know of many catches made on the blue and silver type. A 3 in. (7 cm) size is recommended – smaller ones will take other flatfish such as plaice, but for some unknown reason flounders are not lured in numbers when using small spoons.

Brackish creeks and harbours are ideal spots for trying the flounder spoon, and I have also been successful when working the lure along the lengthy groynes where gullies have been located. Care, however, must be taken to avoid snagging rocks and thick concentrations, of weed. One can also fish spoons from piers if the bottom deck is not too far above the water level, and angling is not restricted to the top promenade only.

One can also fish from the beach using a single trace to a No. 4 hook. The added attraction of a small red glass bead threaded on the nylon, just above the ragworm baited hook, often provides useful catches. It is weighted by a 1 oz (28 g) Jardine lead, and together with a fixed-spool reel for easy casting, the tackle is kept slowly on the move. By keeping it moving one is able to cover more ground, and the bait does not sink into the sand.

As bait for other fish, small flounders are occasionally used for tope fishing, and will also lure conger at times.

It is interesting to note that flounders appear to have a homing instinct, travelling miles to get back to their home waters. Marine biologists have discovered this as a result of tagging, and once I carried out my own small experiment with the permission of the Ministry of Agriculture and Fisheries. I mention that permission was obtained as, obviously, the Ministry does not want individual anglers all over the country carrying out experiments. A number of flounders were netted for me in Poole Harbour, Dorset, by a professional fisherman. They were tagged and released from a Hampshire beach a few miles away in connection with a fishing festival, the idea being that they had a 'price on their heads' if caught on competition day. None were, but eventually they were all recaptured back in Poole Harbour. Not only did they make their way back to the harbour but were caught in the same stretch of water from which they were originally taken. I made it known there was a reward for these fish, and anglers who hooked them helped by returning the numbered tags. Strangely, all these fish were lured by Poole ragworm, which also indicates that local baits are usually best.

Common Sole

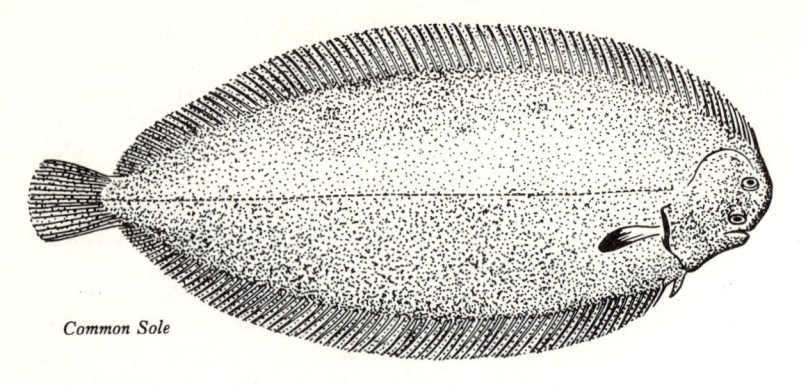

Sole

The common sole is so often regarded only for its food value, and not so much as a sporting fish. Yet given the opportunity this flatfish will give a good account of itself on light tackle. Larger ones are very powerful, arching and stiffening their bodies in an attempt to encircle the line and break it. A sole of around 1 lb 8 oz (0·68 kg) is considered a very good one, although many far larger ones have been taken. Notable specimens include a 4 lb (1·8 kg) fish taken from Clevedon pier, in 1943, by Mr M. Stinton, and a 4 lb 3 oz 8 drm (1·9 kg) fish from Redcliffe beach, Dorset, in 1974, by Mr R. Wells.

This fine flavoured table fish, oval shaped, is usually greyish or brownish in colour, occasionally variegated, with a black spot near the tip of the pectoral fin. Its underparts are white, and the eyes are on the right side. The snout protrudes further than the jaws. They are widely distributed around our coast, although most of the best specimens recorded in recent years have come from the southern half of the country.

Best of the sport is usually had at night, particularly when shore fishing, although sole are landed during daylight. The most successful anglers search for gullies at low tide, taking bearings in order to locate them again after dark. Sole also show a preference for outlets of fresh water in the sea, and some of my best catches have been made in areas where small streams trickle down the cliffside into salt water.

Various baits will lure them, but the top choice is either lugworm or ragworm. For the latter it is best to use three small harbour worms draped from the hook, rather than a single large one. Alternatives are razorfish, slipper limpet, mussel, shrimps and sandeel cuttings. Occasionally one hears reports of sole taking the most odd baits. They have been caught on herring roes lightly tied on the hook with wool, garden worms, small slivers of butchers' tripe, and even a helping of tomato from an angler's sandwich has done the trick. The silver paper dodge often entices fish when used on a single hook trace, especially near harbour entrances. Simply wrap a small piece around the hook shank, leaving room for either a ragworm or lugworm. Lightly leaded, this should be moved very slowly across the bottom. The lead causes a disturbance, and sole, not unlike flounders in this respect, are very curious fish and will soon investigate.

In my experience they move around in pairs, or at least it appears so to judge from many catches. I have hooked one, quickly rebaited to recast in the same spot, and soon reeled in another fish. The pattern has been repeated too often to be sheer coincidence.

At night there seems little need to cast very far, and most of my personal catches have been taken in the first 15 yards (13·7 m), sometimes as close as 8 yards (7·3 m). A gentle, ripple surf movement is best; the type that starts a long way out and glides quickly but smoothly inshore. Few fish are caught in really heavy surf. Sandy beaches are likely to be the most productive, and fish can be hooked from inshore boats, piers and breakwaters.

There are other varieties of sole which the angler will catch, though these are not taken so frequently. The sand sole, with brownish colouring, grows to about 15 in. (38 cm) and has a series of blotches or small black spots over its body. The pectoral fin also has a dark blotch.

The variegated sole, or thick-back sole as it is sometimes called, rarely exceeds 9 in. (22 cm) in length. It is more a reddish-brown colour with several dark crossbands ending in black on the fins.

The smallest is the solenette, often wrongly thought to be the young of the common sole. Average length is from 3 in. (7 cm) to 5 in. (12 cm), and it will sometimes be caught accidentally while using worm baits.

Sole have occasionally been employed successfully as a bait for tope, but their use is not popular. Sometimes the skin is used, and painted red or orange as a lure for pollack and bass by boat anglers. Remove the flesh, leaving the skin to dry. A piece 3 in. (7 cm) by 1 in. (2·5 cm) should be wrapped around a long-shanked hook and kept in position by whipping at the head with monofil. The lure is used from a boat by keeping it on the move at midwater.

Dab

These obliging small flatfish are caught in large numbers from the sandy bays all around our coast. They do not run very large, about ¾ lb (340 g) is the average size fish caught, but they are most accommodating in taking nearly all sea baits one cares to offer them. Specimens taken on rod and line include a 2 lb 9 oz 8 drm (1·1 kg) fish caught at Port Talbot, in 1936, by Mr M. L. Watts; a 2lb 10 oz 12 drm (1·2 kg) fish from the Skerries, in 1968, by Mr A. B. Hare; and a 2 lb 12 oz 4 drm (1·2 kg) fish from Gairloch, Wester Ross, in 1975, by Mr R. Islip.

Known also as the sand dab, it is a rough scaled fish, coloured light brown with slight black or orange markings on the topside, and a bluish-white under-

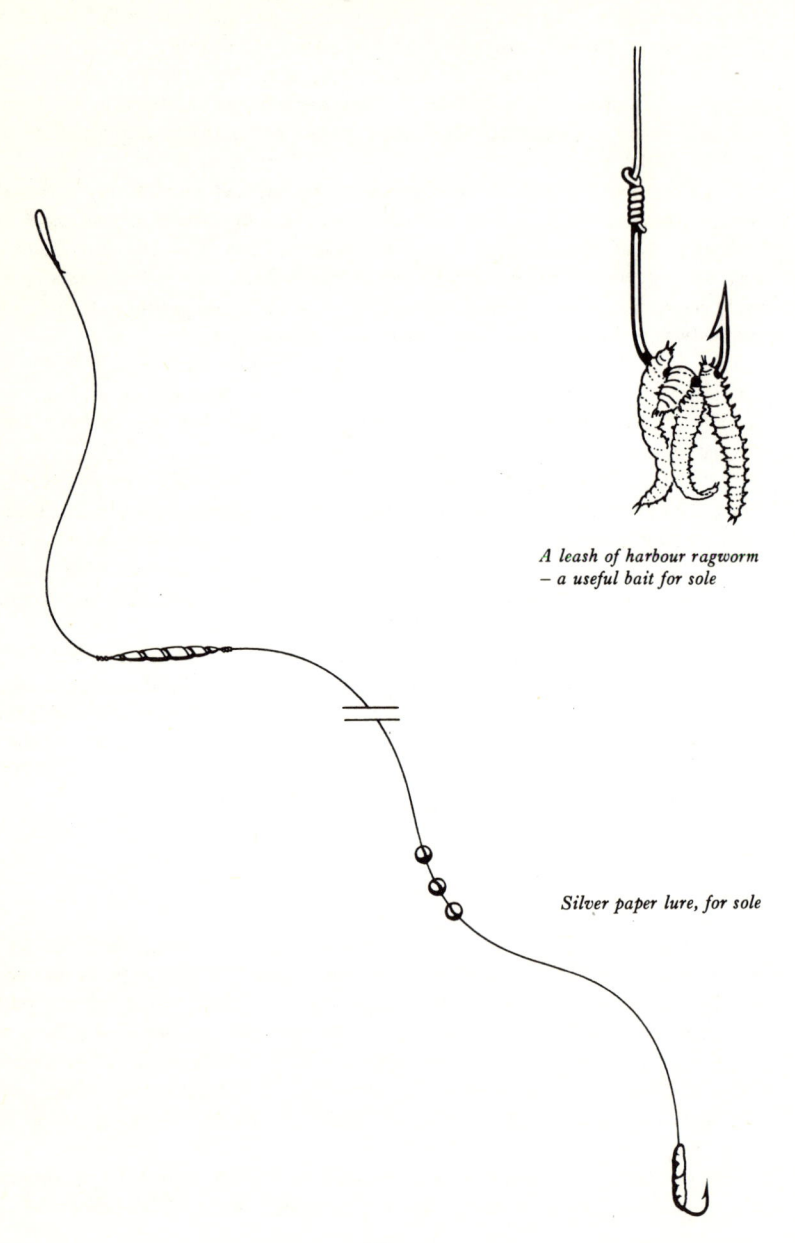

*A leash of harbour ragworm
– a useful bait for sole*

Silver paper lure, for sole

FISHING FOR FLOUNDER, SOLE, DAB, HADDOCK AND POUTING

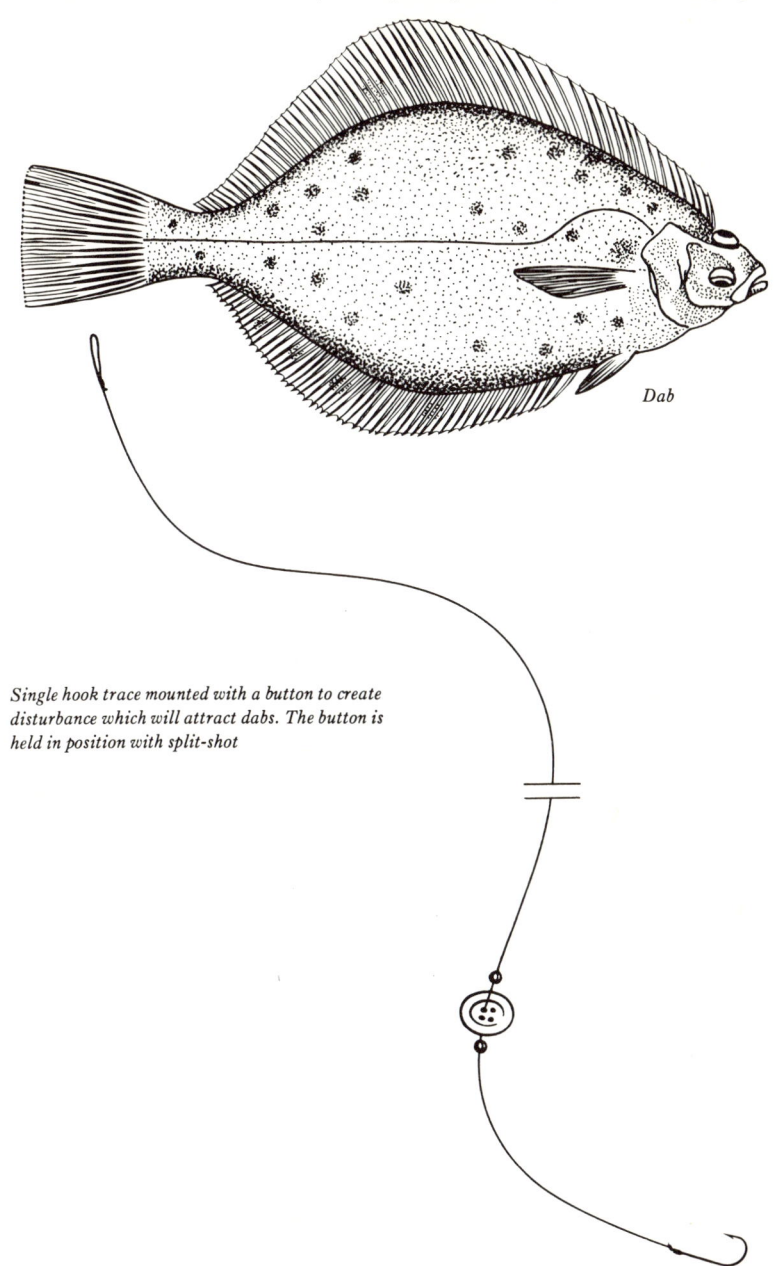

Dab

Single hook trace mounted with a button to create disturbance which will attract dabs. The button is held in position with split-shot

side. The eyes are on the right side; it has a small mouth, and there is a spine which protudes before the anal fin.. It has a more rounded appearance than the flounder, and there is a smooth ridge just between the eyes. Often the orange markings tend to fade after the fish has been out of the water for any length of time.

Most dabs fall to lugworm, ragworm and mussle baits, but they are also lured by razorfish, slipper limpet, rock limpet, shrimps, sandeel cuttings, thin herring strips, and occasionally will take slow moving small spoons. They are caught from boats, piers, breakwaters, and by shore casting.

Dabs are often found in the stomachs of other fish, especially the angler fish and skate. Bass and conger will also take them, and when in the shallows they often fall victim to diving cormorants. They are tasty table fish, but because of an average smallness they cannot be regarded as a sporting species. No great skill is needed to catch them, and at times they will take as many baited hooks as you care to offer, but naturally the lighter one fishes the more chance there is of obtaining some sport.

Although dabs bite fiercely, sometimes their feeding habits are upset by winds, and this is the time when single hook tackle will prove superior to paternoster gear. Like other flatfish they are inquisitive, and if your tackle can be arranged to cause disturbances of the sand this will be a great aid to the fishing. This can be done with a 6 ft (1·8 m) long trace to a No. 4 hook which has a button or milk-bottle top positioned on the trace above the hook. This is kept in position by split-shot.

After casting the tackle has to be given movement to cause the disturbance on the bottom. There is no need to continually reel in, but wind in a few yards, then pause for a minute or two. It is during the pause that the dab is likely to grab the bait. Apart from the shore, this method can be used from piers and breakwaters as long as they are not too high. Otherwise the tackle will fail to lie easily on the bottom.

Like flounders, the dab also has a liking for fresh water. Beneath one pier I fished there was a fresh water outlet. One was assured of fish by casting near the entrance, yet just a matter of a few yards away the chances of making a catch were extremely rare. In one instance I creeled 32 dabs while a tyro nearby who had not quite mastered accurate casting had only two fish during the same period of time.

Often, large catches of dabs are made from inshore boats using the 'bounce' method. A single hook trace is cast shorewards and then retrieved in a series of small jerks. Dabs are not so slow moving as is sometimes believed, and when in the mood will chase a baited hood moved in this way, disturbing the sea bed at the same time.

The dab is found inshore during many months of the year, though autumn usually produces the sweetest tasting fish. They frequently make up winning bags in shore and pier matches from September to December.

FISHING FOR FLOUNDER, SOLE, DAB, HADDOCK AND POUTING

Haddock

Haddock

Although there has been a return of occasional haddock along parts of the south coast in recent years, it is in Scottish waters where they are most prolific. Indeed, many anglers travel to Scotland nowadays just to enjoy the sport of catching decent size haddock.

The haddock is a member of the cod family. It has a greyish brown back shading to silvery white, with a dark lateral line. It has a forked tail which assists in identifying it apart from the cod, which has a square-cut tail. There is an oval black patch on the haddock's shoulder above the pectoral fin, although there are cases of recent ones caught in Scotland in which this distinctive marking is missing.

Notable rod and line haddock include a 10 lb 12 oz (4·8 kg) specimen caught by Mr A. H. Hill, off Looe, in 1972, and a 12 lb 10 oz 1 drm (5·7 kg) specimen caught by Sub-Lt. K. P. White, from the Manacles area, Falmouth Bay, in 1975.

In the south, haddock have fallen to preserved sandeels, smelts and herring strips. They will also take yellow and blue feathers. In northern waters top baits are lugworms, mussels and clams.

Shore anglers can catch haddock on single hook flowing traces, but the best fish are caught afloat; the largest from areas of herring spawn. The inshore fish are usually found around razorfish and mussel beds.

Because of the nature of the sea bed they frequent it is advisable to use reasonably heavy tackle. One cannot better a free-running centrepin reel, and most Scottish anglers favour an 8 ft (2·4 m) boat rod, combined with about 22 lb (9·9 kg) breaking strain line, single trace and No. 2/0 hook. The 4 foot (1·2 m) to 6 foot (1·8 m) trace is joined to the main-line with a swivel, and the rig is fished leger style.

If, after giving the bait a fair trial on the bottom, there has been no result, try raising it a few feet (0·91 m approx.) off-bottom. When you hook a haddock keep a firm grip on the rod, for a large specimen will be sure to do its best to shake the hook free. There is more chance of this happening if slack line is allowed.

From time to time, haddock are reported caught on spinners and rubber and plastic sandeels, so it may well prove profitable around haddock-holding areas of the coast to experiment with a variety of lures.

Pouting

Pouting are caught throughout the year from many coasts, and although the small ones with their bait-robbing tactics are not held in very high esteem by anglers, the larger fish will provide reasonable sport – often when other fishing is proving dull. A particularly outstanding pouting was the 5 lb 8 oz (2·4 kg) fish taken off Berry Head, in 1969, by Mr R. S. Armstrong.

They are known under a wide variety of names, often confusing, for many of them are purely local ones. The selection includes rock-whiting, pout, pout-whiting or whiting-pout, blen, cod-whiting and bream-pout. Sometimes they are called simply 'bait-fish' because of their attractive qualities on the hook. Tope are often caught on them, and conger in deep water wreck marks seem especially keen. Skate show a preference for pouting on evening tides, and they can also be sliced into strips when surf-casting for bass or float fishing for pollack from the rocks.

The pouting is a large-eyed fish with a deep body, and it has a frail barbule on the chin. The lateral line is very curved and seam-like, and on the bottom of the pectoral fin there is a blotch or dark blob. The first dorsal fin is noticeably high pointed, and the tail fin is straight edged. Pelvic fins are long, and the fish possesses fairly sharp teeth.

Colouring sometimes causes a problem with identification. Generally this is coppery, with a slightly olive-bronze overtone on the sides, which are also camouflaged with a number of dark, vertical bands. Frequently these fade at capture, and after being an hour or so out of water seem to be missing altogether. The variation in colour produces fish more orange than copper, and off some coasts they can be a bright yellow shade.

Small pouting are found around rocky venues and wrecks, where they shoal in fairly large numbers, usually keeping company with fish of the same size. The larger pouting move in smaller shoals – from one to two dozen fish.

Pouting can be caught from piers, breakwaters, the shore, and rocky headlands, but to get the best specimens a boat is necessary in order to fish ridges or rocks or near wrecks. In deep water they are able to give a better account of themselves.

For the best sport use the most pliant rod you have, with a centrepin or fixed-spool reel loaded with 6 lb (2·7 kg) breaking strain monofil. The trace should be 6 ft (1·8 m) long to a No. 6 hook and weighted with an easily attached spiral lead.

Baits are legion; pouting are hungry feeders and will take most offerings, especially if you are fishing at dusk. Double lugworm is good, so is ragworm, also squid pieces, slipper limpet and peeler crab. Strips of 6 in. (15 cm) are readily

FISHING FOR FLOUNDER, SOLE, DAB, HADDOCK AND POUTING

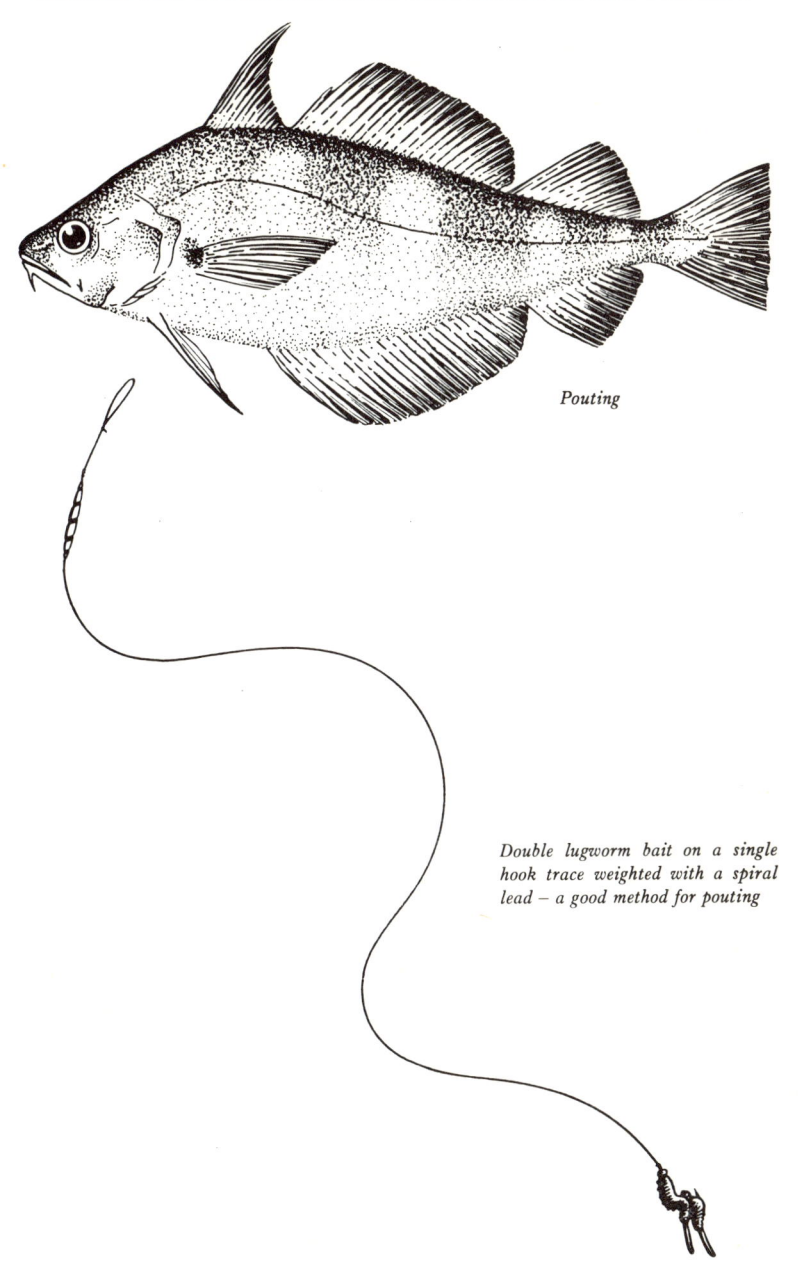

Pouting

Double lugworm bait on a single hook trace weighted with a spiral lead – a good method for pouting

taken, while I have found preserved sandeels very productive on a fast running tide, and mussels useful for pier work. Occasionally they will take peculiar baits. I once ran out of bait and used strips of garfish successfully. A freshwater angler told me of an occasion when he took several large ones on marsh worms. These can be found by removing small clumps of grass from the bank at the river's edge; it is best to use two or three on the hook at a time.

Usually the first tactic of a hooked pouting is to dive deep, trying to find sanctuary in a rock crevice. Some of the big specimens adopt the habit of shaking their heads in an attempt to free the hook – like cod in this respect – and unless a tight line is kept the fish is often successful in disgorging the hook by this method. Usually the head shaking does not start until the fish has its first glimpse of the boat.

Most shore anglers fishing after dark tend to use beach stands or tripods in which to place their rods between casts, but if you want to be successful in hooking pouting it is essential to hold the rod all the time. Many fish are lost because the strike is not made quickly enough – one cannot act fast if the rod needs picking up first.

From the shore, weather does not appear to make a great deal of difference to their feeding habits, providing it is not too rough. If the sea is very flat, it is helpful to give the bait some movement by raising the rod tip occasionally.

Working a bait close to pier piles at night will also locate pouting of larger size. They often nose around the weed-covered piles, searching for mussels and other food. Mussel bait is recommended for pier fishing, and it helps if you introduce mashed mussels as groundbait first. Do not bake or boil mussels in order to harden them off, for this will make a marked difference to the catches. They can be lightly bound on the hook with a strand of wool.

Quite a number of large tope are caught annually using pouting whole or cut into slivers, and no doubt catches would increase if anglers realized their bait value. An indication of how attractive they are to tope can be appreciated from the following sample catches. Michael Taylor had a 41 lb (18·5 kg) tope from Solent waters using an 8 oz (226 g) pouting mounted on a double hook rig; D. T. Lloyd had two, 33 lb (14·9 kg) and 35 lb (15·8 kg), while fishing off Llandudno; and off Hastings a 38 lb (17·2 Kg) fish gave Philip Rogers a 20 minute battle. The pouting he used was two days old, but it still proved better than the fresh herring he had been using previously without getting any runs. Some anglers who have experimented with pouting on shark expeditions off the south coast have captured large blue and porbeagle specimens.

COD FISHING *Cyril Precious*

The cod is a favourite food-fish haunting colder waters from 1 to 8 °C and, being pelagic, spawns heavily, the eggs floating in the upper surface layers at the mercy of wind, storm and tide. The hen fish may lay as many as three million eggs per year, from January to March according to locality, in deeper water of 10 fathoms (18·2 m) or over.

Cod can be hunted all the year round by the sporting angler; from beaches and boats, rocks, piers and estuaries. There is only one species of the true cod (*Gadus morhua*) in the North Atlantic. On the eastern side its range extends from Greenland and Spitzbergen in the north down to a southern limit of 50° N. This species is divided into separate populations known as stocks which differ both in breeding grounds and growth rates.

British anglers are most concerned with the cod from the North Sea which is divided by Flamborough Head into two inshore species-areas: the northern North Sea and the southern North Sea. There is also a central North Sea commercial cod which does not mix in the pre-spawning stage with the previously mentioned two stocks. The largest spawning ground of the northern North Sea cod is the Moray Firth and Firth of Forth to Orkneys area. There is a pronounced summer migration southwards to the Flamborough grounds which are rich in hermit crabs and whelks. This migration culminates in September and October when the fish gather in preparation for the January–March spawning period. The minimum size at which the species can be taken is 12 in. (30 cm), and at this size the codling, as immature cod are called, will be about 18 months old. Growth rate is fairly steady and by the time they attain three years

Cod

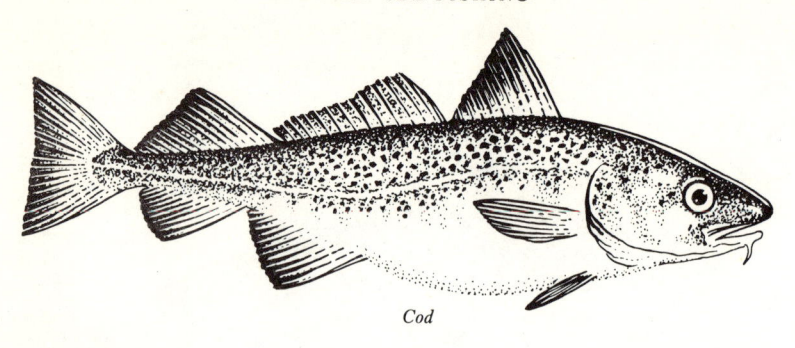

they will have grown to a length of about 25 in. (63 cm). Although some cod spawn at three years, most do so at four years of age.

Codling swarm inshore with the approach of winter in September and October, and the bigger mature cod move in during November and December, remaining until they move offshore to deeper water for spawning. The Yorkshire anglers and commercial inshore fishermen know from long experience that codling are susceptible to prolonged storm weather and that half a gale or gale from between the north and the north-east can shift hugh shoals of these fish from the Flamborough grounds along the east Yorkshire coast where they find their way into the river Humber which is rich in whitebait. About 11,000 tons of sandeel are netted every season in the Humber, which also yields shrimps, prawns, lugworm and ragworm.

Generally speaking, the boat anglers catch more big cod than the shore anglers, and commercial inshore fishermen at Filey have taken cod to 60 lb (27·2 kg) by lining. In the last eight years, since the first edition of this book was published, quite a number of cod weighing between 25 lb (11·3 kg) and 35 lb (15·8 kg) have been caught by pleasure fishermen, but it is surprising to find that at Cold Knap Point along the shore at Barry, Glamorgan, in 1966, Mr B. Jones caught a magnificent cod of 44 lb 8 oz (20·1 kg) *from the shore.*

Boat captures of note include a 53 lb (24 kg) cod taken by Mr G. Martin off Start Point, Devon, in 1972. Spurn Point, at the entrance to the Humber; the Isle of Wight area and further west down the south coast; and the famous Gantocks mark in the Firth of Clyde, are further areas rated highly for the big-cod catches they yield.

Mind you, even 50 lb (22·6 kg) plus cod are comparative tiddlers when compared with the hugh cod weighing 211 lb 8 oz (95·9 kg) taken by line-trawl off the coast of Massachusetts, USA, in 1895. The American cod (which chases and feeds on the shoals of the twaite shad – a member of the herring family known also as the alewife) is resident in waters extending from the southern tip of Baffin Island to North Carolina. Obviously, line fishing from boats, especially over wrecks or rough ground, produces the bigger cod, and the same applies to halibut. Winter fishing from small boats, such as the famous Yorkshire cobles that work out from Bridlington to fish Bridlington Bay and the Flamborough Deeps, is sometimes an unpleasant business and for some reason the British were slow in utilizing big craft for pleasure cod fishing. The Americans are different. They use pleasure steamers for cod fishing in the winter, and a photograph I saw reproduced in *Sportfishing*, the USA angling monthly, depicted such a pleasure steamer — about the size of those that take summer trippers on short, non-fishing cruises from Scarborough and Bridlington — with a row of anglers lining the length of the side proudly displaying scores of big cod between 20 lb (9 kg) and 30 lb (13·6 kg) as well as countless smaller fish.

In Britain, beach and pier and estuary and rock angling for cod seems to be more popular perhaps because they are more reliable pursuits. Smaller craft will not take angling parties out if the sea is running too heavily, but if they will not venture out, then there are sheltered spots in nearby estuaries, bays and rocky areas where cod can be caught. Consider the Yorkshire angler. The Holderness coast is rich in shrimps which the cod gorge upon, but if the sea is too rough due to the wintry north wind, he can fish the sheltered side of Flamborough Head overlooking Bridlington Bay (Sough Landing and Danes' Dyke are two good venues) or transfer to the river Humber at Spurn.

Tackle for shore anglers is becoming rather specialized. Glass rods, multiplying reels and fixed-spool reels are ousting the cane rods and old greenheart rods and centrepin reels along the open coast, but in the rocky areas the famous Scarborough centrepin reel is still used in the lower position on greenheart rods and double-built cane rods.

For fishing the open coasts, glass rods and multiplier reels and fixed-spool reels are excellent — and leger tackle for a swell, using fresh-dug lugworm bait, is very good.

In a rough and choppy sea when fishing from sandbanks, the Holderness tackle is deadly. The spike-grip 6 oz (170 g) lead is wired for 2 in. (5 cm) so that should it become buried in the sand, the line will not fray. The main-line is tied direct to the wire loop. Two imitation booms are made out of the main-line using the blood shrimp knot. This knot is the same as the blood loop dropper knot, but with the loop greatly enlarged and tied in a series of knots, resembling a shrimp. These booms are set about 2 ft (0·61 m) apart and the snoods are about 1 ft 6 in. (45 cm) long, each being equal in length to avoid tangling. Lugworms are used on the 3/0 to 5/0 hooks. Using such a rig in an Inter-Club match I have beaten an entire opposing club of 16 rods! Simplicity and the use of fresh lugworm are so often the key factors of success. But on this occasion I did not use a beachcasting outfit for two reasons. Firstly, I am fortunate enough to be able to cast 100 yards (91·4 m) with a homemade Scarborough reel on a two-piece, 10 ft (3 m), double-built cane rod. Secondly, when the tide comes over the sand-flats and reaches the bottom of the slopes to the beach, the angler often has to fish pools and gullies which have rough bottoms. Here, the glass rod has too flexible a top to pull the lead out fast when a fish is felt. Delay is

Simple free-running leger rig

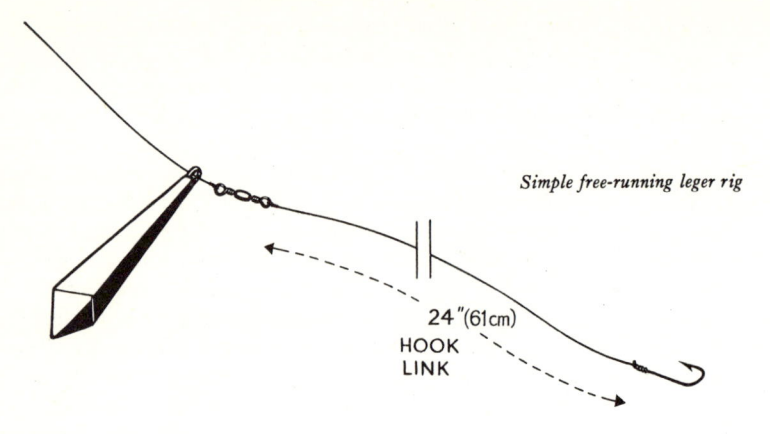

24"(61cm) HOOK LINK

often fatal, as a lively cod will easily shake the hook free, and so for this work I prefer the double-built cane rod which, because each section is only 5 ft (1·5 m) long, is easy to carry when climbing cliffs and the like. The lead used on these rough bottoms is the Scarborough 6 oz (170 g) flat-oval lead, wired as usual. Such grounds as these have to be studied if the angler is to succeed in fishing them.

When an angler studies the grounds, he is trying to find or decide where currents entering the pools and gullies, will scour away the sand and fine shingle bordering the rougher grounds of stones. Here, the feed is washed out of the sand and tries to escape into the protection of little gaps between the stones: a skilled angler will take a dozen codling in an hour from such a spot, then it is all over. The tell-tale marks are there if you know how to read them. Currents cut out little banks of sand, washing the feed into the open where the codling follow like hounds on the trail, closing for the kill. But along the open coast each change in direction of fresh or strong winds will alter the sea bed, so the angler must, to enjoy the best sport, constantly observe and inspect the area lying between high and low tide marks. Unable to see, hear or smell the fish, and aware of the fact that they leave no trail behind them, he relies on his skill in reading the signs of the beach and exposed sea bed to tell him where the fish will come to next time and when they will be on the feed.

The matchman's skill can be matched here by the lone-wolf cod fisherman, but the latter can have the edge on the former quite handsomely. We perceive that clubs are popular because they attract anglers who like competition and company, but there are others who, because of their individual inclinations, or the circumstances of work and life generally, shine best when they are independent – and these are the sea anglers who have the opportunity to dig or catch fresh bait just before fishing, whereas match fishing times will usually decree that the matchman will have to dig his bait the previous day or rely on a bait digger or tackle dealer for his lugworm.

COD FISHING

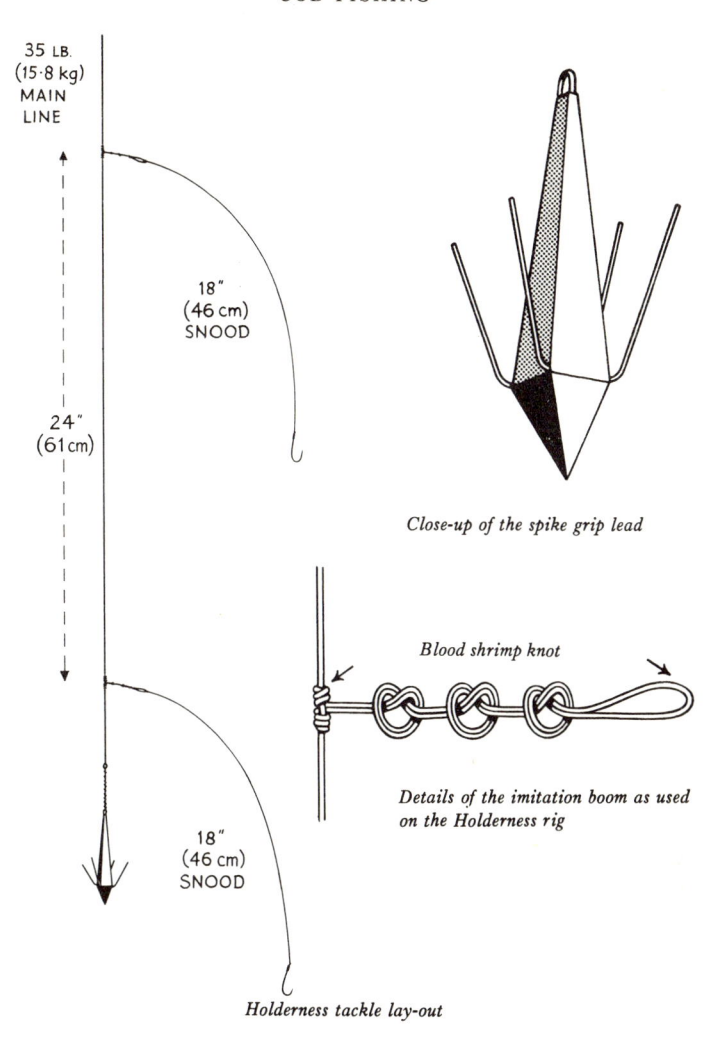

Close-up of the spike grip lead

Blood shrimp knot

Details of the imitation boom as used on the Holderness rig

Holderness tackle lay-out

That fresh lugworm can be more effective is a thing that I have known for 20 years, but only recently did I prove the reason. The club to which I then belonged, fish only the winter season, September to April, and for the rest of the year leaves members free to indulge in other types of angling. I did a lot of lone-wolf fishing, bait digging and research work, and finally wrote a paper on the lugworm *Arenicola marine* which was put on the records of The British Museum in London and the Dove Marine Laboratory, King's College, Cullercoats, Northumberland.

89

During my own personal researches into the lugworm inhabiting the river Humber I came to know that there were different grounds producing different growth-rates of lugworm, but all the preserved specimens of these lugworm which I sent to Dr David George of The British Museum and which are on display there, were found to belong to the one species *Arenicola*. There was the light-coloured lugworm, very poor quality and yellow, grey, pink and orange in colour, dug from the soft sand near the Lifeboatmen's Old Cottages at Spurn; the big, fat, juicy lugworm from behind The Old Den (known to locals as the Mussel Bed) between Spurn Head and Wyke Bight, and the smaller, hardy black lugworm found in the hard, black clays at Kilnsea Corner (Johnny's Point).

The lugworm from the Old Den were taken from a point behind the landward end where two currents met on the inflow and had, in the course of time, deposited a lot of old mussel shells, shingle and some sand in one area which gave forth a rich smell when dug over, just as fertilized soil is strong in the odour of farmyard manure! And this smell seemed to be something to do with the mussel shells, which have a very individual odour. The lugworm is reputed to feed on minute marine matter brought in by the tide, but I suspected that there was something more than this to it. I was worrying over this unsolved problem after a successful fishing trip using this lugworm, and after lighting my pipe, being in thoughtful mood, I took down from the shelf a copy of Charles Darwin's *The Voyage Of The Beagle*. Quietly studying the observations of this great naturalist and marine biologist, I came upon a passage which really made me sit up and take notice. I quote it with the permission of the publishers, J. M. Dent and Sons:

> 'August 14th. I set out on a riding excursion for the purpose of geologising the basal parts of the Andes, which alone at this time of the year are not shut up by the winter snow. Our first day's ride was northward along the sea coast. After dark we reached the Hacienda of Quintero, the estate which formerly belonged to Lord Cochrane. My object in coming here was to see the great beds of shells, which stand some yards above the level of the sea, and are burnt for lime. The proofs of the elevation of this whole line of coast are unequivocal. At the height of a few hundred feet old-looking shells are numerous, and I found some at 1,300 feet. These shells either lie loose on the surface, or are embedded in a reddish-black vegetable mould. I was much surprised to find under the microscope that this vegetable mould is really marine mud, full of minute particles of organic bodies.'

I sat staring at the page. My pipe had gone out. After a little while, I relit it. Who would have thought, when Charles Darwin made this observation and entry in 1824, that nearly 150 years later a Yorkshire sea angler and research worker would use it as a basis for coming to a greater understanding of the growth-rate, and the value as a sea bait, of the lugworm?

So that was it! In addition to feeding on the small forms of marine life brought in by the daily tides, the lugworms behind the Old Den were waxing fat on a diet of organic bodies found in the river bed where they had their homes!

Incidentally, the lugworm must have oxygen, and I always thought that the dark colour of the Kilnsea Corner lugworm which live in beds of black mud, was a response to the colour of its surroundings, but Dr George assured me that the dark colour was caused by de-oxygenation. We live and learn. We perceive how the sea's daily inflow fertilizes the sandflats and estuarine mudflats, and how shells and weeds enrich the sea beds and river beds on which they abound. The seaweeds, known as algae are often rich in protein – this is so in the case of the red weed *Delesseria*, the principal pigment of which is phycoerythrin, which is a water-soluble protein.

Alas, these rich, fat lugworm found in these rich river beds do not have the longevity of the smaller, hardier lugworms found in the harder, mud grounds at Johnny's Point. However, if used a few hours after digging, they do prove an irresistible bait for cod as they are full of rich, fresh blood and digestive matter which the cod cannot normally get. And, as I have discovered from personal experience, when Holderness codling are full of shrimp they will take these big, fresh, juicy lugworm when they will hardly look at any other bait.

So we see that the lone-wolf sea angler can operate at deadly efficiency when he knows where to get the best lugworm and is able to use them perfectly fresh – which is must one of the many reasons why some sea anglers do not belong to sea angling clubs!

Estuary fishing for cod can be undertaken during daylight hours just inside the heads of estuaries like the river Humber at Spurn Point, where the fast run of the ebb, especially in calm weather, brings the fish close in to the river bank where they feed well during a period lasting about one hour either side of slack water. In the dark hours, there are places along the river banks where the cod will come in on the big tides, such as at The Old Battery, Sunk Island, on the northern bank of the river Humber, or along the river wall opposite the fish docks at Grimsby.

But there are other venues such as Dungenness, made famous by long distance casting expert Leslie Moncrieff and his fantastic cod catches from the 'Dustbin' mark. Many anglers visiting such venues lack the essential beach-casting ability to get the very best from the fishing. It is a good idea to buy a top quality beach casting outfit, and then to practice and practice with it until you can get a good distance time and again without tangling up.

A major difficulty arises when putting the line smoothly on the reel. Unless this is done correctly, without twisting it, the line cannot be expected to come smoothly off the reel when casting. Monofil lines are mainly sold on spools of 100 yards (91·4 m), but you will require at least 150 yards (137·1 m) of line on a multiplying reel, and a big Scarborough centrepin can accommodate 200 yards (182·8 m). Now, you can buy two 100 yard (91·4 m) spools connected, but it is not so simple to transfer their contents to the reel. I do it this way. Cut two strong cardboard discs 2 in. (5 cm) larger in diameter than the spools and fix them to the sides of one of the spools with Bostik. Obtain a length of thick dowel rod

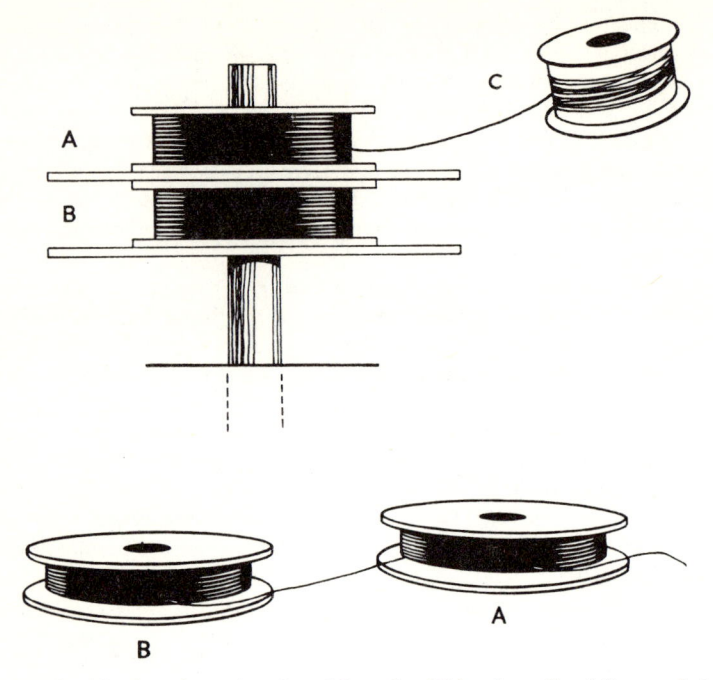

Transfer of line from the spools to the reel drum. Spool B has the cardboard discs attached, and is mounted first on the dowel rod. Spool A is placed on top and its line wound off on a spare spool, C. This is then transferred from spool C to spool B, and from there to the reel drum

and shape one end so that it will fit tightly through the hole in the line spool. Fix the dowel in a vice, or some other retainer such as a clamp, and push the second spool on top of the first. Now unwind the line from the top spool to a spare spool and then back on to the first spool which has the cardboard discs fitted. With all 200 yards (182·8 m) on the one spool, the dowel is shaped down more so that the line spool is just free to rotate. Mount your reel on a rod butt and wind the line on to the reel's drum or spool.

A multiplier with a plastic spool should have a base of linen backing wound on first, and be loaded with a really soft brand of monofil line. A Scarborough reel, on the other hand, requires a stiffer less-stretch brand of line. Alvey reels, in my experience, work best with lines of minimum diameter.

After many years of practical fishing I now consider the following outfits suit my needs:

1. Beachcaster – Sportex 12 ft (3·6 m) fibre-glass. Multiplier. Sportex Perlyl 35 lb (15·8 kg) breaking strain line. 6 oz (170 g) lead.

60 LB (27 kg) MAIN LINE

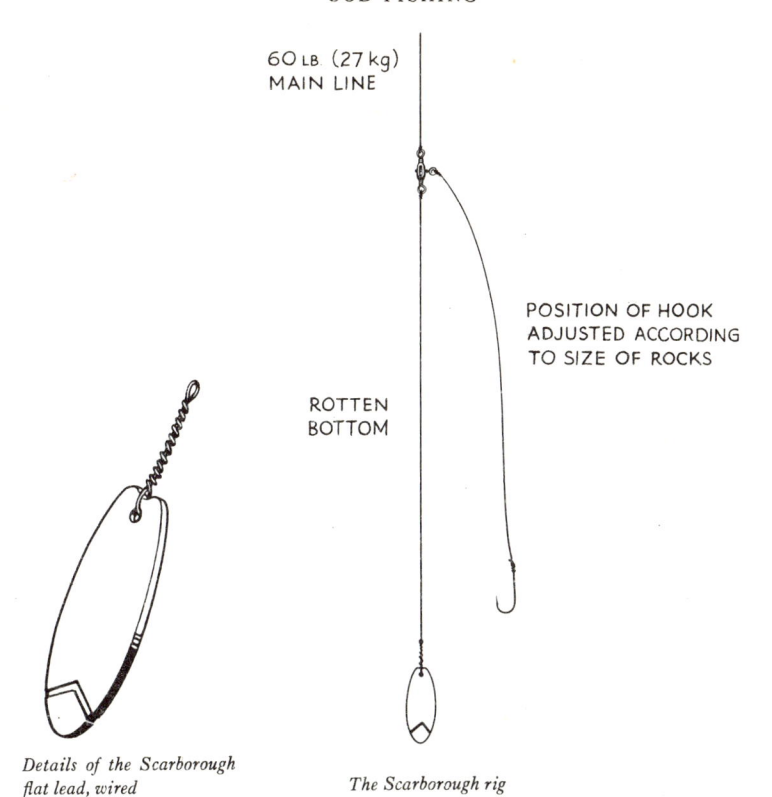

POSITION OF HOOK ADJUSTED ACCORDING TO SIZE OF ROCKS

ROTTEN BOTTOM

Details of the Scarborough flat lead, wired

The Scarborough rig

2. Double-built 10 ft (3 m) cane rod (mine is an old Marco design). Scarborough 7 in. (17 cm) reel. Harelon 33 lb (14·9 kg) breaking strain line. 6 oz (170 g) lead. With this outfit (reel in the low position) I can cast 100 yards (91·4 m).

3. Alvey Estuary Special reel. Fluor 28 lb (12·7 kg) breaking strain line. 4 oz (113 g) lead. Used in the low position on either of the rods already mentioned.

The individual angler should also try to find a rod to suit his physique. A tall person with long arms can use his reel in the high position on the rod quite easily, whereas a short person with short arms will require the reel to be fitted in a lower position.

I am purposely leaving rock fishing to be dealt with after boat angling, because pretty much the same tackle and bait can be used for both types of sport.

Boat angling can be dangerous in the winter. And as an ex-riverman and commercial boatman I can say that most inshore commercial fishermen in Yorkshire prefer a wooden, clinker-built boat with a well-shaped stern. The Yorkshire coble, safe yet fast, is a classic example of its kind, but the best ones are still built north of the Humber. The dangers of getting into and out of a harbour can be witnessed at the mouth of the river Esk at Whitby, between the piers. Handle a boat carelessly here, at the wrong state of a big tide, and you are in real trouble. The entrance to the river Humber, made dangerous by the shallows known as The Binks and The Outer Binks, is beset with tide-rips and the Spurn lifeboat is the only permanently-manned lifeboat in the country.

The clinker-built boat, derived from the Viking ships and so called because the planks overlap, has stability, strength, and the necessary weight to enable her to ride the waves safely, A well-shaped stern will mean that she will also answer the tiller quickly, even at low speed. A fibre-glass boat is lighter, livelier, much more prone to keel over if a mistake in handling is made, and is not so safe when there is too much weight in one place. The old whaling boats, which were hulled with only half-inch (12 mm) pine, were fast and safe but are rarely seen nowadays. Marine plywood is pretty strong material, but has to be kept well painted, and these boats are also on the light side. I much prefer the clinker-built boat. She is more stable and sits well in the water. Such boats, from the 12 ft (3·6 m) pleasure boat to the Yorkshire coble, are widely used along the treacherous east Yorkshire coast and do not get into trouble.

Pleasure anglers on this coast, who have to land and launch from open beaches, do not use such things as echo sounders and radar equipment for obvious reasons. Such expensive gear could get damaged, and very easily, too. Big craft which operate in big areas, carry echo sounders to locate wrecks lying well offshore in deep water and which are not buoyed, but very few pleasure anglers can afford the expensive upkeep of such craft. In any case, whether or not you need an echo sounder also depends on what sort of a fisherman you are.

Here I am reminded of a Hull trawler which got into a spot of bother in Icelandic waters and sailed south with not enough fish aboard. On her way home, she hunted for fish in traditional grounds off the Scottish coast but got nothing. She was equipped will all modern devices for finding and catching fish, but she got nothing, because the fish were simply not there to pinpoint. Let me put it this way: in an area where there are shoaling fish moving about a lot, an echo sounder is going to be useful, but in another area where the local wrecks are marked by buoys and where fish gather in interesting sections of the sea bed, the working man will not spend money on an echo sounder – he can catch plenty of fish without one. If you have plenty of cash and like to splash it about, you are free to do what you like with it. On the other hand, if you are finding life a bit of a grind, you will have to count every penny you spend. See what I mean?

Good boat tackle need not be expensive. But it must be on the strong side. Big centrepin reels are still popular, so are cane rods (when you can get them) and so are the old greenheart rods. I have a 10 ft (3 m), two-piece greenheart rod, (made for me by Mr Dyson when he had a tackle shop in Wright Street, Hull), which has for 26 years served me well in both beach and boat fishing.

I made my own centrepin reels, in local evening institute classes.

Lines of 40 lb (18·1 kg) to 60 lb (27·2 kg) breaking strain and heavy leads are always in demand, especially over rough-ground marks where big cod gather. The Filey cod of 60 lb (27·2 kg) mentioned earlier could have been caught by a pleasure angler fishing from a small boat – a sobering thought for anyone contemplating using lighter kit.

Offshore tide-runs are strong on a big tide and heavy leads are then required to hold bottom. The fish, though, have a habit of feeding well on the top of the tide (high water) when the sea is quieter. I must explain that the tide-runs along the Yorkshire coast, for example, move from north to south on the inflow and from south to north on the ebb, thus when the inflowing run slows down there is a quiet, high-tide period before the ebb run gets under way.

Here again, we can do a little research work to enable us to understand the habits of the cod more fully. We have previously described the cod as a pelagic fish, being spawned prolifically in the form of eggs which drift at the mercy of wind and tide and storm. From its earliest beginnings, therefore, the little grey-black globule of life inside the egg is literally as well as metaphorically cradled in the bosom of the deep, and thus the little fish inherits this tendency to drift along until it is big enough to make its way out of the tide-runs. Then, when it is a mature fish of 7 lb (3·1 kg) to 8 lb (3·6 kg) weight, it migrates long-distances to spawn before returning to its home grounds.

I have explained how the British cod migrate south from the Moray Firth and Firth of Forth area to Flamborough to spawn. The Arctic cod, the Skrei, migrate each spring to the coast of Norway to spawn. The American cod and the Canadian cod also go on migrations. Even the Scarborough rock-codling, which are reddish brown on the back, sometimes move offshore into the tide-runs after the sile in the late summer – I know because I have taken them on spinners when they have been mixing with the mackerel shoals. Thus, we see an easy way of boat fishing for cod.

Smaller boats are quite suitable for inshore fishing as far out as about $\frac{3}{4}$ mile (0·402 km) in the tide-runs on neap tides. The outboard motor should be kept in first-class trim, and the anchor and rope must be strong and reliable, too. Room for two sets of oars can be found in a 14 ft (4·2 m) craft, and it is obligatory to carry a white light. Favoured grounds are found in the vicinity of buoyed wrecks, where the sea bed holds big whelks, attractive as feed for cod. I shared for many years a small, clinker-built boat which was well shaped in the stern and very beamy, with plenty of keel. From this stable craft we took lots of cod from marks no deeper then 9 fathoms (16·4 m). Our bottom tackle was generally a single hook on a trace held well down. Interesting to note that many of the fish, when gutted, were found to be full of red shrimp. For bait we used inshore shrimp, lugworm, and mackerel and herring strips.

A good plan, therefore, is to emulate the fish and drift, giving the boat to the tide, to the marks – meaning that if, for example, there is a wreck to the south, you should launch the boat at slack water on a neap tide, take it out into the tide-runs and then motor down with the tide to the wreck on the inflow, catching cod on the top of the tide and returning with the ebb. This is a very safe method and it is also easier on the engine (and fuel consumption). It is wise to play safe. Below the waterline, the wooden planks in the hull, known as the bottoms, should be kept well tarred, and those above the waterline should be painted orange or white, which will show up well against the dark sea, so that any boat in the vicinity can soon tell if you are too low in the water and need aid. Remember also that a coat or shirt waved at the end of an oar is a recognized signal of distress.

Before every trip a weather forecast should be obtained, and knowledge about winds which produce dangerous ground swells on big tides should never be forgotten. Along the Holderness section of the Yorkshire coast the north-west wind produces sufficiently bad swells to get small boats into trouble. Out at sea, keep an eye open for these ground swells: there, the waves will be small and a long way apart, but by the time they are rolling on the beach they will be closer together and 5 ft (1·5 cm) or 6 ft (1·8 m) high. The skyline should also be watched for heaving waves which denote a swell coming in, and great care needs to be taken not to go too far out on the big tides when the tide-runs will be extra strong.

Failure to look after yourself may result in a serious mistake and someone may not come back – at least, not alive. Every year aspiring boat anglers who live inland come to the seaside with a boat and get into trouble. The risk is just not worth it.

Avenues can be used, it must be firmly said, which can prevent these tragedies. The best thing to do is to decide where your nearest, well-known boat-fishing centres are situated, and then to book a place in a boat at the weekends or join a boating club. The latter course is cheap enough, and as time goes on and you gain experience you will be able to have a boat of your own or share one. Just you try buying a boat and looking for a crew when it is known that you are a greenhorn!

The big snag with boat fishing in the winter is only too well known. You arrange for a trip in a boat, drive 60 miles (96·5 km) or 70 miles (112·6 km) to the coast, and then find on arrival that the sea is too rough for the vessel to be able to put out from port. Hopefully, somewhere in the vicinity there may well be a sheltered area where shore angling will be rewarding enough as a satisfactory substitute.

The next step, therefore, is obvious. You visit the tackle shop locally and buy a book about the area's fishing, or write to the Town Hall for a guide. You find out where bait can be dug or gathered, and you ferret out the best harbour or estuary or rock-fishing venues. This means that if your boat fishing trip has to be cancelled, you can do some useful fishing just the same. There is a bit of an adventure in all this, and it will bring out in you the same rare qualities that Scouting does. You will soon get to know your way around. Rock fishing, however, may take rather longer to master.

Rock fishing, in fact, certainly does take some mastering, so we might just as well discuss the pros and cons, because this sort of cod fishing can be very rewarding indeed at times. Some rocky grounds are not as forbidding or as difficult to fish as they look. Saltwick Bay to the south of Whitby; The Rock by South Cliff at Scarborough; Green Rock at Filey Brigg, and South Landing and Danes' Dyke, Flamborough – all these look rather difficult to fish, but when you use a flat-oval Scarborough lead, a 55 lb (24·9 kg) breaking strain line, and a centrepin reel in the low position on a greenheart or double-built cane rod, you soon find that things are not so bad after all and that before the sport is over you have a useful cod or two – cod which enjoy rich feeding and are just as rich in the flesh. Mussel bait is not difficult to get, and a hook above the lead will mean that amongst the stones or small rocks your hook will not drop down a lot lower than the lead and get fast.

If the ground is not too rough there is no need to put the single hook too high above the lead. Along the worst rough areas of Filey Brigg expendable tackle is used, locally known as a rotten bottom rig. The main-line is heavy, say 60 lb (27·2 kg) breaking strain, tied to a three-way swivel. Between the swivel and the lead is a line which is of much less breaking strain – the rotten bottom. The hook is fixed by a snood to the side-eye of the swivel. Using this set-up, if a cod is hooked and the lead becomes snagged, the rotten bottom is broken under rod pressure so that only the lead, and not the fish, is lost.

Never forget, when using such tackle, that you must not fish with a *tight* line, as this drags the lead into holes and crevices. Some people never seem to take kindly to rock fishing for years. I know I never did, but at least I did consider it a challenge and ended up by winning big inter-club matches at both Filey and Scarborough. If others could succeed, I said, so could I – and I did. And so, too, can you – if you are willing keep at it for long enough. The experience will also broaden your outlook on sea angling, and provide an extra variety in your sport. An all-round and experienced cod fisherman is always at an advantage at a time when there are more and bigger cod amongst the rocks than there are further out on the sand, for then he can do so much better for himself than the man who has never mastered rock angling.

The following comments should give a fairly balanced picture of the angler's cod year. In September, when the codling shoals move in, they have a habit of going to the rocks, and in this month the big Yorkshire and All England Codling Championships are fished at Scarborough. Winds from the north-east will also bring the cod down to the Holderness section of the Yorkshire coast (Barmston to Spurn). If the sea is calm, the rock and beach fishing may be below average, but the boat fishing may well be much better. There are boat classes in both the Scarborough and Bridlington Sea Angling Festivals. In October, the cod and codling will already have moved in nicely. By November, we see more of the bigger cod, and in December they are really in with a vengeance. The boat fishing may drop off as the fish come closer in, chasing the inshore migration of feed. In January, the big cod prepare to move offshore to the deep spawning areas, but there will be hordes of immature codling from about 1 lb (0·45 kg) to 7 lb (3·1 kg) for the beachcaster and rock angler. In this month the cod often begin moving to the sand from the rocks after fresh feed. February is also good for smaller, inshore fish, but the boats can do well if the weather holds, as too much fresh water from drains, streams and estuaries drive the fish out to where the salinity content of the sea is better. In March, sport begins to drop off along some rocky coasts, but often remains good over sandy bottoms now that the common shrimp is migrating inshore. April sees rock fishing quiet, beach fishing falling off, but sport from the inside of the estuary head can be reasonably good. In May, the beach angling finishes, and from then till September, the boat fishing offshore provides the sport.

Cod fishermen must study the data for the feed. In the autumn, cold weather can drive the crabs offshore, also the shrimps, but in the spring the common shrimp migrates inshore in large numbers. Favourite feed in the summer is the offshore shrimp. The herring shoals appear off the Yorkshire coast about Hull Fair time, in mid-October, and the sprat season lasts from November to March. Alas, the movements of the sprat shoals are often unpredictable. February to March is the time when we see the little crabs coming inshore. Whiting spawn during the New Year, and the eel-pout bring forth their young during December and January.

All this information gives the angler a sound idea of the reasons for cod moving about from place to place during the year. In my opinion, the best baits are peeler crab in season, hermit crab and fresh lugworm.

All through the year, we can hunt for cod from beaches, rocks, estuaries and out in the boats along the tide-runs. The dedicated cod angler will tell you that his sport is as good as any and that if there are days when the total bag is rather light, there are other days when so many fine fish are taken that it becomes very much a fag to carry them home.

Fishing of all kinds is like that, but to me cod fishing is much more rewarding in experiences than most other kinds of sea angling.

THE WRASSE FAMILY *Trevor Housby*

Although there are half a dozen species of wrasse in British waters only the ballan wrasse, corkwing wrasse and, possibly, the cuckoo wrasse are of any real interest to the sea angler. The gold-sinny wrasse, rainbow wrasse and scale-rayed wrasse are all far too small to offer any sort of sport on rod and line. Few sea anglers can distinguish one species of wrasse from another, with perhaps the exception of the cuckoo wrasse whose extra-bright colours and unusual markings make it a rather distinctive creature.

In the case of the male cuckoo wrasse, the body colour is a brilliant yellow-gold overlaid with streaks of bright blue. The female – at one time regarded as an entirely separate species – is basically pink with a series of dark blotches along the back. Compared with the rest, the corkwing wrasse is more sombre but easily identified by the dark vertical bars which cross its flanks.

The ballan wrasse – the largest wrasse species in British waters – is a magnificent fish which varies considerably in colour from one locality to the next. However, the most common pattern, found on nearly all big ballans, is a combination of turquoise, red, and white.

The wrasse family is widely distributed around the British Isles, particularly in rocky areas, for they are true rock-fish which seldom thrive in open water. Generally speaking, they are most prolific along the south and south-western coasts, although I have caught wrasse in northern waters off Scotland. The range of the species in home waters is difficult to ascertain with any degree of accuracy for few indeed are the anglers who rock-fish along the Scottish coastline, and hence many likely areas remain unexplored. On a recent trip to the Orkney

Islands I found that shore anglers often encounter wrasse. Large specimens, however, are uncommon.

For many years the British wrasse record was held by an alleged 12 lb 12 oz (5·7 kg) ballan wrasse taken by F. A. Mitchell-Hedges at Looe in 1912. Several years ago this fish was dismissed from the record lists after careful examination of its stuffed remains revealed it to be obviously far smaller than the inscription on its case had led people to believe.

Wrasse have made a truly remarkable comeback during the past decade and heavyweight specimens – mostly caught from West Country and Channel Islands venues – are now once again a regular part of the summer fishing scene. Fish to a little over 8 lb (3·6 kg) in size were caught during the summer of 1976 and I do not think it will be too long before a 10 lb (4·5 kg) plus wrasse hits the headlines.

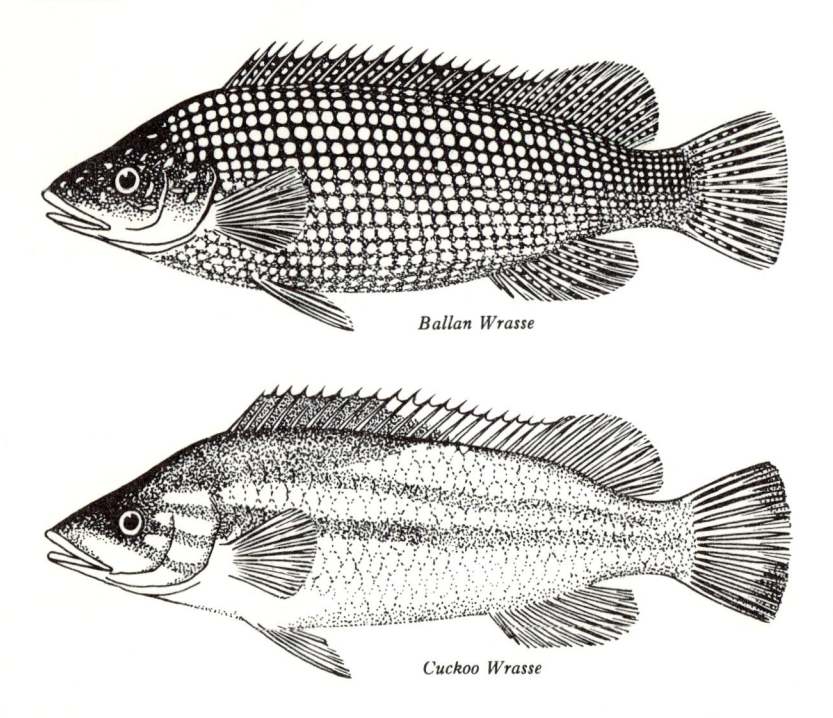

Ballan Wrasse

Cuckoo Wrasse

Beginner or expert, wrasse have much to offer the sporting angler. They feed greedily and even on hot days, when little else is willing to take bait, wrasse will oblige. Very little skill or knowledge is required to catch them and they make an ideal quarry for the novice sea angler. Really large wrasse, though, are a different proposition; a great deal of skill and indeed patience being required for their capture. It takes a very good angler a lot of dedicated effort to be successful, and in my book a wrasse specialist who can get among the big fish regularly is a man to be admired.

Of course there will always be days when wrasse seem to go mad, taking any and every bait which is offered to them. Such a day is a comparative rarity, but if you are on the spot at the time it will certainly be a session to remember. I recall one occasion when I landed exactly 40 wrasse over 4 lb (1·8 kg) each, and 12 of these topped the 6 lb (2·7 kg) mark. It was the finest day's wrasse fishing I could ever hope to experience.

Where to find Wrasse

Wrasse, typical rock dwellers, seldom venture far from the safety of large, underwater obstructions – rocks, the base of stone jetties and shallow water wrecks are all likely places to find wrasse. If the obstructions are heavily weeded it is also a good sign, for the species has a distinct liking for weed which provides both cover and food in the form of small crustacea of many types which live among the fronds. Deepish rock gullies set between high rock walls and sunken reefs are other likely wrasse-holding marks, and each spot should be thoroughly explored by the wrasse angler. In the West Country, the stone jetties of the fishing villages provide the wrasse family with perfect homes. For the angler unable or unwilling to go clambering over slippery rocks this jetty fishing is comfortable sport, with always the chance of an extra large specimen. One can also go boat fishing for wrasse, but there is little real advantage when one considers that they normally live and feed within easy casting distance from the shore.

Handling Wrasse

Because of their bright, angry-looking colours and sharp dorsal spines, wrasse have gained a reputation for being poisonous. This is utter rubbish. The sharp spines can easily cut if you are careless enough to let them, but the risk is not very great. Far too many anglers treat wrasse as dangerous and beat them to pulp before attempting to remove the hook. One cannot eat wrasse, but they do give sport, and the correct drill is to return them to the water as little harmed as possible. Wrasse which have fought hard on light tackle need time to recover, so hold each fish gently upright in the water until it is able to swim clear. Out of water, wrasse seem to fill up with air rather quickly, but a period of nursing helps them to adjust and get rid of this extra buoyancy. This is more humane treatment than allowing them to float away on the surface to be pecked to death by sea birds.

The bright colouring and heavy scales give them ample camouflage and protection among the jagged rocks and heavy weed. Thick lips and neat teeth are obviously designed to suck and crush crabs, molluscs and marine worms – I have a theory that wrasse of all sizes feed over beds of mussel; often I have caught specimens and on investigating the stomach contents for research purposes, found them to contain whole or partly crushed mussels which have obviously been torn from their natural moorings.

Tackle

Wrasse can be taken on any type of tackle, but the best of the sport is only to be had with light gear – as light, that is, as conditions allow. I have fished for big wrasse all round the British Isles and through trial and error have reached conclusions regarding the right tackle for the job. My standard outfit consists of a 10 ft (3 m) hollow glass carp-type rod, matched with a medium size fixed-spool reel loaded with 10 lb (4·5 kg) to 12 lb (5·4 kg) breaking strain monofil. At one time I used a shorter rod, but I soon discovered that it was almost impossible to control a big fish which decides to take cover in the rocks beneath one's feet. So I discarded the short rod in favour of a carp rod, which has since proved to be ideal. This weapon will handle float, leger and paternoster rigs with ease, and for all-round wrasse fishing I would consider it hard to better. Many anglers of course use standard beach casting tackle for wrasse catching. I am not in favour of this. You will catch fish certainly, but they will hardly be able to display their fighting qualities. No doubt it is the use of excessively heavy gear which has given wrasse the reputation of being non-fighters. A reputation, in my opinion, which is completely unfounded. On a carp rod, a wrasse of 4 lb (1·8 kg) class will put up a very stout if not prolonged struggle.

Both rod and reel will take a fair hammering when you are fishing from the rocks, so after each outing it pays to give the tackle a thorough inspection. Particular attention should be paid to the rings and ferrules on the rod and the moving parts of the reel. Clean *all* salt away with fresh water and lightly oil the reel after it has been dried. Because the majority of this fishing is undertaken among jagged rocks and barnacle-encrusted reefs, monofil line is subjected to some mighty rough treatment. Apart from a regular inspection it is a good idea to cut off the last few yards of the line at the conclusion of each fishing trip. A worn line can mean a lost fish, so never take chances! If you carry a spare spool you will be able to change a suspect line as required. Make absolutely certain that the discarded line is either burnt or rolled up and taken home for destruction. Under no circumstances should loose nylon monofil be left lying over the rocks or for that matter be thrown into the sea. Birds get tangled up in monofil very easily and unless found and released quickly they die a most painful death – ripping and tearing themselves in frantic efforts to escape. Worse still, monofil does not rot. Single lengths can kill over and over again.

During the seasons I specialized in wrasse fishing, I constantly reviewed my ideas on terminal tackle and floats in particular, which I used a great deal when hunting these fish. I discarded, with very few exceptions, all the floats labelled

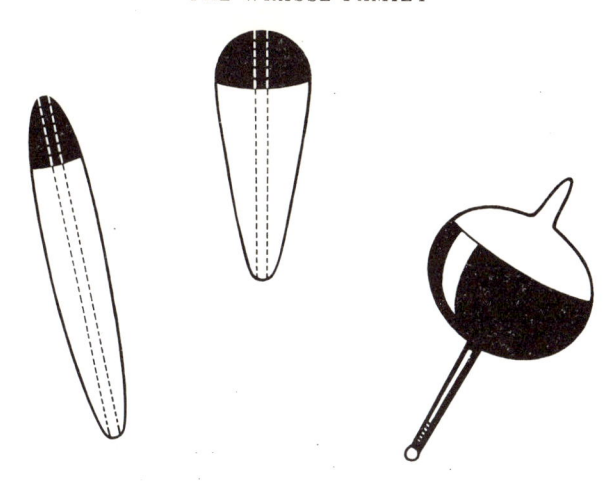

Left *and* centre, *good wrasse floats*. Right, *a badly shaped float which is unsuitable for sea fishing*

'sea float'. They were badly designed and far too bulky for the job in hand. Why it is that sea floats are designed to support about 8 oz (226 g) of lead and with the shape of miniature lighthouses, I cannot say, but the fact remains that many float makers still continue to produce floats which are totally unsuitable for most types of sea fishing. Long, streamlined balsa or plastic designs are far superior to the standard 'bungs' which still find their way into anglers' tackle boxes. Where wrasse are concerned, the lighter and more delicate the float, the more confident will be the bite indication. A float capable of supporting $\frac{1}{2}$ oz (14 g) of lead is all one needs when wrasse fishing. I seldom bother to carry fixed floats, preferring the sliding types which can be regulated to stop at the correct depth for the gully being fished.

Wrasse have thick leathery mouths and once the hook is in past the barb it is unlikely to come adrift. To ensure good hook penetration a top quality make should be used. My personal favourite is the bronze, Model Perfect eyed hook. Before use a hook should be given a final 'edge' with a few rubs on a carborundum stone.

Tackle when shore fishing for wrasse should be kept to a bare minimum. This will allow freedom of movement to cover the maximum amount of ground and so get the best from the fishing. My own kit consists of the following items: rod and reel, and shoulder bag containing a spare spool of line, a selection of size 2, 4 and 6 hooks, a box holding a selection of leads, sliding floats, set of scales, split-shot, swivels and elastic bands for making float stops. I also take along a landing net with a telescopic handle which acts as a wading staff when crossing shallow rock gullies.

Float Fishing

Float tackle is ideal for fishing a level-bottomed gully. With the bait suspended some 6 in. (15 cm) to 12 in. (30 cm) off-bottom it is possible to work the tackle completely round a gully, presenting the bait in a most natural manner to any wrasse feeding in the vicinity. Wrasse in feeding mood will take a baited hook in no uncertain manner, making the float abruptly vanish beneath the surface. Such

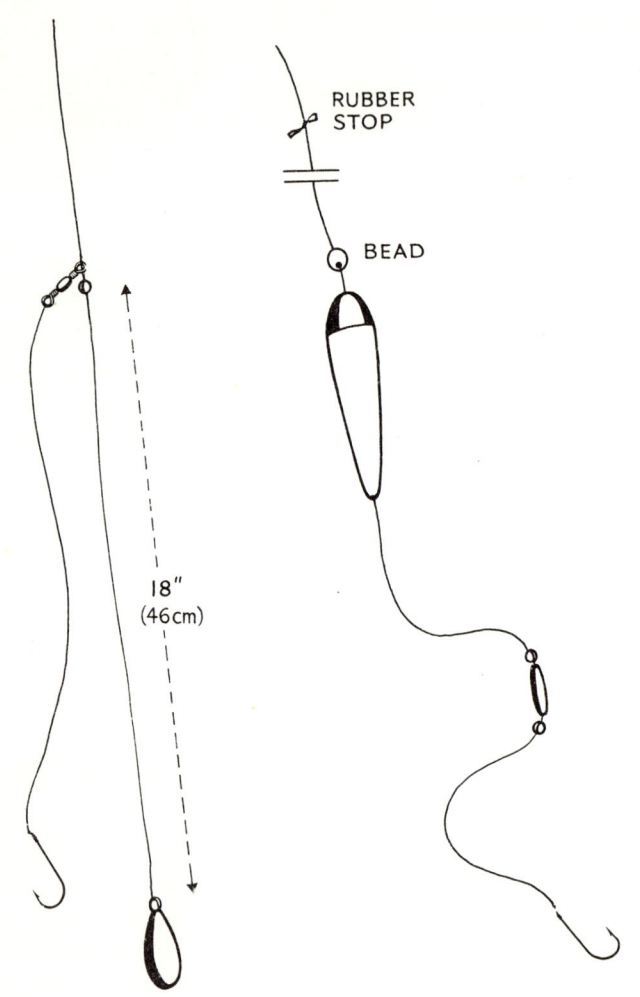

Right, *typical wrasse float tackle* Left, *paternoster rig for fishing ledges and weed-covered rocks*

bites are easily hit and very rarely is a fish missed. At odd times the float will bob up and lie flat on the surface; this is caused by a wrasse taking the bait and swimming upwards. The 'flat' float is a sure sign that the bait is well inside its mouth and a strike should be made without delay.

Choice of baits when float fishing is very much a matter of personal choice. My own experience leads me to believe that for all-round sport, lugworm and ragworm are best. At the same time, though, I have proven to my own satisfaction that the average wrasse taken on worm baits is rather on the small side, and so I now use them only as a stand-by. On the subject of worms, I have used garden worms quite often for wrasse and found them equally as effective as marine

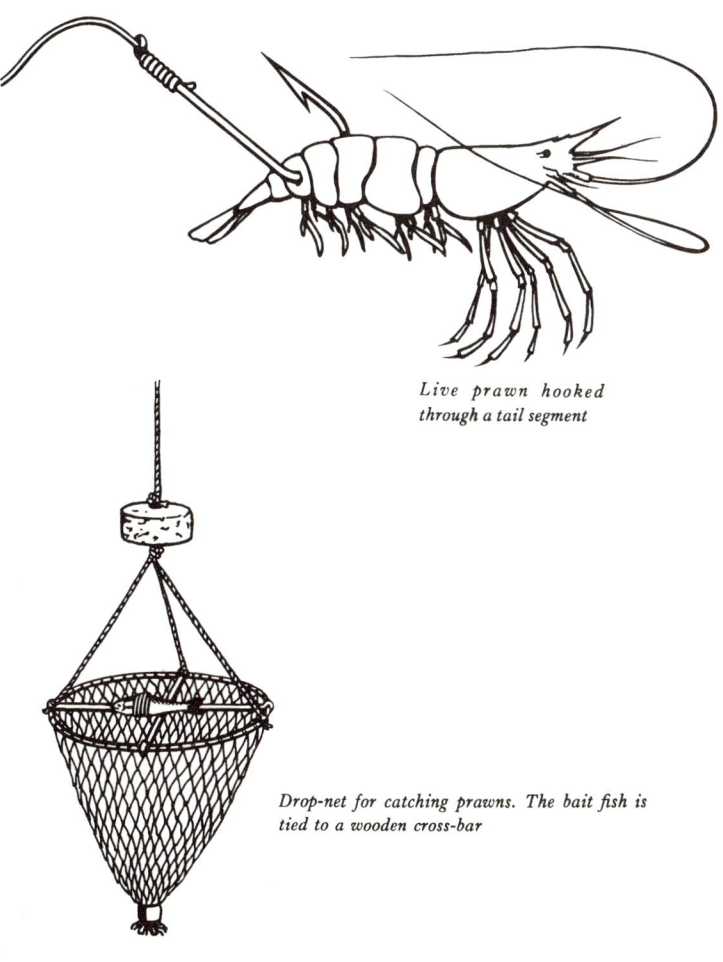

Live prawn hooked through a tail segment

Drop-net for catching prawns. The bait fish is tied to a wooden cross-bar

worms. Also, contrary to popular belief, garden worms remain quite lively in salt water for long periods.

However, for float work I very much prefer the natural prawn. Where rocks are covered with a thick growth of weed, prawns are usually prolific and half an hour with a baited drop-net should produce enough of them for a full a day's fishing. Collecting prawns is a simple enough job, but keeping them alive can be a problem. A large container is required, and it is vital to change the water at frequent intervals – once it is allowed to become stale the prawns will quickly die. A dead prawn is still a quite effective bait, but not half as enticing to a wrasse as a live one. When using a live prawn as bait the hook point should be passed completely through one of the tail segments. This hardly damages the prawn and allows a high degree of movement. Prawns are absolutely perfect for wrasse and often account for the better quality fish – I have had several over the 7 lb (3·1 kg) mark on this bait.

Float tackle is little use where the sea bed is uneven. The float would need to be adjusted for depth in each section of the gully or it would alternatively be dragging the bottom or suspending the bait well above the wrasse.

The Leger

I have tried leger tackle for wrasse on many occasions and found its suitability to be strictly limited. It works well over sandy-bottomed weed-free areas where wrasse pick up much of their food from the bottom, but in weedy or snaggy conditions the leger lead frequently gets hung up and once that has happened a break is an inevitable consequence. I have caught some fine wrasse on leger tackle while jetty fishing in the West Country over sand and mud bottoms.

The most practical leger weight is a ¾ oz (21 g) coffin lead – the type once widely used by freshwater anglers. These weights hold the bottom well and seldom move with the action of the tide. For wrasse fishing the lead should be stopped approximately 18 in. (45 cm) from the hook. Worms or mussels make good baits for this style of fishing.

The Paternoster

Where wrasse are located among a jumble of ledges and weed-grown rocks, the only practical type of terminal tackle to use is a paternoster. Not, I hasten to add, one of the multi-hooked, steel-booms type so popular with pier anglers! No, the wrasse paternoster is a much more delicate affair and easily made up. The simplest way of doing this is to take a 12 in. (30 cm) length of monofil and tie a tiny barrel swivel to one end and a hook to the other. Pass the end of the main line through the swivel eye and run the hook length some 18 in. (45 cm) up the line before stopping it with a single swanshot. Finally, tie a suitable lead to the loose end of the main line.

THE WRASSE FAMILY

The advantage of this tackle lies in the fact that no matter how much variation there is in depth, the bait will always be located just above the sea bed where the wrasse mostly feed.

A good bait for this type of fishing is a hard-back crab – about the size of a 50p piece. These are easily collected, simple to keep, and tough enough to withstand hard knocks against the rocks. To hook on a live crab, the hook point is passed through the bait's shell from the underside so that it protrudes from the back. Mounted in this fashion a crab will stay alive and kicking for a considerable period. One other good bait worth mentioning is the common limpet.

Bites on the paternoster are usually registered by two or three sharp tugs followed by a hard pull. Wait for that final pull and rarely will you fail to hook the fish.

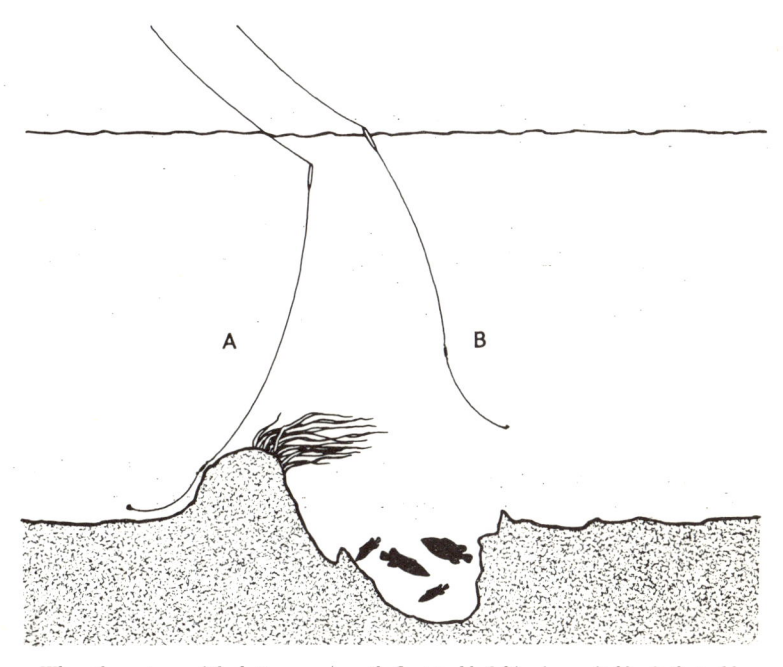

Where the contours of the bottom vary greatly float-tackle fishing is unsuitable. A, the tackle drags and produces false bites. B, it is set too shallow and hangs well above the fish

SHARKS AND SHARK FISHING
Kevin Linnane

Shark. Since the year of *Jaws* the very word conjures up all sorts of images in the minds of non-anglers. They can see 30 ft (9·1 m) monsters cruising around the ocean devouring people and boats, like children eat sweets. Shark fishing to these people is something carried out with harpoons, rifles and explosives. It is somewhat of a disappointment to them when they realize that for shark fishing around Britain and Ireland all that is required is a relatively light rod and reel and a little bit of know-how. Of course, we are not dealing with great white shark because they simply do not come so far north, but what we do have are blue shark, porbeagle shark and occasional mako and thresher sharks. The only shark in these waters that is anywhere near the size of the great white is the basking shark but, mercifully, he is not a huge dangerous thing as he is strictly a plankton feeder – a perfectly harmless leviathan if left alone.

However, as a result of *Jaws* two things have happened. Firstly, many thousands of new 'shark anglers' have come on the scene. These are largely non-anglers who simply want to catch a few shark. They arrive in shark angling centres like Looe and Kinsale and simply make use of existing facilities. They hire out waterproofs, a set of tackle, and book a seat on a charter boat. The rest is in the hands of the skipper who takes them out to the right locations, lays a rubby-dubby trail, mounts the bait, sets it at the right depth, tells his client when to strike and finally boats the fish. All the angler will have done is 'caught' a shark of 60 lb (27·2 kg) to 80 lb (36·2 kg) of which he is justifiably proud. He cannot know that the hired tackle would be more suitable for fishing shark of 500 lb

(226·7 kg) or what is involved in attracting the shark to the vicinity of his bait. I mean no disrespect to these people but I do not really believe they are shark anglers. The true angler is the skipper.

The second thing that happened as a result of *Jaws* is that it instilled a new instinct in the minds of many genuine anglers. These people are now fishing for and catching shark in places that a few years ago were totally ignored. These people succeed because they know something about the shark they are seeking, particularly their feeding habits and distribution.

Of the true sharks that are available in the north-eastern Atlantic, the blue shark is by far the most common. Like Continental tourists they arrive en masse

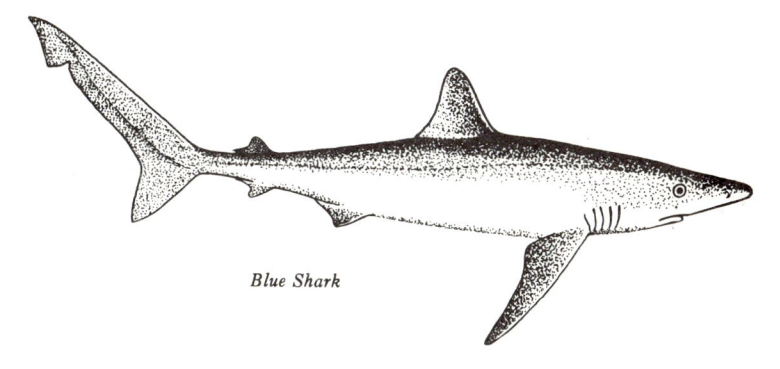

Blue Shark

about the middle of June and remain until the end of September or October, depending on weather conditions. They appear to come in from the south-west, reaching Cornwall and the south-western Irish coast at about the same time. From here, as the water heats up, they spread up along the west coast of Ireland as far as Co. Donegal and I think that we will shortly find out that in fine summers they reach even the west coast of Scotland. On the south coast of Ireland they spread east past Dungarvan but they appear to stay well away from the Irish Sea, possibly because of a slight difference in salinity. From Cornwall they spread up the Channel as far as Tor Bay and north along the Welsh coast as far as Cardigan Bay.

They feed mostly on pelagic species like mackerel, herring and garfish, but will dip down to the bottom occasionally for a feed of whiting, haddock or whatever else they may come across. They are reputed to have a preference for cruising around the oceans in the top 30 fathoms (54·8 m) but some research results are now showing that they occasionally feed deeper then 100 fathoms (182·8 m). However, everybody is quite adamant that they dislike shallow waters, seldom coming inside 12 fathoms (21·9 m). I certainly would not dream of fishing for them in less than 20 fathoms (36·5 m).

The blues we get around the British Isles are quite small by world standards. In southern waters, blues can reach 400 lb (181·4 kg) but The Irish Specimen

Fish Committee has set 100 lb (45·3 kg) as their specimen weight and this is generally accepted as being a good fish.

Although blues as large as 206 lb (93·4 kg) have been taken in Irish waters, and as large as 218 lb (98·8 kg) in English waters, the average fish boated weighs about 40 lb (18·1 kg). Identification of a blue does not present any problem. Its dark, indigo blue back, bright blue sides and pure white stomach cannot be mistaken for any other shark in these waters. For colour-blind anglers, its teeth are triangular and serrated on each side.

The distribution and habits of the porbeagle are not nearly as well known. They have a much wider range than the blue but numerically they are spread

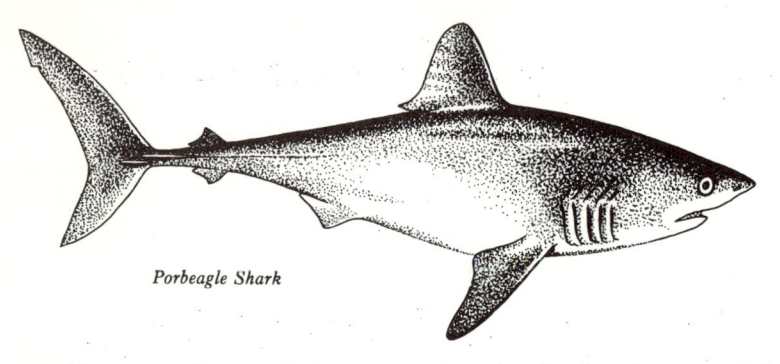

Porbeagle Shark

much thinner over the ground. At some stage or other they have been recorded from almost every stretch of water around the British Isles, from the north of Scotland, the North Sea, the Channel, the Irish Sea and from all around the Irish Coast. There are certain places, however, that they appear to 'adopt' as feeding grounds and they concentrate in these hotspots in large numbers at times. I am thinking of such places as the Isle of Wight and the Clare coast. Over the years these two areas have produced thousands of fine fish but in the last three or four years very few fish have been recorded. The Clare coast produced only about 20 fish in 1976, and I have heard of very few being taken from the Isle of Wight marks. I cannot pretend to understand why this should happen but it is certainly beginning to form a pattern. In the 1930s, Achill Island off Co. Mayo was considered to be the home of the porbeagle, but since then there has been practically nothing. It is beginning to look as if they frequent an area for only a short time before abandoning it in favour of a new feeding ground.

Another interesting thing about porbeagle is that certain size groups appear to adopt different feeding areas. During the good years in Achill, Dr O'Donnell-Brown and his party were taking very big fish. In the course of one month's fishing, six of the fish they landed were over 300 lb (136 kg) and the smallest they encountered was 210 lb (95·2 kg). The same applies to the Isle of Wight. When Dick Downes was running a charter business operating out of Yarmouth, he found that the 200 lb (90·7 kg) plus fish kept strictly to a very small area. Once he went outside the area he met the smaller fish of between 80 lb (36·2 kg) and 100 lb (45·3 kg). On the Clare coast the normal fish was between 80 lb (36·2 kg) and 120 lb (54·4 kg) with only the very occasional one beating 150 lb (68 kg). All this suggests some kind of age segregation which is as yet not fully understood.

Porbeagle, as well as liking deep water, are quite prepared to venture into very shallow areas. I have seen 100 lb (45·3 kg) plus fish in 2 fathoms (3·6 m) of water and a few years ago Jack Shine, one of the finest shore anglers ever to fish the British Isles, was catching 100 lb (45·3 kg) plus porbeagle regularly from the shore in Liscannor Bay in 6 fathoms (10·9 m) of water. I have taken most of my porbeagle on the Clare coast in about 12 fathoms (21·9 m), not more than half a mile (0·804 km) from the shore. Porbeagle feed on mackerel, herring, pollack, coalfish and anything else they may come across. The Irish records include a specimen weighing 365 lb (165·5 kg), while in English waters specimens of 400 lb (181·4 kg) plus have been taken. A porbeagle of 465 lb (210·9 kg) was caught in 1976 by Mr J. Potier, fishing a newly discovered area off north Cornwall.

The identification of a porbeagle must be observed carefully because it can easily be mixed up with a mako. The porbeagle is a thick-bodied fish with a brownish grey back and white underside. Its eyes are fairly large and it has long, smooth, lanceolate teeth which have at their base tiny secondary cusps. The mako is slightly more slender and its back is a deepwater blue. The more specific differences between the two species are the lack of the little basal cusp in the mako's teeth, and also the mako's lack of a secondary keel which the porbeagle has on each side of its tail column.

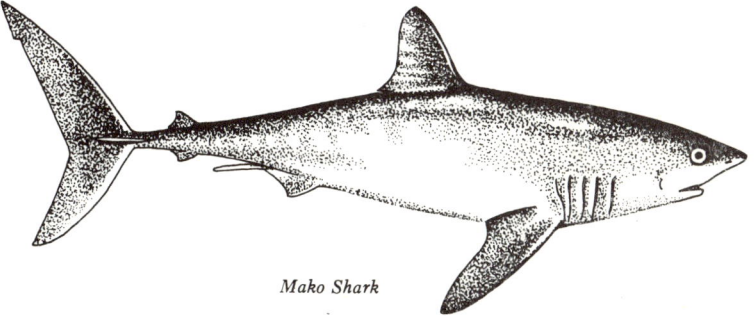

Mako Shark

If an angler hooks a mako it is something he will never forget. When even the most experienced shark anglers lie in bed at night, allowing their fancies to take flight, they dream of an encounter with a mako of a few hundred pounds. (136 kg approx.). It is renowned the whole world over for its fighting ability; time and time again leaping well clear of the water in between clutch-burning runs. Unfortunately for us there are not many of them about. They are truly oceanic sharks which roam around the warm oceans and rarely go deeper then 10 fathoms (18·2 m). They feed on mackerel, herring and bonito, and so far have only been recorded from the mouth of the Channel and the south coast of Ireland, although I have reason to believe that they are not infrequent visitors to the west coast of Ireland. It is most likely that the British Isles are the northern extremity of their range. There is very little known about the habits of the mako, but there are suggestions that they like to hang about the reefs where there is plenty of food available. Certainly there have been quite a few taken around the Manacles, but mostly they have been encountered by accident while fishing for blues. The I.G.F.A. record for the mako is 1,061 lb (481·2 kg). In English waters the largest taken at the time of writing weighed 500 lb (226·7 kg) – by Mrs J. M. Yallop, off Eddystone Light, in 1971 – but I have a feeling that this weight will be smashed before very long.

The fourth shark I would like to discuss before getting down to tackle and tactics is the thresher or fox shark. It is easily identified by its extraordinary tail, which is extremely long and scythe-like and makes up approximately half the total length of its owner. Very few have been landed on rod and line in the British Isles, but they are frequently seen in estuaries. This shark is generally considered to be a warm water species, and is usually encountered close to shore.

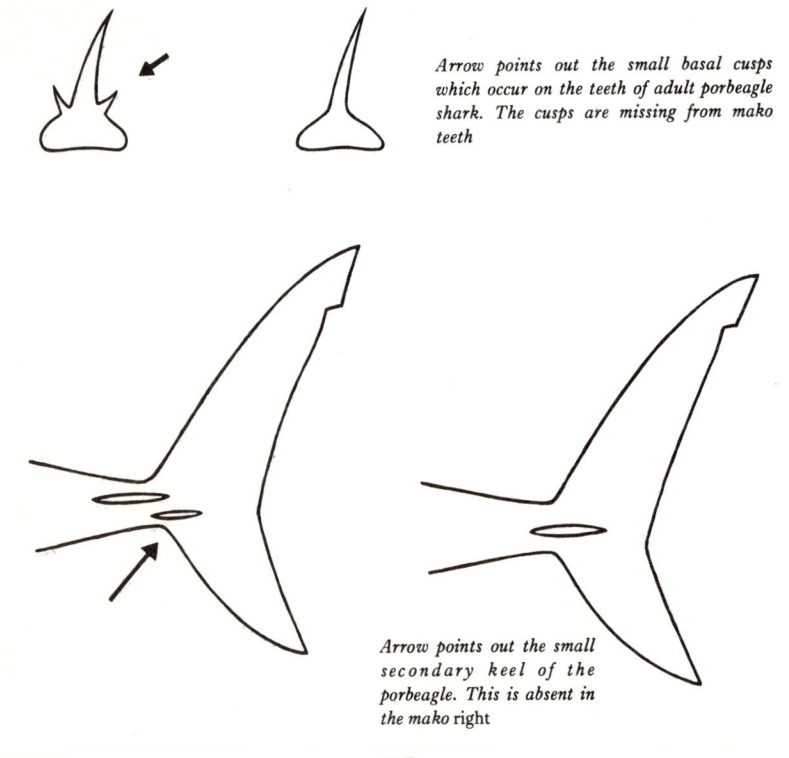

Arrow points out the small basal cusps which occur on the teeth of adult porbeagle shark. The cusps are missing from mako teeth

Arrow points out the small secondary keel of the porbeagle. This is absent in the mako right

It is reputed to swim round and round a shoal of mackerel or herring until they are herded into a tight group, and then to lash at them with its tail to stun and injure as many as possible – which it then mops up at its leisure. There is really very little known about the habits of the thresher around these islands, and only when a lot more of them have been caught will we be able to begin to piece together their life history. We know that they grow large as the I.G.F.A record

Thresher Shark

stands at 729 lb (330·6 kg), but so far the largest taken in British waters weighed less than 300 lb (136 kg).

There are a few other sharks which have been recorded but are not of any great interest to anglers. The six-gilled shark is more like a large dogfish than a true shark. It lives on the bottom and is more likely to be caught by skate and halibut anglers than by shark anglers. There are a number of Irish records, the largest of which scaled 154 lb (69·8 kg). The unmistakable hammerhead is a very rare visitor, but one was hooked in Galway Bay a few years ago and lost at the side of the boat. The greenland shark is a huge, lazy beast that is not uncommon in Scottish waters, but I have never heard of one being hooked.

At least 90% of shark angling carried out in these waters is strictly for blue shark only. As the chances are quite slim of connecting a 100 lb (45·3 kg) plus fish, we should gear our tackle accordingly. The equipment one hires at the normal charter centres is usually much too strong, but it must be added that there is a good reason for this. This type of sharking is very much a commercial proposition and the charter skippers have long since found out that heavy equipment in the hands of 'amateurs' is far less likely to be returned broken than is light tackle. Apart from economics, there can be no justification for catching 50 lb (22·6 kg) blue shark on 9/0 reels loaded with 120 lb (54·4 kg) breaking strain line. It is not very sporting, to say the least. For four years I was employed by the Inland Fisheries Trust to tag large numbers of blues off the south and west coasts of Ireland. With two assistants and a 33 ft (10 m) boat we tagged more than 40 per day on many occasions and our record was established off Co. Kerry where we tagged blues at the rate of 11 per hour. Our normal gear during this exercise was a medium Hardy boat rod and a 4/0 Penn reel filled with 56 lb (17 m) breaking strain line! For pleasure fishing I replace the 4/0 Penn with an ABU 10000 CA filled with 35 lb (10·6 m) braided line, and find this quite adequate.

The make-up of the trace is of vital importance to any shark angler. Very often a blue, or indeed a porbeagle, when tiring, will roll up in the trace. Since the skin of a shark is as abrasive as the best quality sandpaper, it is essential to have a very long trace to avoid getting broken up. Many people use about 20 ft (6 m) of wire for this purpose, but I find that 5 ft (1·5 m) or 6 ft (1·8 m) of 200 lb (90·7 kg) breaking strain wire and approximately 10 ft (3 m) of very heavy 300 lb (136 kg) to 400 lb (181·4 kg) breaking strain monofil is much better. I prefer this type of trace for two reasons. First, it is much cheaper, and second, it is far easier to handle. I have a definite preference for cable-laid wire which is not nylon covered, as tatty bits of nylon hanging off the wire, after one or two fish, has a slightly unnerving effect on me. All connections should be crimped if possible, and the hook, about size 9/0 or 10/0 should be kept needle sharp. Very little else is required in the shark angler's armoury, apart from a few floats – balloons or detergent bottles – to keep the baits suspended at selected depths, a few leads to counteract the drift if it is moving too fast, a good, strong gaff and a pair of wire cutters.

Bait presentation for blue shark does not present any problems. Because of the amount of care that some people take in mounting their baits, I can see eyebrows being raised, but it is simply not necessary. I have heard different people, at different times, insisting that the only way to be sure of hooking a blue is by mounting the bait (it is usually a mackerel) with the head down, the head up, the hook sewn in, the hook-point projecting a ¼ in. (6 mm), and many other variations. The truth of the matter is that if a blue, under the effects of rubby-dubby, decides to take a bait, it will do so regardless of the way it is mounted on the hook. The miser in me refuses to allow any more than half a mackerel for any blue. I simply cut a mackerel in two along the backbone, stick one half on the hook and tie it up with a piece of cotton. This method works well enough for me to recommend it to you without reservation.

If somebody were to go out into the Atlantic and let out a baited hook in the hope of catching a blue, he would probably have to wait for a very long time. There may be many thousands of blues in any area, say off Looe, but they are spread thinly over the sea. They are continually roaming hither and thither in their relentless quest for food, and the chances of one of them just happening across a particular mackerel with a hook in it are, consequently, very small indeed.

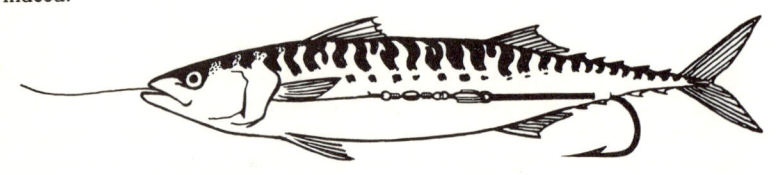

A popular method of mounting a mackerel bait

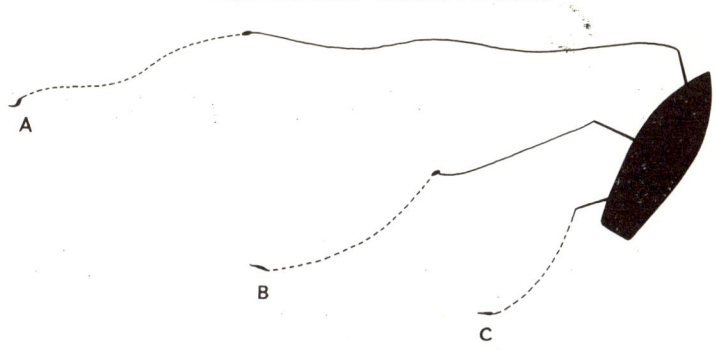

Fishing a drift. Bait 'A' is 6 fathoms (10·9 m) deep; bait 'B' 4 fathoms (7·3 m), and bait 'C' 2 fathoms (3·6 m)

This is where the rubby-dubby comes in. It attracts shark to the vicinity of the baits by making use of their wonderful sense of smell. The system is basically quite simple. A concoction of minced-up mackerel, bran and fish oil is suspended in a net bag over the side of a drifting boat so that, as the boat rolls, the bag, which must be kept topped-up, dips in and out of the water. As the boat drifts on, a thin trail of highly smelly material is laid along the surface of the sea. Some of the blues which are roaming about are bound to swim into the trail and follow it up in the hope of an easy meal. The first sight the fish gets of this meal is a mackerel, or a section of mackerel, suspended in the water. Usually, it will leisurely take this offering, and then find itself hooked. But then again, it may pass it up as being below its expectations and swim right along the trail as far as the boat, where the scent disappears. Then, and this is important to remember, it may well turn around and go down the trail until the scent becomes faint; turning once more and coming back up again. This pattern we established during tagging operations; some fish remaining on the up-and-down course for four or five hours.

The system of tagging we developed in 1972–73 gives ample proof to this fact, but there is not, unfortunately, space enough to describe it here.

But let us return to the angler who is sitting in a boat waiting for his float to bob up and down. If he is lucky, there will only be two or at the most three floats out. Any more will cause chaos, and will certainly not catch any more fish in a day's outing. The three floats should be separated as much as possible; each fishing at a different depth – say 2 fathoms (3·6 m), 4 fathoms (7·3 m), and 6 fathoms (10·9 m), at distances of 20 yards (18·2 m), 40 yards (36·5 m), and 60 yards (54·8 m) from the boat. The reel should be on very light drag with the ratchet on. The first indication of a take may be the float bobbing up and down, or the line may start tearing out setting the reel screaming. At this point the reel should be thrown out of gear, and the fish allowed to take line until it is moving away from the boat. Then the reel is switched into gear, and the fish struck hard. The fish should be played carefully but firmly, making sure not to allow it any slack line, and adjusting the drag as required, until the boatman or a companion can grab hold of the top of the trace. At this point the reel should be thrown out of gear. What is to be done next I shall deal with later.

So far I have been dealing strictly with blue shark, but the principles are the same for fishing any of the other species with rubby-dubby attractor. Only the strength of the tackle differs. If porbeagle are expected then a slightly stronger rod is necessary; matched with a 6/0 reel and 60 lb (27·2 kg) to 70 lb (31·7 kg) breaking strain line. In the unlikely event of somebody being lucky enough to expect a big mako it is advisable to use the strongest possible rod and a 9/0 reel filled to capacity with 120 lb (54·4 kg) breaking strain line.

The first shark I ever caught was a porbeagle, and that was almost 20 years ago. Since then I have been fishing porbeagle for pleasure and tagging purposes as often as I possibly can because they are such fantastic fish. They are not nearly as reliable as the blues – one does not catch a porbeagle every day one tries, even in the most productive locations – and pound for pound they fight so much better. Up to a few years ago I fished conventionally with rubby-dubby tactics, but one day, for a variety of reasons, I tried trolling and found that it clicked, too. Since then I have always trolled for them, and have discovered it to be a far more effective method than the traditional style. The reasons are straightforward enough. Whereas the blue is primarily a scent-feeder, the porbeagle, although also having a good sense of smell, is primarily a sight feeder. It may also be aware of vibrations, although I cannot prove this. I use the same tackle and trace as I would for rubby-dubby, but I mount the bait in a special fashion.

The mackerel is filleted along the backbone from the tail to the back of the head. The backbone is removed, and the hook is passed through the mouth and oesophagus until it is hanging free between the two fillets. A piece of light copper wire is then passed down through the skull, between the eyes, through the mouth and out through the lower jaw. This wire is then crimped to the main trace, in front of the mackerel. It serves not only to keep the bait's mouth closed, but also to prevent the bait sliding down to the hook. When this rig is drawn through the water it 'swims' in an amazingly life-like fashion. The bait is towed at about 2 knots, 80 yards (73·1 m) to 100 yards (91·4 m) behind the boat, searching at about 1 fathom (1·8 m) depth. A 6 oz (170 g) spiral lead, attached to the trace, will bring it down to about 3 fathoms (5·4 m) depth, but I have found this an unnecessary practice. On the Clare coast this system of sharking is lethal, but I cannot say this about other areas for the simple reason that I have not had an opportunity to try it. Only two rods can be fished on the troll, but these two baits entice fish up from 20 fathoms (36·5 m) on a sandy or rocky bottom.

Trolling has many advantages over rubby-dubby fishing. Only half a dozen mackerel are required for a day's fishing, and the horrible smells of rubby-dubby are abolished. The most important advantage, however, has nothing to do with comfort. It is statement of fact that most porbeagle are taken within half a mile (0·804 km) of the shore. This applies to north Cornwall, Galway Bay, the Clare

Three mackerel mounted 'bunch of bananas' style

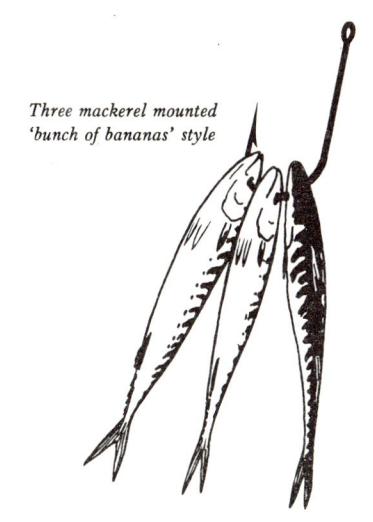

coast, and even the Shetlands which is producing fish over 400 lb (181·4 kg). How often can a good trail be laid along the base of a cliff? Not very often because the wind controls the direction of the drift. Trolling allows the angler to work 100 yards (91·4 m) off the rocks all day, if he so desires, regardless of wind direction. I, for one, would dearly love to try out this system off north Cornwall and Devon. I know it would be very successful – that is, if the porbeagle have not decide to shift feeding grounds by the time I get around to it!

I have never heard of any angler around these islands going specifically fishing for mako. All mako captures have been accidental hookings during blue shark trips; mostly during rough weather when the boat was drifting along at a fair rate of knots. This, of course, would mean that the baits were moving at the time they were taken!

Blues glide in lazy fashion through the water. They are not built for speed and endurance. In fact they are quite weak fish, with highly developed olfactory lobes and, most likely, poor eyesight. They are excellent scavengers. The porbeagle, on the other hand, is built for speed and strength, and has excellent eyesight. He is a tough, powerful predator who chases live food and kills it fast. The mako is even more advanced. Pound for pound a much stronger shark than the porbeagle, and very much faster, too. Everything points to it being a superb and ruthless predator; and the most effective way to catch him, in my opinion, is by trolling. I think it would be well worth somebody's time and effort to spend a week or so trolling around the Manacles with mako specifically in mind.

Finally, we come to decision time. A shark of any species is churning the water into foam at the side of the boat and the trace is held firmly in the gloved hands of the boatman. Those of you who shout 'gaff' should pause and consider. What good is a dead shark, apart from making an impressive photograph? Why not instead reach for the wire cutters and say: 'Well fought, shark, maybe we'll meet again when you have grown even larger.'

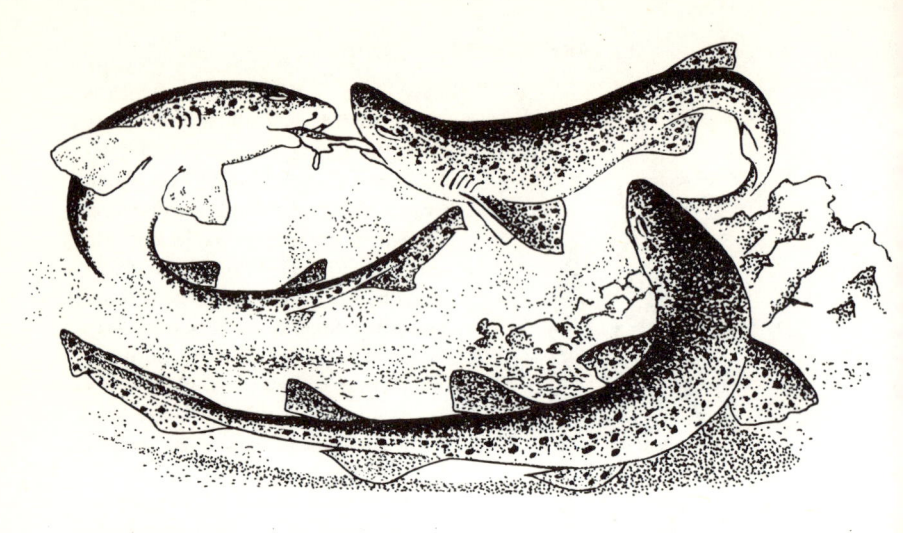

THE DOGFISH *Winston Hall*

Although I have fished from boats, piers, promenades, rocks and beaches all round the British Isles and parts of the Continent for the better part of a lifetime, I realize only too well that I still have much to learn about fish and fishing. However, when it comes to the subject of dogfish I can cast modesty aside without a twinge of conscience.

Since retirement I have settled on the shores of Bantry's Bay in Southern Ireland. Only a mile (1·609 km) from my home is an ex-Royal Navy refuelling jetty, and from it, virtually throughout the whole year, weather and time permitting, I can catch dogfish one after another until the monotony of the exercise bores me to distraction.

Neither dogfish nor their near relatives the shark family are particularly lovable species, and, frankly speaking, I can think of little to say in their favour.

They are named dogfish from their habit of hunting in packs. The term wolf-fish would be even more applicable, although dogfish packs are truly immense and a far greater threat in the sea than ever are the wolves on land. Individually ferocious and voracious with insatiable appetite, a single pack of dogfish leaves a trail of devastation behind it. Its passage is marked by wide corridors of ocean floor denuded of feed and all but the largest and most powerful creatures. In the absence of free-swimming prey, a pack will turn over the bottom with the efficiency of a four-furrow plough. Worms, molluscs – everything edible is taken, leaving an area totally empty.

From a biological viewpoint there is not all that much difference between dogfish and sharks. Indeed, of the four species commonly termed 'dogfish' by sea anglers, only the greater spotted dogfish and the lesser spotted dogfish truly own

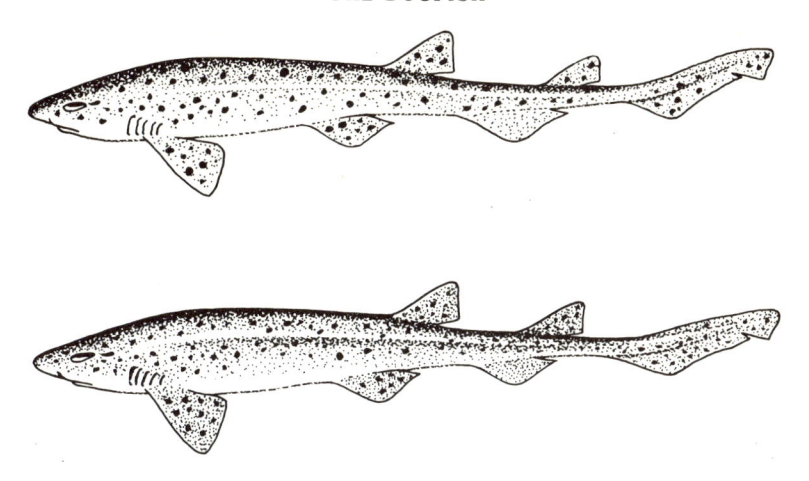

Top, *lesser spotted dogfish* Bottom, *greater spotted dogfish*

the classification. The spur dog is, in reality, a spiny shark. The smooth hound is a shark, pure and simple.

The lesser spotted dogfish, *Scyliorhinus canicula*, alias rough hound, robin huss and sand hound, is generally regarded as an out and out pest. This species, and its bigger brother, *Scyliorhinus stellaris*, better known as the larger spotted dogfish, nurse hound or bull huss, are more alike than any two species have a right to be. Accurate identification has fooled many with knowledge well above average, and it is small wonder that officials responsible for specimen fish awards are constantly plagued with unintentional false claims. What the claimants honestly believe to be lesser spotted dogfish of specimen class, only too often turn out to be undersized greater spotted dogfish. As the terms 'lesser' and 'greater' imply, the essential difference between the two species is one of size. The lesser reaches a maximum length of around 30 in. (76 cm). A full-grown greater may well double that figure. Unfortunately, as we have already noted, size in itself can mean nothing. To use an Irishism, a small 'greater' may well prove considerably smaller than a large 'lesser'.

Generally speaking, the lesser spotted dogfish is covered with numerous small spots. The greater spotted dogfish wears a pattern of larger, less sharply defined spots, which are fewer in number. But as with all generalizations, conclusions so reached can be dangerous. The skin of the lesser spotted dogfish is rougher than that of the greater, but perhaps the most reliable distinguishing features lie in the shaping of the nasal flaps and in the positions of the anal fins.

Wherever our coast offers sizeable stretches of open, sandy beaches, lesser spotted dogfish may be expected; and invariably, when they do turn up, they form shoals so large that they are regarded as pests. The east coast, English

Channel, Irish Sea and Atlantic, abound with them. Des Brennan, speaking of the Irish waters, once confided to me: 'Our lesser spotted friends are too plentiful, literally everywhere, both in deep and shallow waters.'

Most Irish club officials echo this sentiment. At times, they claim, lesser dogfish are around in millions. To quote various friends in Eire: 'A bad dogfish year can ruin serious angling'. 'They'll not let a bait stay on the bottom for a second after touching it.' 'We'd like to ban them from all competitions, but if the dogs are around, you can be certain that nothing else will be caught that day.'

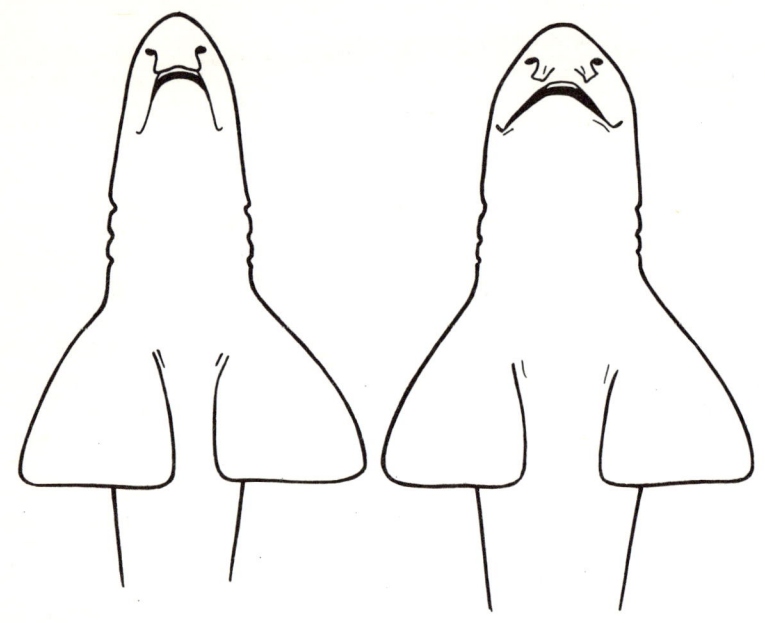

Nasal flaps, and mouth comparisons. Left, *lesser spotted dogfish* Right, *greater spotted dogfish*

Although only a minority of anglers pleasure fish specifically for any of the species, lesser spotted dogfish are often sought during festivals and other competitions. This, not for their sporting qualities, not for food, simply for their dead-weight value on the scales. When a shoal of dogfish is beneath the boat the problem becomes not one of catching the pests but of avoiding them. From a sporting point of view, the over-rewarding task of dropping a sinker to the bottom for the baited hooks to be grabbed by perhaps three dogfish at once, inevitably soon palls on all but the most blood-thirsty fanatic. Those who have yet to get among a shoal of feeding dogfish may doubt this. They should, nevertheless, remember that the larger and more voracious shoals are most likely to be found in deep water – often when the angler (particularly the competitive angler) is set up with heavy tackle in expectation of really big stuff. Consider too, that baits for big-fish angling will consist of whole or halved mackerel, which bait is by no means always available in unlimited supply, and you will concede the annoyance they can cause.

The lesser spotted dogfish is undoubtedly the easiest of all fish to catch – whether on rod or professional long-line. Incidentally, the greater spotted dogfish, spur dog and smooth hound, have little to offer in the way of sporting qualities other than sheer weight. Only by fishing the lightest outfit will the serious angler consider himself entitled to self-congratulation by reason of numerically large bags.

Due to the dogfish's habit of frequenting deep water with the accompanying strong tide-runs, it is unfortunately rarely possible to use really light tackle. Lesser spotted dogfish will, however, freely venture into shallow estuaries and protected bays. In such places, when physical surroundings and formations inhibit tidal currents, it is possible to use ultra-light sea and normal freshwater gear. This can be used as effectively for boat fishing as it can from the shore. For such fishing, either a running leger or a trace rig will prove satisfactory, but owing to the sharp teeth and rough hides of dogfish, hook snoodings should be of at least 12 lb (5·4 kg) breaking strain monofil, and preferably of 15 lb (6·8 kg) strength.

A problem with using a very light rod is lack of power. The jaws of a dogfish are as tough as rubber, and the rod may not have enough backbone to drive the hook home. The answer lies in withholding the strike and allowing the fish to swallow the hook – not to my mind a sporting method of the first order. However, those choosing this approach should lose few fish – providing a long-handled landing net is at the ready.

When fishing for lesser spotted dogfish in shallow water a spinning outfit provides a much more pleasing approach. They are, however, a bottom-feeding clan, and an artificial lure must be worked accordingly.

Approaching the question of a normal bottom tackle for dogfish fishing, I find that conventional bottom rigs answer well enough. My choice is a simple two-hook paternoster fitted with three-way swivels in place of booms and size 1/0 hooks.

There is nothing very complicated in fishing for lesser spotted dogfish. The bite is usually of the emphatic double-knock variety similar to, but more powerful and slower than that of whiting. Reaction should not be over smart. Do not worry, though, about a missed strike, as an interested fish will invariably oblige with a second, even a third go at any bait remaining on a hook.

This brings us to the subject of baits, and quite honestly I have rarely known dogfish to refuse anything. Only in times of desperate food gluts are they likely to prove choosy. However, asked to list baits in order of preference, I would place first small, whole fish. Mackerel, herring or pilchard strip, cut to resemble small fish, would follow. Next I would put lugworm and ragworm, then shellfish, with mussel possibly at the bottom of the list. But bait priority among any of the dogfish is so low that no angler with a single bait in his box need despair.

Thinking of the scavenging habits of dogfish, I am reminded of a friend of mine, Dick Watts, telling me that a run of dogfish along the east midlands coast is nearly always immediately followed by a run of whiting. Puzzled as to why this should be, I finally evolved a feasible theory. Is it not possible that such voracious feeders as the lesser spotted dogfish could also be dirty feeders – dirty that is in the sense of leaving uneaten scraps floating around behind them? Whiting, after all, are notoriously off-bottom feeders. I wonder – do they follow the dogfish after the manner of jackals trailing a prey? Another less attractive suggestion is that the whiting are possibly motivated by the same urge that compels birds to follow migrating herds of vegetarian animals?

Commercially, the value of lesser spotted dogfish flesh varies greatly according to locality. The Home Counties offer the best outlet. There the fish are sold in fish and chip shops under the rather misleading name of 'huss'. Wet fish shops include lesser spotted dogfish under the more appealing title of 'rock salmon'. The demand is considerable and one professional skipper tells me that he spends the summer months long-lining for dogfish out of Grimsby. I have also seen large quantities of lesser spotted dogfish landed at Looe. Like the Grimsby fish, these are dispatched to the London market.

On the quayside at Looe, I have joined crowds of holiday spectators around the fish sheds where dogfish have been under preparation for dispatch. Each fish is impaled by the head on a fixed hook. The flenser makes things look easy; with a slick cut in the skin below the head and a single jerk ripping the skin from the body. It is remarkably like peeling off a sock by turning it inside out. Actually, the fried flesh of the lesser spotted dogfish is perfectly palatable and very good eating. Apart from the long, cartilaginous spinal cord the fish is virtually boneless. The flesh should not by choice be eaten the same day as caught and never when tainted with ammonia.

Conservation-minded anglers need not worry about killing dogfish for eating purposes. They are far too widespread and numerous to ever be severely decimated by rod and line fishing.

Before dismissing lesser spotted dogfish, it is necessary to warn the uninitiated about careless handling of any specimen captured. The skin is rough as a rasp, and was indeed used by seventeenth-century cabinet makers as sandpaper. The beautiful finish on many pieces of the period tells its own story.

While being unhooked, a dogfish will twist and writhe like an eel, and may easily skin the wrist or hand of an angler who does not take sufficient care. Aware of this danger, many an angler who should know better has treated live dogfish with inexcusable brutality. Even professional angling skippers have been known to tread a dogfish under a seabooted foot in order to tear out a huge 8/0 or 10/0 skate hook. All so unnecessary when a blow on the head from a priest before unhooking makes the whole task cleaner and more sporting.

Most anglers see little point in returning lesser spotted dogfish to the water alive. Few sportsmen actually enjoy killing rats — but it must be done. If you feel you must return your fish, a dogfish can be safely handled by grasping its body immediately below the head, doubling up the tail and clamping it against the body with the thumb. This requires practice and a firm grip. A thick cloth will be found helpful.

Notable lesser spotted dogfish captures include a 4 lb 8 oz (2 kg) specimen taken by Mr J. Beattie, off Ayr Pier, Scotland, in 1969, and a 3 lb 12 oz 8 drm (1·7 kg) specimen taken by Mr A. Gibson, from the Firth of Clyde, in 1967.

Greater Spotted Dogfish

The greater spotted dogfish is better known in the south as the bull huss, and in the north as the nurse hound. For angling purposes we may regard it as a different sub-breed rather than a different species. Size apart, the main variance to concern us lies in where to search for it. While the lesser is addicted to open prairies of clean sand, the greater is more of a deep water fish, favouring rock, mud and scree bottoms. It is every bit as voracious, greedy and gregarious as its smaller brother, and no less of a pest. One way and another the species has been thoroughly blasphemed. Even the staidest of biologists have no hesitation in calling the breed lousy — using an adjective rather than an epithet. A single fish carries as many parasites as a sea-urchin has spines; these minute creatures must torment it to the point of madness. Some cause little but discomfort; others, such as gill worms, behave like leeches, feasting on the blood stream of their unfortunate host and eventually causing serious damage.

Bull huss have a preference for warmer waters, and marks influenced by the gulf stream, even if only slightly so, are densely populated. In Sussex, the area around Littlehampton is one of their happiest hunting grounds. Chesil Beach and West Bay are other well-populated areas, as are suitable bottoms off the Devon and Cornish coasts. The big-fish hunter should also try his luck in Ireland, where Dingle, Valentia Island and Courtmacsherry have yielded many outstanding specimens.

Wherever bull huss are fished for, little specialization in tackle or methods is called for, but since deep water demands heavy leads the fishing rarely lends itself to light gear. Either a stoutish paternoster or trace will do for the business end, but I believe a running leger to be the best rig. The great thing to remember is that, unlike those other dogfish we have under consideration, bull huss are inclined to mouth the bait before properly taking it. When using a running leger this can make the setting of the hook a bit of a tricky business.

Time after time a fish will take only part of a bait without getting the hook properly between its jaws. It then hangs on with the tenacity of a bulldog and fights all the way up. Consequently, the angler is convinced that his fish is 'on', and confidently retrieves, but the fish, on seeing the boat (or is it when reaching the surface?), will release its hold, leaving the angler with nothing but a badly mangled bait. This infuriating experience I have suffered many times with ling and conger as well as with big dogfish, but with the former two species it is hard to avoid, owing to the 'too much fish and too little hook' sort of baits needed.

When fishing specifically for greater spotted dogfish, chances can be increased by threading small slivers of fish bait on a long-shanked hook. Any size hook between 1/0 and 8/0 will serve, but in my experience the smaller the hook the better the method works. Two double-bait hooks rigged pennel-tackle fashion is another useful rig of my own design, that often succeeds when other set-ups fail.

As with the lesser spotted dogfish, bait selection is of no great importance, but here again whole fish is undoubtedly best of all. Strips of fish – mackerel, herring, pilchard, etc. – come a close second.

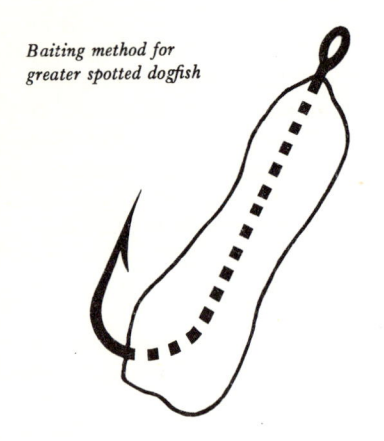

Baiting method for greater spotted dogfish

I firmly believe that where any member of the shark family is concerned, rubby-dubby is of more importance than a wide selection of baits. All these fish are exceptionally sensitive to scent in the tidal stream, and will follow up a trail to its source even over a distance of several miles. A splendid rubby-dubby consists of mashed fish (preferably of the more oily species) mixed with either sawdust or bran. Fish oil or slaughterhouse blood should be added when obtainable. No real need to follow the traditional practice of tying the sack to the anchor cable; simply bend a 6 ft (1·8 m) length of line to the sack's neck and lower it overboard. Keep it on the tidal side, or the end of the boat, to avoid snagging it during fishing.

Bull huss weighing over 21 lb (9·5 kg) have been caught from both British and Irish waters, but fish of this class are quite exceptional. A bull huss of 12 lb (5·4 kg) or over is a very good fish indeed.

Spur Dog

Before moving on to the spur dog, or piked dogfish, *Squalus acanthias*, and the smooth hound, *Mustelus mustelus*, it is as well to discuss the points of difference between these species. Fortunately, these are sufficiently wide to prevent any real confusion. Ironically, it is between the smooth hound and the tope that mistakes in identification are most common.

In colour, the tope lacks the whitish spots common to both the spur dog and the smooth hound. Differences are also apparent in the positionings of the first

THE DOGFISH

dorsal and the pectoral fins. In the smooth hound, the first dorsal is situated slightly behind, but partly above the pectorals. In the tope, fin placings are more positively separated, with the pectorals being well in front of the first dorsal.

The tope's teeth are triangular and pointed, while those of the smooth hound are flat 'grinders'. However, an even greater difference to the casual observer, is the shaping of the tail fin.

The spur dog, on the other hand, is quite unmistakable. Its colour may be dark grey, brownish or slightly blued. It has white or grey spots, although these, at times, can be so faint as to be hardly discernible. In comparison with the rest of the small sharks, the back of the spur dog gives a less streamlined (slightly humped) impression. However, since it is the only dogfish to possess spines – situated on the leading edge of each dorsal – these offer a positive means of identification.

At first sight these spines, or spurs, appear innocent enough, but do watch for them! Careless handling can result in dangerous wounds in which blood poisoning may develop. Take no liberties. Kill the fish immediately it is boated, and before handling nip off the spurs with sharp pliers, and throw the spurs over-

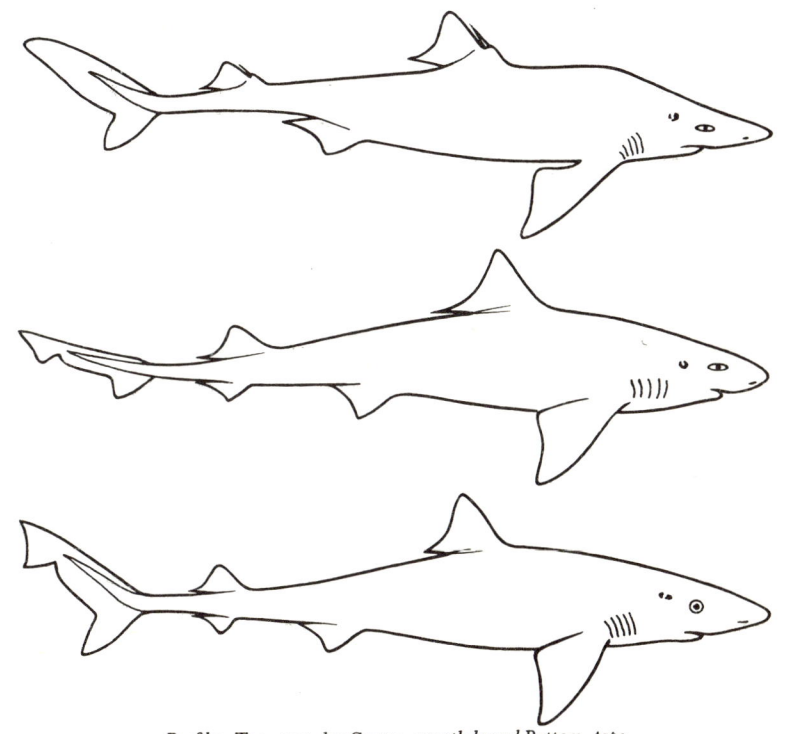

Profiles. Top, *spur dog* Centre, *smooth hound* Bottom, *tope*

board. However, do not remove the spurs if you intend returning the fish alive.

Spur dogs are found in both deep and shallow water. This means adapting tackle to meet existing conditions. A line strength of 18 lb (8·1 kg) to 20 lb (9 kg) is sufficient, but considerably heavier terminal gear should be fitted to counteract the abrasive nature of the spur dog's skin.

Specialized tackle for spur dog fishing is as unnecessary as for any of the dogfish group, but to get the best out of a not particularly sporting species, light leads and a long, flowing trace are advisable providing conditions allow. Nevertheless, since spur dogs will often feed a little off bottom, a stout, boomed paternoster will – if the shoal is extensive – more often than not account for a fish per hook. That is, of course, if you enjoy such fishing.

Wherever lesser spotted dogfish are known to visit, spur dogs may also be expected to turn up. The packs are every bit as numerous, every bit as mean (in the American sense of the term) and every bit as destructive to other sea life as their lesser cousins. In other words, if a shoal is beneath your boat you can expect to catch little else until you move marks.

Michael Kennedy, a well known Irish angler, explained to me that spur dog packs work the Clew Bay, Co. Mayo area on a sort of annual rota system. Some years they are so plentiful that one needs merely to drop a three-hook trace into the sea, to pull up as many fish. Back in 1959 the glut was so great that spur dogs became regarded as less than vermin. The bay was a veritable paradise for anyone seeking large bags of easily-caught big fish. During the following three years, hardly a spur dog ventured into the bay. Then 1963 saw a return of the species, with numbers as overwhelming as ever. The pattern apparently still continues.

To digress a little, it may be of interest to mention that Michael Kennedy has succeeded in putting lesser spotted dogfish to good use. He got the idea when a 100 lb (45·3 kg) plus, rod-caught common skate, hanging from his mast head, disgorged half a dozen freshly swallowed lessers. Taking the obvious hint, he has since used whole dogfish as bait for skate (also monkfish) with considerable success.

Spur dog reach weights exceeding 20 lb (9 kg). A 20 lb 3 oz (9·1 kg) specimen was taken in 1972 by Mr J. Newman, fishing off the Isle of Wight to the south of the Needles Lighthouse.

Smooth Hound

The smooth hound is the least important of the dogfish in British waters. Strictly speaking, it has no business to be so classified, as it is essentially a true shark. There are really two species of smooth hound found off our shores, but they differ so little from each other that identification is a matter of specialized knowledge mainly based on the shapes of the skin denticles which take the place of scales in normal fish.

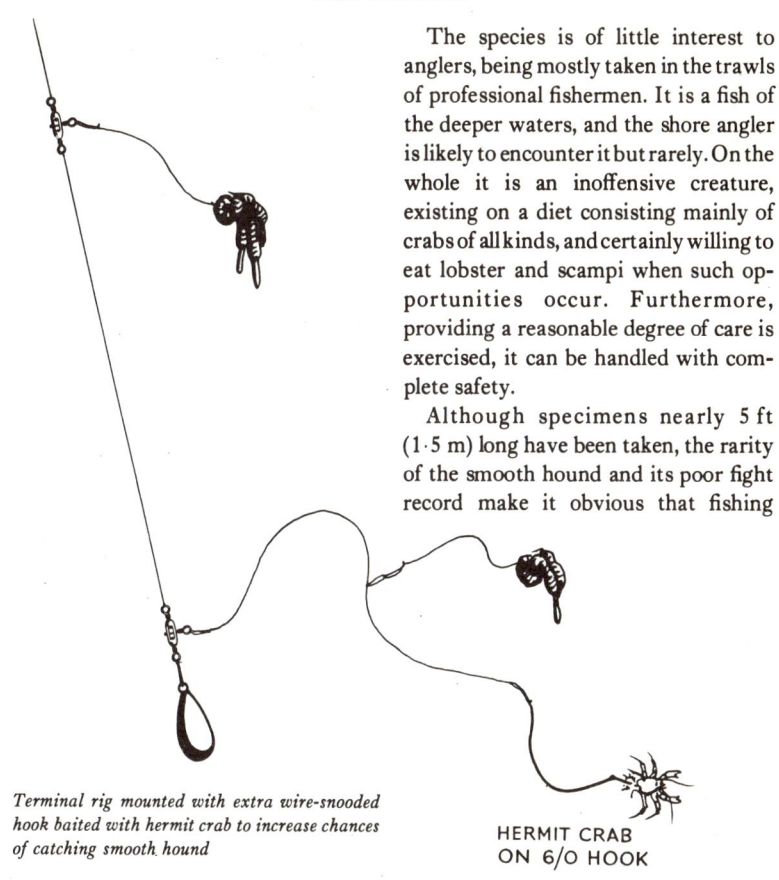

THE DOGFISH

The species is of little interest to anglers, being mostly taken in the trawls of professional fishermen. It is a fish of the deeper waters, and the shore angler is likely to encounter it but rarely. On the whole it is an inoffensive creature, existing on a diet consisting mainly of crabs of all kinds, and certainly willing to eat lobster and scampi when such opportunities occur. Furthermore, providing a reasonable degree of care is exercised, it can be handled with complete safety.

Although specimens nearly 5 ft (1·5 m) long have been taken, the rarity of the smooth hound and its poor fight record make it obvious that fishing

Terminal rig mounted with extra wire-snooded hook baited with hermit crab to increase chances of catching smooth hound

HERMIT CRAB ON 6/0 HOOK

specifically for this species can be an unrewarding business.

The cod angler keen to capture a smooth hound might do worse than add a wire-snooded hook baited with hermit crab to the end of his trace – which should prove equally attractive to cod. The smooth hound is very fond of hard bottoms of clean sand, and is caught as often from marks of this type located off the Essex and Suffolk coasts to the north of the Thames Estuary, as anywhere else. Good cod grounds these, and venues where inexpensive experiments with the smooth hound might pay off – and with this species research could be a most rewarding business, for little is really known of the angling possibilities involved.

Notable smooth hound captures include a 28 lb (12·7 kg) specimen of *Mustelus mustelus* taken off Heacham, in 1969, by Mr A. T. Chilvers, and a 23 lb 2 oz (9·1 kg) specimen of *Mustelus asterias* taken from the beach at Bradwell-on-Sea, in 1972, by Mr D. Carpenter.

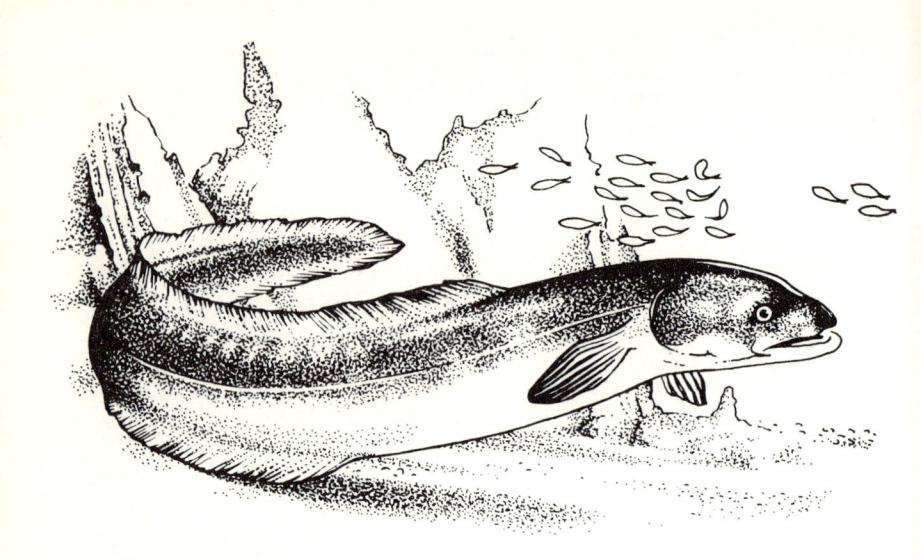

CONGER FISHING *Bruce McMillen*

The conger is a muscular, immensely powerful fish, and the tackling of a really large specimen will tax the energy of any angler. The species is found in many areas of the world and in all British Isles waters. It is said to spawn once only, in depths exceeding 1,000 fathoms (1828·8 m), and then to die. The male is believed to attain a maximum weight of only 7 lb (3·1 kg), so that, in view of this, all large conger are essentially females. Moveover, it has been said that the females sometimes eat the males! And I recall the claim of one old Manx fisherman, who stated that he had found a 5 lb (2·2 kg) conger inside a 28 lb (12·7 kg) female of the species.

Conger vary in colour according to their surroundings. Some are greyish white, others blackish grey, or even camouflaged with a mottling of several shades of these colours. The underparts vary from greyish white to almost pure white. Teeth are sharp and powerful, with a tremendous cutting potential.

Conger grow to huge size. In 1974, Mr R. B. Thomson caught a specimen weighing 102 lb 8 oz (46·4 kg) from a mark off Mevagissey, Cornwall, and in 1976, Mr R. Potter boated an even bigger one, scaling 109 lb 6 oz (49·6 kg), out from Plymouth, Devon. Yarrell (1836) mentions a conger of 130 lb (58·9 kg). In 1959, an 87 lb (39·4 kg) specimen was found alive and stranded in the Welsh Dee. According to Bickerdyke (1885) a conger in Southport Aquarium attained a weight of 90 lb (40·8 kg) in five and a half years, which would seem to suggest that under certain conditions the growth rate of these fish is very rapid.

Many divers examining wrecks and breakwaters (both of which are favourite haunts of conger), have reported seeing specimens exceeding an estimated 100 lb

PLATE 9

Barnstable angler, Bob Maunder, with a truly outstanding conger of 70 lb (31·7 kg) The line he used had a B.S. of 45 lb (20·4 kg), which makes the capture even more remarkable

Photo:
Bruce McMillen

Angling magazine editor, Brian Harris, with a very fine bass which pulled 10 lb 2 oz (4·6 kg). It came from an estuary mark where the fish lie in fast water, only about 2 feet deep on the ebb

Photo: B. Farey

PLATE 10

Tony Dolman unhooks a good ballan wrasse caught from a rock-hole along the wild coastline of Co. Kerry, Southern Ireland. Note the thick, tough lips of this species

Photo:
Trevor Housby

Small pollack taken on the feathers

Photo:
Ernest Merritt

Above left:
The late Mr G. Davies displays a 16 lb (7·2 kg) specimen turbot caught from the famed Shambles mark

Photo:
E. H. Harding

Above right:
Plaice 4 lb 4 oz (1·9 kg) from Poole Harbour, the location of many big plaice captures

Photo: *D. Davis*

PLATE 11

Ken Townley displays a top-quality ling of 33 lb (14·9 kg). The specimen was lured from a wreck mark out of Fowey, Cornwall

Photo:
Trevor Housby

An excellent shore-caught flounder
taken by Ernest Merritt

Photo: Ernest Merritt

A big porbeagle shark alongside the boat off the Isle of
Wight. Although played-out and very tired, a beaten
shark remains a dangerous customer and requires very
careful handling   *Photo: Trevor Housby*

PLATE 12

Clive Gammon
fighting a blue sh
off Kinsale, Coun
Cork. Boatman in
picture is Jerry
O'Donovan

Photo: Des Brenn

PLATE 13

Digging for lugworms, the most popular of all the sea baits, at Robin Hood's Bay, Yorkshire

Photo: Ernest Merritt

A black lugworm

Photo: Ernest Merritt

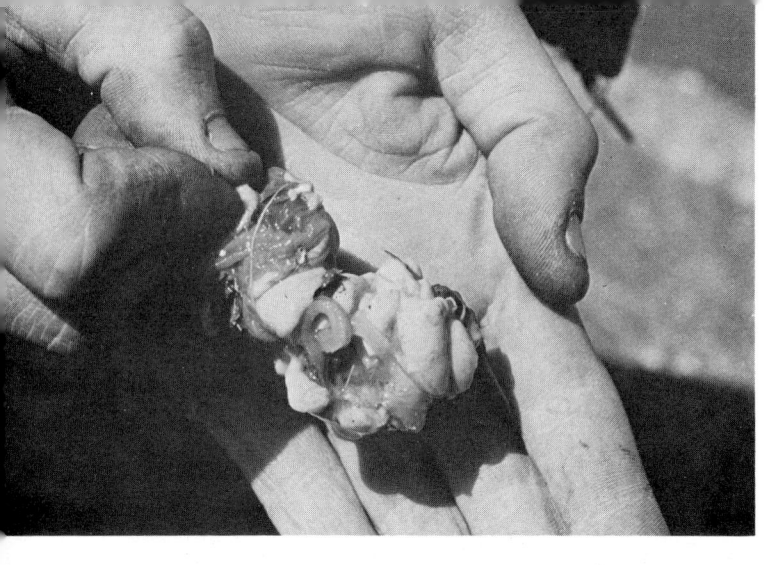

PLATE 14

Left: Mussel-baited hook – a large helping for a big (

Photo:
Ernest Merritt

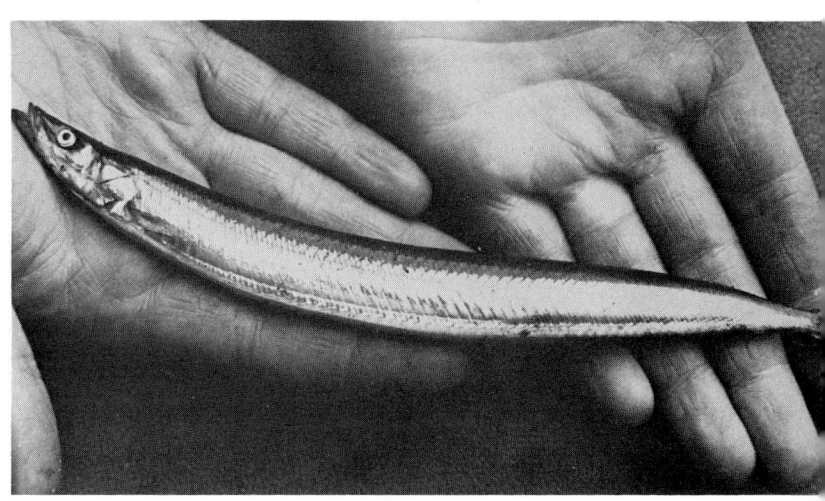

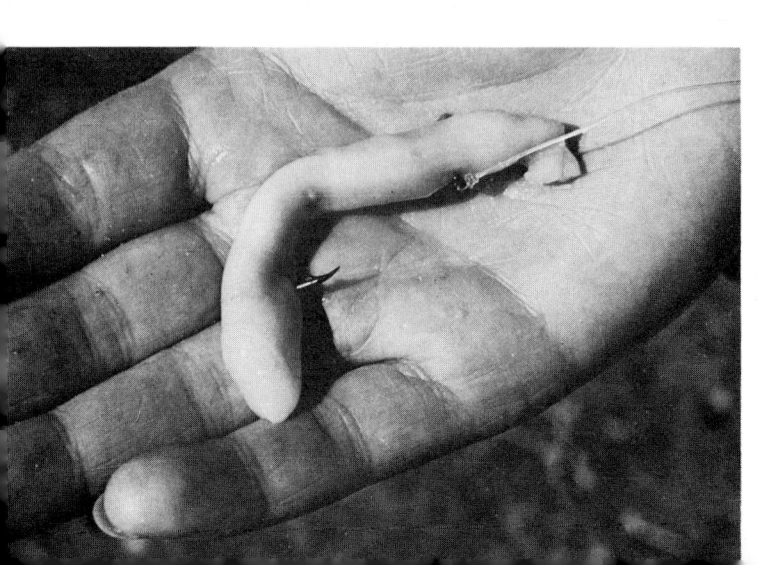

Above: A sandeel first class bait for many species of f but particularly fo bass

Photo:
Ernest Merritt

Left: A hook bait with razorfish

Photo:
Ernest Merritt

PLATE 15

Netting shrimps. The youngster in the picture is dealing with a sting fish by using an old table fork

Photo:
Ray Forsberg

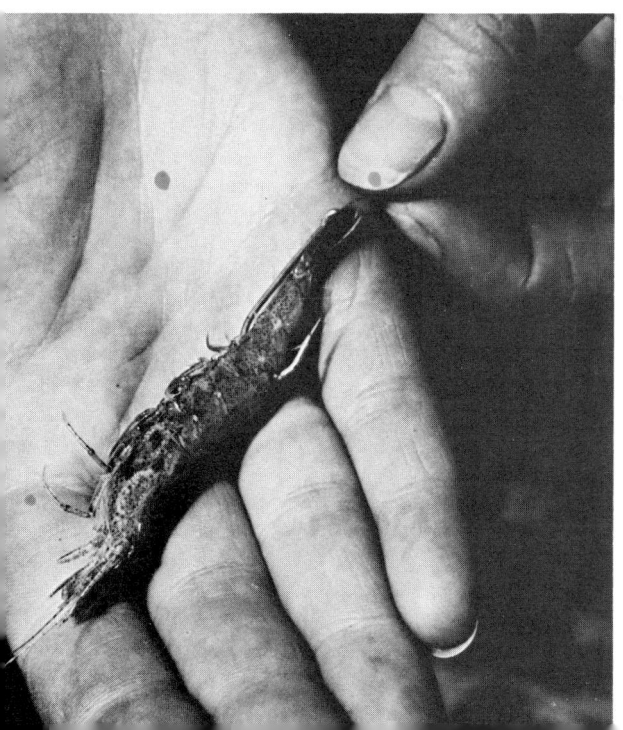

A shrimp bait mounted with the hook passed correctly through a tail segment

Photo:
Ernest Merritt

PLATE 16

Collecting peeler crabs at low water. It is a good idea to make a mental note of the rocky ground when bait hunting, to help in successfully fishing the area later on

Photo: A. Nevison

Southern I.T.V. angling personality, Jack Hargreaves, out off the Isle of Wight, baits-up his skate tackle with a mackerel

Photo: Trevor Housby

(45·3 kg) in weight, but they wisely avoid tackling these monsters owing to possible hazards – such as those connected with possible severage of air-lines, etc.

Some years ago I heard of a diver who had the fright of his life when he came face to face with an enormous conger, gazing malevolently at him through the porthole of an old wreck. The diver insisted that so huge was this fish, its head had actually become jammed in the porthole! Now, considering the average diameter of a ship's porthole, this fish would – if the diver had spoken the truth – have surely been the 'daddy' of all congers. Maybe he was right, but I have not heard tell of any diver subsequently going down in order to prove or disprove the story.

There are certainly many legendary stories concerning conger, and these have doubtless been responsible for the fired imaginations of specimen-conger hunters. Conversely, such stories have also scared some anglers badly enough to keep them well away from conger and conger fishing for the rest of their lives. Of one thing there can be no doubt – a truly large conger, hooked on relatively light tackle, will put up a tremendous fight before it can finally be subdued or, as often is the case, it breaks free. An angler engaged in wreck fishing, may be faced with the daunting task of trying to dislodge a hooked conger which has power-dived back to its home within the wreck. Then, no matter how heavy the tackle, the conger is more likely to win the day.

In my schooldays, the idea of conger fishing certainly stirred my youthful imagination. An uncle of mine would sometimes take me on conger expeditions, which were always conducted at night after the village pub had closed! I well remember those thrilling evenings when we would depart the shore full of anticipation, returning on many occasions with literally a boat-load of sizeable conger weighing anything up to 50 lb (22·6 kg) apiece. This was a somewhat hazardous business, as it often involved hugging the rocky headlands and bays of the Manx coastline, where occasional huge pinnacle rocks rose sheer from deep water to near-surface. Miraculously, even on the darkest of nights, we always managed to avoid these dangerous pinnacles, some of which would only just be submerged. We did, however, at times experience some frightening moments.

In those days, our sole means of artificial illumination invariably consisted of either a parafin lamp or an electric torch. One night, a particularly lively conger caught the lantern with a mighty swish of her tail, sending it flying overboard and into the sea! On another occasion, an over-excitable member of the party sought to transfix a conger with his knife, and in the semi-darkness drove the blade clean through the side of his rubber boot, only just missing his foot!

Many lessons emerge from such experiences. For example, when night fishing for conger, there should always be a reserve source of artificial illumination available, and such illumination should be entirely adequate for what may sometimes develop into quite a dangerous situation. It is also wise for the tyro to leave the handling of a boated conger to someone more experienced than he.

Some angling writers are inclined to mislead their readers into believing that daylight fishing for conger is not productive, and that these fish should be sought only at night. Admittedly (particularly in relatively shallow waters) congers feed more avidly during the hours of darkness, but some excellent catches of specimen-sized fish are regularly taken during daylight hours, from both shallow and deep water marks.

One lovely, sunny afternoon, again during my schooldays, I approached some friendly boatmen on the beach of a Manx bay famous for its conger. I asked them for a boat, and for an empty herring barrel complete with lid. My light tackle evoked some humour, as also did my request for the barrel. 'You'll never catch conger on that tackle, Mac! And what do you want the empty barrel for?'

Some hours later, a jubilant, but rather tired young angler returned to the beach. The now curious boatmen lifted the barrel – which I had weighted with stones – out of the boat. 'What the hell have you got in it, Mac?' Inside the barrel lay four conger. They scaled precisely 112 lb (50.8 kg). After that successful episode, I always felt that the boatmen treated me with an extra degree of respect for having managed both the heavy boat and the struggling congers single handed.

The light tackle caught the conger, and the barrel kept them from slithering all over the deck. An old barrel or, alternatively, an empty sack serves the dual purpose of keeping the boat clean and tidy and holding the catch.

In order to kill a conger, it is essential to drive a sharp-pointed knife through the spine, just at the back of the head. Although this is intended to kill the conger, it does not always do so, but it is, nevertheless, a far better method than hammering the fish on the head and then assuming it to be dead when very often it has just been temporarily stunned. By all means stun the fish before driving the knife-blade in, as this will help make the task less difficult.

Conger can inflict particularly painful wounds, and here is an example of its abilities in this respect. While seeking edible crabs on a rocky beach, I inserted my hand into what appeared to be a crab-hole. My index finger was promptly grabbed by something which was certainly *not* a crab. The pain was intense, to say the least, but I had no alternative other than to withdraw my hand very gradually from the hole, with the 'something' still clamped tight to the throbbing digit. 'It' turned out to be a conger, which was promptly dispatched by a friend and weighed in at 7 lb (3.1 kg) – only a relatively small fish, but what a bite! My badly lacerated finger ached for weeks before it healed, a constant reminder that, when 'crabbing' under rocks, you should *never* insert a hand into what appears to be a crab-hole. The conger inside might prove to be something appreciably heavier than 7 lb (3.1 kg) and you may not be able to withdraw your hand – a nasty state of affairs if you happen to be on your own facing a rapidly rising tide.

The following incident shows another characteristic of these fish. While angling at low water from a sandy beach which was interspersed with large boulders and pieces of rock, I hooked a conger. After playing the fish for some time it finally, and to my utter amazement, came right out of the water and slithered up the beach behind me, actually landing itself!

In 1881, at Colwyn Bay, North Wales, a porpoise was observed to be chasing a conger, which eventually came out of the water and began to climb the sloping beach, where it was captured by a spectator.

From these observations it would appear that conger in relatively shallow water, will vacate their natural habitat in an effort to escape from danger.

I have been in the fortunate position of being able to observe the habits of conger in clear water, alongside a privately-owned old stone jetty, where some huge specimens could be seen in the act of vacating their hidey-holes in the jetty structure and moving out over the sea bed. At that time of tide the water would be less than 2 fathoms (3·6 m) in depth.

Efforts to tempt these fish with a baited hook proved abortive, until I hit upon the idea of dropping the offering right on to their noses. This action seemed to annoy them, for it certainly proved successful. It was quite a thrill to see these large creatures actually swallowing the bait, and then to await the terrific flurry of activity which inevitably followed. I do not think they were really interested in feeding, but I do suspect that the very act of placing the bait virtually in their mouths just made them feel that they had to grab it.

I recall hooking one of these fine specimens and pumping it to the surface. Lifting the fish from the water to the top of the jetty was an arduous job, so I asked a boat angler fishing nearby if he would kindly gaff and boat the fish for me. He replied quite vehemently that he would not. He was actually afraid of the conger – as indeed are a great many anglers when they bring one of these troublesome fish into the boat.

One can quite understand the fears of anglers inexperienced in conger fishing when a sizeable specimen is boated, and so it is advisable to take the following precautions.

First, as soon as the fish is brought aboard, let the boatman or the most experienced angler in the boat take care of subduing it. As already mentioned, a heavy blow on the head (or on the tail) may be given to temporarily stun it, but afterwards it should be killed with a knife-point as previously suggested. Leave plenty of space on the deck, for the purpose of dealing with the fish – the threshing tail can wreak havoc with such things as loose fittings, lines and ropes, and, indeed, the ankles of any angler with which it may come into contact.

The conger gaff *must* be really strong, for the twisting action of these fish can easily distort a light instrument beyond recognition. The same action can also put excessive strain on the angler's wrist, and even unscrew a detachable-head gaff completely. There are few suitable gaffs available on the market at the present time, and therefore the best plan is to construct your own by purchasing a heavy-gauge, lash-on type gaff-hook and binding it to a stout pole.

Even better still is a gaff with a swivel head, which allows a large conger to spin and thrash about – but without imparting a twisting effect on the handle of the gaff and therefore the angler's grip. My own swivel-head gaff is fitted with a *barbed* hook which has a gape of 2¾ in. (7 cm). The diameter of the metal is ½ in. (12 mm). The barb assists in holding a conger firmly on the hook as it swivels round.

In order to avoid the accidental loss of the gaff when tackling a fish, secure a length of Courlene or similar line to the gaff-handle, looping the other end of the line to your wrist or, alternatively, to a convenient point in the boat. Then, if the conger does manage to swim away with your gaff, it cannot take it very far. Always keep the point of the gaff-hook really sharp, and when gaffing a fish, endeavour to get a good hook-hold in its vent – a most vulnerable part of the conger's anatomy when it comes to subduing its struggles.

It may not, of course, always be possible to insert the gaff into this exact position, but a most important point to remember is that the gaff must be driven hard into the fish. The actual gaffing operation is not usually carried out by the captor (unless he happens to be alone in the boat) because he will find himself fully occupied in manoeuvring the conger into a gaffing position alongside the boat. Once the fish is close in, maintain a tight line, otherwise the conger will almost certainly start to spin violently in its struggles to get free, rolling any loose line around itself. The gaff-handler should waste no time in getting the fish into the boat and under control.

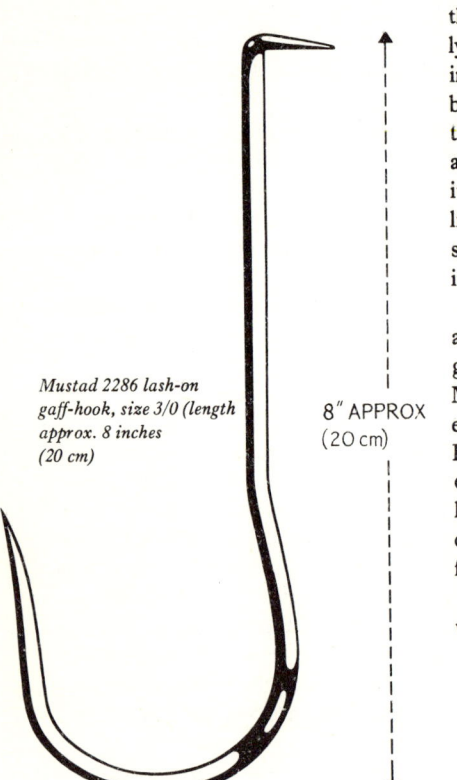

There is some controversy among anglers concerning the ideal size for conger hooks. Is there indeed an 'ideal' size? Much depends upon the size of fish to be expected and the type of bait to be used. Personally, I have found the 'swivel-eyed' conger hook, size 5/0, to be entirely adequate for all but really monster congers, which are best tackled with a forged hook, size 10/0 at least.

The trace should be of stainless steel wire cable, and between 12 in. (30 cm)

Mustad 2286 lash-on gaff-hook, size 3/0 (length approx. 8 inches (20 cm)

8" APPROX (20 cm)

CONGER FISHING

and 18 in. (45 cm) long. At the top of the trace secure a good quality swivel, size 3/0 or larger, and to this swivel attach a stainless steel screw link fitting for quick attachment and detachment from the main line. This will obviate the necessity for immediate removal of the hook from a captured conger. Carry plenty of spare traces – you may well need them if you locate a stock of conger indulging in a feeding rampage.

The shape and weight of the sinker is a matter for individual choice, but always remember that the stronger the tideway, the heavier will be the sinker needed. Over rocky ground a more streamlined sinker will prove easier to retrieve. In all cases it is advisable to attach the sinker to the line or to the trace by means of a relatively weak piece of line, which will easily break to release main-line and trace should the sinker become wedged in rocks, caught in heavy weed, or jammed in the structure of a wreck.

For conger fishing, the main-line should be from 40 lb (18·1 kg) to 80 lb (36·2 kg) breaking strain – or even heavier, and of braided nylon, braided

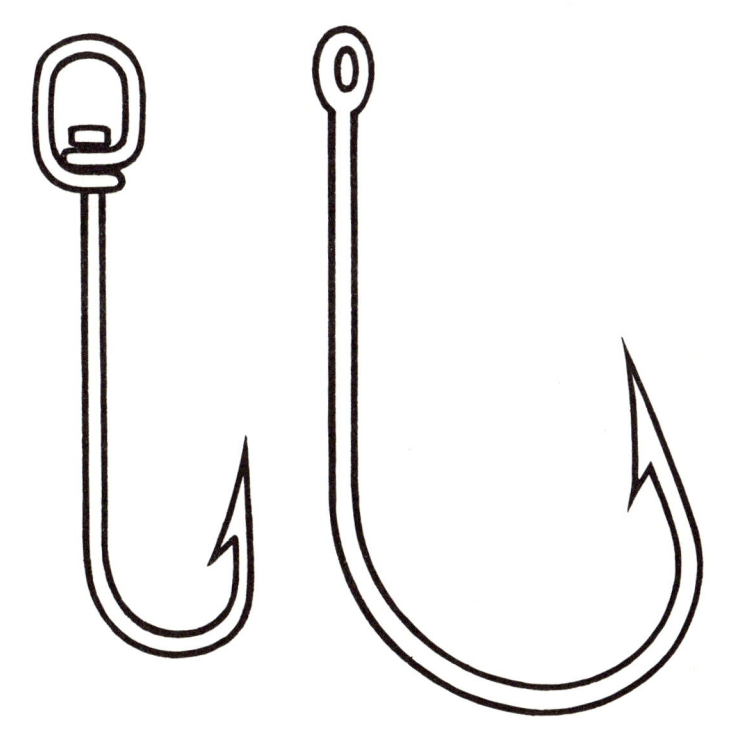

Conger hooks Right, *Mustad Sea-Master hook, size 11/0* Left, *swivel-eyed conger hook, size 5/0* *(actual size)*

Terylene, or monofil. Terylene is considerably more waterproof than nylon, with less tendency to stretch. I prefer it for conger fishing. Remember too, when deciding upon line strength, that there may literally be a tug-of-war between yourself and a very determined conger with her tail firmly wedged in a rocky lair or in a wreck. Under such circumstances, the wisdom of selecting a line of high breaking strain becomes readily apparent. It can easily make all the difference between your boating or losing what could be an outstanding specimen – even a record-breaker. It is also important to note that under stress, monofil will weaken considerably, often being reduced to a fraction of its original breaking strain rating. For this reason, when big conger are the main quarry, use braided Terylene (preferably) or braided nylon, rather than monofil.

It must be mentioned that braided lines present more resistance to the current than does monofil. In consequence, the angler fishing a braided line in a strong flow, will require a much heavier sinker to reach bottom than the angler using monofil.

Selecting a suitable rod and reel depends not only on the size of the conger you expect to catch, but also the nature of the ground over which you will be fishing.

For searching a strong tideway, in relatively deep water, some anglers prefer to use metal lines. Such a line enables the bottom to be reached easily with a light sinker, and there are other advantages, too. Personally, however, I do not favour metal lines because of their tendency to kink. When fishing a metal line it is essential that the rod is fitted with roller-type butt and end rings.

Ideally, from the light tackle viewpoint, a sandy or muddy bottom is to be preferred, although it will not be so prolific with conger as will a rocky area or a wreck. The more rocky the area, the heavier must be the tackle, and for wreck-fishing – which produces some truly massive congers – extra-heavy gear is strongly advised.

Always ensure that the spool-capacity of your reel is entirely adequate for your requirements, *without filling the spool*. You will find it well-nigh impossible to level-wind the line on to the spool when playing a struggling conger and allowance must be made for this. A 'pile-up' of line in the centre of the spool could possibly lose you a fish through the reel jamming-up tight. In this connection, I fail to understand why it is that tackle manufacturers do not design a heavy boat reel with an automatic level-wind mechanism similar to that fitted on some lighter reels.

While 100 yards (91·4 m) of line is perfectly adequate for some types of conger fishing, it would obviously be entirely inadequate for deep-water work – for instance, searching a wreck lying in 60 fathoms (109·7 m). The reel, therefore, must be capable of carrying the amount of line needed, *with room to spare*.

When selecting a reel, check that both the reel and its spool are constructed to withstand the tremendous stress and strain associated with conger fishing. For boat fishing choose a reel with a relatively low gear-ratio. It is my personal choice to use a big multiplier; other anglers prefer a centrepin type; both reels have their merits. The multiplier, for instance, is normally fished uppermost on the rod. This not only reduces strain on the rod rings, but also enables the angler to exert greater leverage with the reel in this position. The slipping-clutch and free-spool features are also distinctly advantageous. A merit of the centrepin type is that its direct drive assists greatly in pumping a heavy fish hooked in deep water. On the other hand, a centrepin reel must be fished under the rod, thereby putting a strain on the rings. It is also difficult to brake the drum as it revolves rapidly to the efforts of a fast-moving fish – a task which often leads to severely bruised knuckles.

A typical rod for conger fishing has an overall length of about 7 ft (2·1 m), preferably with a one-piece top and a short, detachable handle. A ferrule in the centre of the rod's length not only spoils its action, but is also a weak-spot which may break when imposing great pressure on a big conger.

An ideal design, in my opinion, is the ABU Pacific 650, which is relatively lightweight, of tubular glass, and fitted with roller-type butt and end rings. A less costly rod I recommend is the ABU Pacific 630R – an ideal partner for the moderately-priced Ambassadeur 12 reel. For heavier types of conger fishing, I suggest the Pacific 650 matched with the Ambassadeur 20 reel, or with one of the Policansky range of reels (featuring a lever-operated clutch instead of the usual star-drag).

It is important to ascertain that your rod is fitted with sufficient rings to prevent the line from chafing against the length of the rod when it is curved over to the weight of a heavy fish. I consider that a 7 ft (2·1 m) boat rod should have at least five rings, excluding the end ring. Ring lining is another vital point. Stainless steel is a reasonably satisfactory material, but it is subject to grooving, particularly in the end ring. Porcelain rings should be avoided – no matter how well they may be protected. This material is especially vulnerable to breakage, and to minute cracking which will quickly fray the line. Fortunately, these rings have now been largely displaced by modern lining materials such as hard chrome, Sintox, Regalox and Agatine, etc. Nevertheless, even these synthetics should be hooded or otherwise protected as a precaution against accidental damage.

The end ring should be fully reinforced and of the roller type – in fact my ideal set of rings for a boat rod consist entirely of rollers. While these are normally regarded as 'shark rod' rings, they are eminently suitable for the best possible type of conger rod.

Useful accessories include a rod-socket to relieve the strain of tackling the heavier specimens, and a complete harness (by no means essential) for maximum comfort. Other items include a heavy priest for stunning the fish, a sharp-pointed knife for killing, a pair of long-handled pliers for removing the hook (after the fish is dead), and a large sack for holding the catch.

Here are some good conger baits: sandeel, mackerel, herring, pilchard, pouting, whiting, squid, cuttlefish, bunches of ragworms and lugworms, and various crustaceans – notably soft and peeler crab. All baits should preferably be fresh. As in tope fishing, whole fish baits should be mounted on the hook with the head positioned downwards.

Although conger may be taken in every month of the year, by far the most productive period is summer to autumn. My best catches have invariably been made in hot, calm weather. Their feeding habits seem to be influenced by sudden changes of temperature and the onset of a rough sea. Extremely cold spells often result in numbers of dead conger being washed ashore.

The effects of low temperatures were once vividly demonstrated to me during a very severe winter. I was fishing a stone jetty; full of holes and cracks, and the haunt of many large conger. And looking over the side of the jetty at low water, I noticed the head of quite a big specimen protruding from a hole in the wall above the surface of the water. This is not an unusual sight at low water, but somehow this particular conger appeared to be quite inert, while its eyes had a glazed, white appearance. Taking to a boat, I managed to get close alongside the fish. It was stone dead and literally frozen!

The slack periods of the tide associated with high and low water are particularly productive for conger. Normally, neap tides are better than springs, probably due to the slacker currents of the neaps.

The bite from a conger varies between a gentle, almost imperceptible tremor on the line, to quite a hearty tug. Do not be too eager to strike, but when you do so, be sure to strike firmly, rather than quickly. Immediately you feel the resistance of the hooked fish, exert a steady pull, using the brake of your reel to full advantage, in order to minimize the possibility of line breakage. Do not let the conger 'run' just as it chooses, or no doubt it will seek refuge among the rocks or in the wreck, and there remain. The only possible way to dislodge a conger which has 'gone to ground' is to exert a steady pull until it either tires (hopefully) or the line parts (sadly).

When you are fortunate enough to be able to play a conger in the normal way, it will very likely resort to violent spinning tactics before it is ready for the gaff — one good reason for fitting the trace with efficient swivels. If you are inexperienced, be guided at the gaffing stage by the boatman or an experienced angler. Alone, of course, you will have no alternative other than to boat the fish yourself. Keep cool and do not try to rush matters. A conger may appear to be tired, but it might just spring to life again and give you quite a shock! Remember too, that not only do the powerful jaws and the sharp teeth present a problem, but also the thrashing tail which, in a large specimen, can easily cause severe bruising or a fractured limb. Altogether, reason enough for treating this powerful adversary with respectful caution.

TURBOT AND BRILL *Leslie Moncrieff*

There was a time in my younger days when the size of the catch rather than quality signified angling success. In competitions, or simply out for a day's pleasure fishing, the main aim was to drop anchor on rough, broken ground, and then make every effort to fill the boat with fish in the fastest possible time. To be honest, many of the dogfish, pouting, pollack, bream and whiting, not only required little skill to catch, but in quantity were well above the needs of the table – a waste of fish in fact. These days, a good deal older and perhaps a little wiser, the satisfaction I derive from angling comes from a specialist's approach towards certain species better known for their size and quality rather than sheer force of numbers.

For me the pleasure comes as much from the anticipation and planning as it does from the actual act of catching fish. Interest soon wanes if the angling is 'easy' and one catches large bags trip after trip with little real effort or thought – common enough with such species as dogfish or mackerel for instance.

Throughout the year, as sea temperatures rise and fall, many species of fish visit our shores and find ideal environments for breeding and feeding. The initial shoals of black bream arrive on the rocky, inshore reefs during late April and early May. The plaice, fresh from the spawning grounds and ravenous, feed heavily on the mussel beds; conger, back from the deeper, warmer waters, find shelter in the sunken wrecks dotted along the coastline.

But what excites my imagination more than all else is the spring return of the turbot and brill to the sandbanks. In my opinion these two species require tremendous understanding before one can expect reasonable success. My fin-

Turbot

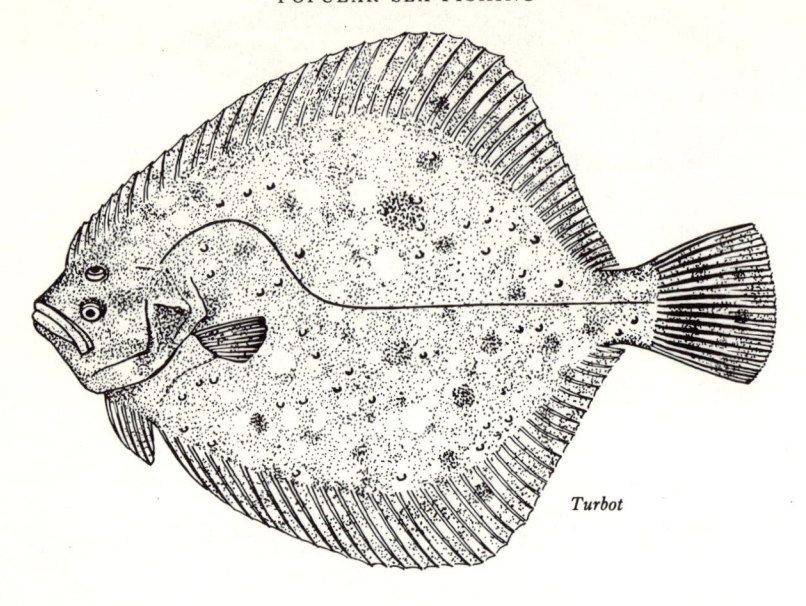

dings on the subject of their capture are based on personal experience over a number of years, during which time I made a study of the habits of turbot together with an analysis of recorded catches.

The turbot is not a deep water fish, and it is rare to take them in depths greater than 50 fathoms (91·4 m). Indeed, the majority of commercial catches are caught from marks of less than 20 fathoms (36·5 m). My own records compiled over many years show all my catches to have been made on or close to sandbanks in depths between 4 fathoms (7·3 m) and 12 fathoms (21·9 m).

This species has a broad, diamond-shaped form with no scales on the eyed side but instead a number of blunt, bony tubercles or spines. The mouth is very large and in keeping with a species which relies almost entirely on a small-fish diet. One could easily insert a hand into the maw of a big turbot, although I hasten to add that this is not advised, for the teeth are numerous and razor sharp. The lateral line curves strongly over the pectoral fin, and the long dorsal extends on to the head. The blind side is opaque white, and the coloration of the back or top side is dependent more on locality than any other factor. There are various shades of brown, marbled and speckled with light and dark tones so that, when the turbot rests on the bottom against shingle, sand or shell, it forms a wonderful camouflage pattern which blends perfectly, making the fish almost invisible.

Turbot have a wide distribution from the Mediterranean to the southern North Sea, being particularly plentiful around the south and west coasts of England and Ireland. The average size is between 10 lb (4·5 kg) and 18 lb (8·1 kg), anything over being considered an outstanding capture. Notable specimens include a 32 lb 4 oz (14·6 kg) fish taken by Mr D. Dyer off Plymouth, Devon, in 1976; one of 31 lb 4 oz (14·1 kg) taken by Mr P. Hutchings from a mark near the Eddystone Light, in 1972; and a 28 lb 8 oz (12·9 kg) shore-caught specimen landed at Dunwich, Suffolk, in 1976, by Mr J. Dorling.

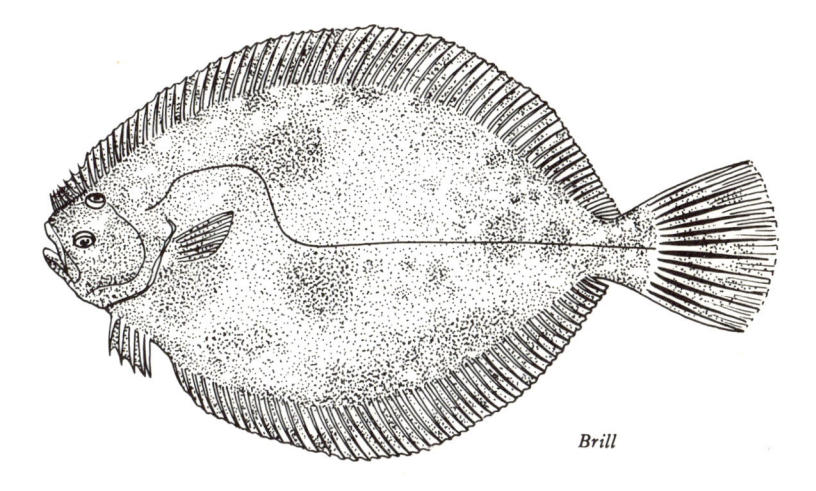

Brill

The distribution, haunts and habits of the brill are similar to those of the turbot, and both species are often caught from the same mark. The brill's spawning period, from March to August, is a little later than that of the turbot which is February to mid-July. In shape the brill is more oval – narrower in relation to length. Unlike the turbot, the eyed surface is smooth with no tubercles and is covered with cycloid scales. Coloration is rather similar to that of the turbot, although a little greenish in tone and with more pronounced mottling.

Brill do not grow as big as turbot and one of 10 lb (4·5 kg) is considered an excellent specimen. A particularly outstanding brill weighing 16 lb (7·2 kg) was taken in 1950 by Mr A. H. Fisher while boat fishing off the Isle of Man.

I was fortunate to be born at Folkestone where, only a few miles offshore (4·8 km approx.), are the giant sandbanks, the Varne Bank and Colbart Ridge – the habitat of big turbot and brill. Out of school hours, my parents had little trouble in finding me, for harbour and fish market attracted like a magnet. I would watch completely fascinated as the commercial fishing boats left for the grounds, to return later with boxes of conger, skate, turbot and brill.

However, it was not until the mid-1940s that I was able to satisfy the great longing to fish these famous offshore marks. After several fruitless months it became obvious that enthusiasm, great as it was, would be no substitute for skilled experience, and that a careful study of turbot movement and habit was essential to success. Now, after many years chasing these elusive fish, I have been able to establish, at least to my own satisfaction, a definite series of rules which I must observe to be successful.

Many turbot are caught more by accident than design, but I am quite confident that their catching can be made more of a certainty if anglers developed a greater understanding of habits, and made more use of Admiralty charts to locate suitable sandbanks.

Feeding habits are significant, for unlike humans their food is not consumed at regular intervals, but in conjunction with the strength and state of the tide. As mentioned previously, turbot are almost exclusively fish-eaters, and from stomach examination their main diet appears to consist of sprats and other immature fish, and sandeels. Worms I have rarely found, which is interesting and is doubtless the reason why, when I have used this bait and turbot have obviously been present, there have been no takes.

During slack water they lie semi-dormant on the bottom, but with tidal increase during the ebb and flow they are stimulated into activity – in many cases, using the element of surprise, they will rise suddenly and attack small fish unable to cope in the stronger tidal water. A further interesting fact is that they completely lack fear of any sudden movements of the bait. This is natural enough considering their predatory feeding habits, and is a great help to the angler, who, if he misses contact on the first strike, can drop the bait quickly to the bottom. Turbot will return again and again until they are hooked or are able to pull the bait free.

I am not in agreement with the view that fishing slack neap tides is more profitable than the strong spring tides. When the tide strengthens and the bait streams away, the majority of sea fish, but especially turbot and brill, are stimulated into active feeding.

Anglers often maintain that it is difficult to hold bottom in strong tides, no matter how great the amount of lead used. This could well be true of deep water, for it is the water pressure on the surface area of the line which is responsible. But on the sandbanks, in depths between 4 fathoms (7·3 m) and 10 fathoms (18·2 m), this pressure is minimized, and in my experience it is rarely necessary to exceed 14 oz (396 g) of lead, even during heavy spring tides, to hold the bottom.

Choice of bait is an important consideration. I would say the best of all is sandeel. These tiny creatures abound in rivers and estuaries of the West Country, where many fishing boats are fitted with livebait tanks continually aerated and supplied with a regular change of salt water, in order that the sandeels can be transported alive and fresh to the fishing grounds. In other areas, on rock and shingle foreshores they are less plentiful, but fortunately for the turbot and brill angler, the majority of sandbanks, like those off Folkestone, are simply alive with them.

Jigging with feathered hooks is an effective method of catching sandeels, but rather than the large hooks normally used for mackerel and pollack, I prefer to make up special sets from small freshwater hooks and shorter feathers. These I find result in a greater number of sandeels being taken.

Filleted flanks from freshly caught mackerel are also excellent bait. Cut into strips 1 in. (2·5 cm) wide and full length, they are hooked twice only through one end leaving the free section to waver and twist in the tide, very much like a sandeel.

If neither of these baits is available, the immature fish of most species can be used. I prefer a small whiting or pouting. It is essential when mounting these fish to locate the hook in the mouth, for most fish – including turbot – tend to avoid the sharp spines on the dorsal fins by taking small fish head first.

Before discussing suitable tackle it would be best to make some mention of turbot behaviour when hooked. In slack water they can dive very strongly, but all things considered it would be wrong to praise their fighting qualities too highly. Yet it would not be wise to treat them with impunity, for they are wily enough, when hooked in strong tides, not to expend their strength unnecessarily in violent movement. Instead, they direct their vast body area against the tidal current, imposing a great deal of pressure on both angler and tackle. Under these circumstances the body weight of a turbot is magnified several times and tackle strength must be judged accordingly.

A hollow glass rod with a one-piece tip for uninterrupted action, and about 6 ft 6 in. (1·9 m) long designed with a testing action of 18 lb (8·1 kg), is quite suitable. The reel should have a handle which disengages when line is taken, otherwise the knuckles can be rapped quite badly by a fast-moving fish. In this respect, the multiplier is undoubtedly the favourite.

Main-line needs to be around 35 lb (15·8 kg) breaking strain, with traces and snoods made from 50 lb (22·6 kg) breaking strain. There is good reason for this terminal tackle increase: a turbot lying back against the tide can, in a very short time, cut through a light line as it grates against its sharp teeth. The heavier 50 lb (22·6 kg) breaking strain helps to reduce this wearing to a minimum. Braided lines of terylene or nylon can be used for the main-line. With virtually no stretch in these materials the bites are more pronounced and the hook can be struck home with greater power. I, however, prefer monofil for its elasticity value, which, coupled with the cushioning action of the rod tip, imposes far less strain on the hook-hold while a fish is being played. With a big-mouthed species like turbot there is little need for small hooks. A size 6 or 7 is the calibre you will need for this fishing. I use three distinct types of terminal rig – all based on the firm conviction that turbot and brill respond best to moving baits.

The first of these is a two-hook flowing trace, the main line passing through a running boom attached to the lead, so that any interested fish is free to pick up and move off with the bait without feeling any resistance from the weight. The trace, roughly 6 ft (1·8 m) long, is clipped to a link swivel attached to the end of the main-line. Should a fish be deeply hooked, the trace can easily be removed and replaced by another without any loss of time – a vital factor in brill and turbot fishing. Weights should be as light as possible according to tide strength, and judged to allow the bait to be moved down the tide.

A sink-and-draw technique is useful in strong tides. In this case the terminal tackle consists of a single hook on a 6 ft (1·8 m) nylon snood, and is again attached to the main-line by a link swivel. The weight, either of the spiral or barrel type is attached to the main-line above the link and bent half-moon shape to avoid any tendency to spin in the tide. By lifting and lowering the rod tip the bait can be kept on the move and worked well away from the boat.

In a weak tide, in order to get the bait to cover as great an area as possible, I sometimes use this same single hook rig with a float attached above the lead and controlled by a stop, set to allow the bait to drag along the bottom and so encourage the turbot to attack. Remember, bait movement is exciting to turbot and brill which *expect* potential food-fish to move off quickly as they approach.

Drift fishing is a very effective method of luring both species. Its successful operation is dependent not only on the strength and direction of the tide in relation to the sandbank, but also on wind force. The boat needs to be repositioned at frequent intervals otherwise you can quickly be carried off the mark and away from the fish.

Many turbot are taken in strong tides and once hooked they adopt the same attitude as the skate – curling up against the flow. With fish of over 18 lb (8·1 kg) it is sometimes difficult to break this hold and line simply cannot be recovered. In such a situation it is a good idea to let out a short amount of line suddenly. This controlled release will often break the turbot's posture, and if the line is then recovered immediately it will not be able to return to this same method of resistance and can be played in the normal manner.

If a gaff must be used, avoid damaging the flesh by body-hooking. The gaff point should be inserted either in the mouth or at a point just below the head. To safeguard the flesh from blood contamination, bleed each fish by making an incision about 3 in. (8 cm) long on the top side near the tail and allow the blood to drain away by hanging the carcases.

The turbot is a species limited in distribution. Many are found in estuary waters where it is significant that sandeels and immature fish are usually present. To be certain, however, of locating brill and turbot in any quantity it is advisable to study the Admiralty charts and pin-point the shallow sandbanks in deep water – their true habitat.

I have already mentioned the Varne bank and the Colbart Ridge, but there are many other marks of equal importance, including the Shambles off Weymouth, and the Skerries out from Dartmouth. Although sandbanks maintain a regular position, defined in many cases by lightships and buoys, their structural composition often varies.

The Varne Bank, for instance, is formed from sand, pounded rock hard by tide and wave action. The Shambles, on the other hand, is composed of sand, shingle,

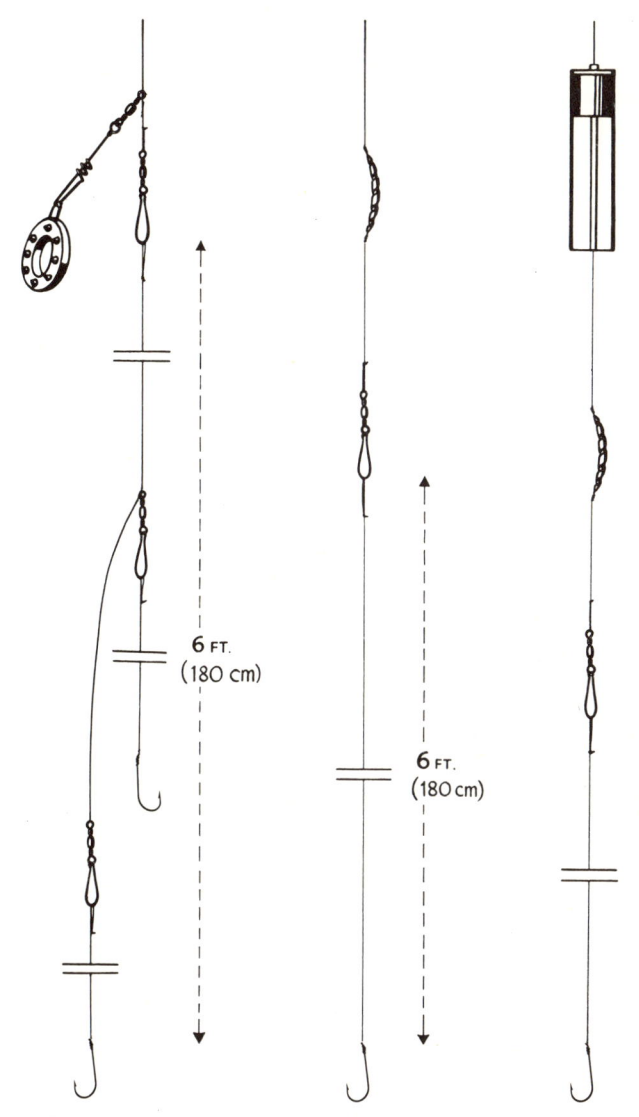

Left, *two-hook trace and running boom* Centre, *single-hook rig for sink and draw technique:* Right, *float rig for weak tides*

and large quantities of broken shells torn from the mussel beds further out in the deeper water by gales and storms. The surface of the bank is constantly moving as strong tides rip gullies from one point, to build ridges elsewhere. Although sandbanks may differ in some respects, in others they are almost identical – rising from deep water to within a few fathoms (5·4 m approx.) of the surface. All are subjected to strong tidal movements, and populated with sandeels, and mackerel, too, at certain times of the year.

This, then, is the type of environment which attracts turbot and brill. It has also been established that clear water is desirable, and that the most favourable conditions occur during periods of settled weather following gales.

From my own experience there is no doubt that success will only come when the angler is thoroughly acquainted with the art of sandbank fishing. This entails not only an understanding of tackle and methods, but also an intimate knowledge of turbot movement in relation to the tide. Take the Varne Bank as an example. Situated 8 miles (13 km) out from Folkestone, the bank is roughly 7 miles (11 km) long and a few hundred yards (274·3 m approx.) wide. The bank lies in 16 fathoms (29·2 m) of water, the sides rising steeply to the edges which, in some instances, are less than 4 fathoms (7·3 m) beneath the surface – during low water spring tides it is often possible to spot the bait lying on the hard, clean sand below. The bottleneck formed between the French and English coastlines at this point creates extremely fast currents.

Although the length of the bank runs roughly in the direction of the tide at a compass bearing of 220 degrees, this is not strictly true, for the tide is bent at this point, sweeping diagonally across at 235 degrees. Naturally, this deep fast water moving against the bank becomes compressed and deflected upwards. The speed as it now races across the top of the bank is greatly accelerated, smoothing the surface of the water and causing giant eddies and swirling currents to form. When again it meets the deeper water on the far side, the sudden check in speed causes a back wave to form which outlines the contours of the bank.

The angler should anchor and position the boat so that he can present the bait half way down the slope at a depth of 8 fathoms (14·6 m) – the area I have found most successful for turbot and brill. This would seem to suggest that both species lie in ambush below the edge of the bank where they are sheltered, to some extent, from the force of the tide. Sandeels and small fry unable to cope with the strong water movement are swept over the turbot and brill which rise up, grab the victims, and drop back again ready for the next attack.

During my early visits to the Varne Bank I concentrated my fishing on the shallow water at the very top. I took plenty of fish including plaice, dabs, whiting, dogfish and cod, but only the occasional turbot or brill. As time went by I noticed that the French long-liners fishing the mark would always set their hooks during slack water along the down-tide edge of the bank. Later, the tide increased, sweeping the baits down the incline towards the waiting fish. Then the lines were recovered and, often, I was surprised at the quantities of turbot

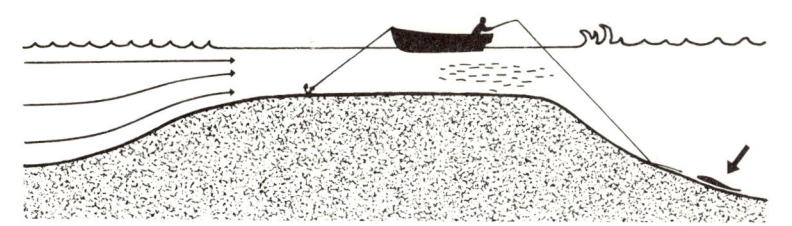

The boat is positioned so that the baits can be presented half-way down the slope, where the turbot and brill lie in ambush ready to grab sandeels and small fry as they are swept to them in the strong flow

and brill they hauled inboard.

From these observations I started to fish in the same area and found immediate success. I recall one memorable occasion when I netted five turbot in two hours, the best weighing 18 lb (8·1 kg).

Although the edge of the bank is easily located during strong tides by the water disturbance, this guide is not so apparent during weaker tides. Then it becomes essential to use an echo sounder to find the correct fishing position.

Groundbaiting is effective without any doubt. Pounded fish mixed with bran, pilchard oil and dried blood will do, emptied into a fine mesh bag – onion sacking or prawn netting being most suitable – and tied to the cable a few fathoms above the anchor, thus allowing the rise and fall of the boat to distribute the contents down the tide to the waiting fish.

Patience is the key to turbot and brill fishing. You may sit for hours without so much as a knock, but then, as the tide reaches a certain speed, the fish begin to feed and take the baited hooks. Perhaps for an hour they will be caught in quick succession before the bites cease as suddenly as they began.

The movement of turbot and brill on any sandbank is unpredictable. On the Varne Bank my best catches have been made between October and late December. On the Shambles, the months of April, May and June fish well, and of course the reports of turbot from the famed Skerries appear in the Press from spring to autumn.

A word of warning. Fishing the sandbank marks should only be attempted from a boat of sound construction in settled conditions. In troubled weather, with high winds battling against a strong tide, the shallow waters, obstructed in their movements, erupt in a turmoil of agitation. Under these conditions, fish, I can assure you, are absent, having taken shelter in the deeper waters. If experienced boatmen consider weather conditions wrong, take such advice seriously, for judgement of sandbank fishing should be left to those with long experience.

Although sandbanks are undoubtedly a favourite environment for turbot, a survey of their distribution would be incomplete without a mention of the exceedingly large specimens taken by anglers fishing the deep-water wrecks of the West Country – many of these fish scaling more than 25 lb (11·3 kg).

It has been suggested that their presence is accounted for by the inability of the commercial fishing boats to trawl these confined and dangerous areas; stocks, therefore, remaining undisturbed. Although valid to a point, I feel that other factors may play a more important part.

The majority of the wrecks in Devon and Cornish waters rest on a sandy sea bed. Echo sounder tracings show that many of these rusting hulks, by baulking the natural flow of tidal water, have altered the contours of the bottom. For example, around many of the hulls, the fast water has scoured out a deep channel – a favourite haunt of conger – while often just clear of the wreck shallow sandbanks will have formed.

Any obstruction located on this flat, sandy sea bed, attracts and holds a wide variety of predatory species, such as conger, ling, pollack, coalfish, cod and turbot. These different species, of course, feed in different areas of the wreck; conger tend to roam around the scour line at the base of the hull, others patrol much higher in the water, swimming either in the hull itself or in the jumble of its superstructure. As well as larger fish, shoals of smaller fish are also present, seeking protection from the hull, and on these the larger fish prey.

In my experience, the turbot, so neatly camouflaged as to be almost invisible, lie in wait some distance from the wreck itself – perhaps on the undulating shallow sandbank. Although ungainly in appearance, they are surprisingly fast and powerful, and as the water flow reaches a certain strength they begin to feed from ambush, rising suddenly to pick off unwary small fish which have wandered too far from the protection of the wreck.

PLAICE FISHING *Sid Cloke*

The 'deep sea' angler, powering out to the offshore conger and ray grounds armed with his strong tackle, is apt to regard with a certain faint contempt the plaice angler peacefully fishing the harbour or estuary as he passes by.

There is really no justification for this distain at all. In fact, at the end of the day, it is often revealed that the plaice angler has had the better of the day. Content to pursue his quarry in more peaceful waters he enjoys the best of both worlds – comfortable fishing, and a chance to exercise his skill with excellent sport as the end result – for there can be no argument about it, plaice *can* and *do* give splendid sport on the right tackle. Moreover, the plaice angler also has the last laugh when it comes to cooking and eating the catch.

Aesthetically, the plaice is a most attractive species; the Beau Brummel of the fish tribe – sedentary, a trifle portly, and very colourfully attired. Few anglers who have seen the fat shape of a large plaice, with its vivid orange spots and its ivory-like fins extended, weaving up through sparkling water to the net, can forget the thrill of the experience. Nor can they forget the heavy, thrusting dive a plaice makes once it nears the surface and senses danger. Although that dive can soon be over, its strength is such that the unprepared angler can be broken, particularly if his tackle is not in the best of shape.

The plaice is one of the most widely distributed of all British fish, from the south of these islands to the north. It occurs in vast quantities in the North Sea, the Irish Sea and the English Channel. There are also heavy local populations: fish that are spawned, mature and breed in a relatively circumscribed area of the coast, instead of migrating to the big spawning grounds in the North Sea, east of the Dogger, off Flamborough and the Isle of Man, and possibly to the Hook of

Holland. Tagging has disclosed that many plaice do make this journey from quite remote areas, but many others, especially those in the Channel, are content to stay at home.

Plaice grow slowly for the first three years, then in the fourth year they double their weight. The greatest average increase occurs in the fifth and sixth years. At three to four years old the average length is 10 in. (25 cm), at four to five years 13 in. (33 cm), and with a life-span of something like 30 years a female in top condition which has escaped anglers and trawls can measure 40 in. (101 cm) or so and weigh perhaps 14 lb (6·3 kg). Plaice as large as 11 lb (4·9 kg) have been taken in the nets in such areas as Poole Harbour, Dorset. A specimen weighing 7 lb 15 oz (3·5 kg) was taken on rod and line in 1964 by Mr I. B. Brodie boat-fishing at Salcombe, Devon.

Incidentally, plaice mature at an average length of 15 in. (38 cm) (it varies slightly with different areas) and if one considers the N.F.S.A. minimum of 12 in. (30 cm) and the statutory minimum of 11 in. (28 cm) for trawlers, it seems obvious to me that both are too low. In my opinion, to properly safeguard stocks the minimum should be 16 in. (40 cm), so that every plaice surviving natural hazards and reaching maturity has at least one or two opportunities to spawn.

Spawning takes place over about four months. On the east coast of Scotland plaice spawn from December to May; in the Channel from December to April, although early spawners will come inshore to summer feeding grounds during March. Thus, in southern coastal waters, there are eight months during which plaice can be caught – although few are in peak condition until August at least.

Most anglers know where plaice can be taken in their own areas, and I could be accused of teaching 'old hands' to suck eggs if I gave detailed advice on finding fish locally. It is a fact, however, that plaice have been found in recent years concentrated in unexpected areas, simply by following certain basic guides.

During the summer months, plaice favour a depth between 10 ft (3 m) and 15 ft (4·5 m), a bottom of sand, marl or clay, and, in the open sea, rocks or rough ground nearby. There is good reason for this; the basic diet of the mature plaice is shellfish, especially cockles and mussels, and where better to find such life than in the conditions indicated? Once a sea bed of this type has been located it is almost a certainty that plaice will be found in residence. In most harbours, of course, shellfish and crabs abound everywhere, so that plaice can be widely spread about, though even here they definitely favour certain spots.

It is more or less a waste of time to fish for plaice on shingle or extensive rock. In such areas they would be unable to follow their regular habit of burying themselves in such a way that only their eyes are visible; taking a rest, in fact, while still maintaining a constant watch for edibles passing by. The odd plaice does, of course, stray over shingle, to be caught as a bonus by the angler seeking other species.

With apologies to the shore angler, beach fishing for plaice can be dealt with quite briefly.

Providing suitable plaice areas are within casting distance, and the right bait is used, plaice are caught with any other species that may be around. A trace rig will be found more suitable than a paternoster, although a light monofil paternoster can be successful anywhere. If you must use a boom use a French type. The most useful tackle I know for plaice is a simple 3 ft (0·91 m) trace with a size 1 hook and a 4 oz (113 g) running weight stopped with a swivel, or perhaps a Kilmore link for the lead. The actual weight used is, of course, dictated by local circumstances or weather conditions. Only in a fast tide have I found it necessary to change to a hook above the weight, and then only in certain conditions to avoid the trace wrapping itself up the line.

Recommended baits for shore fishing for plaice are lugworm, ragworm, slipper limpet, razor fish (where such occur naturally or where it is known to be a successful bait), cockle and sometimes small clams. One of the finest plaice baits, the mussel, cannot be used with much confidence when casting because the shellfish is so soft it is apt to fly off the hook. I have never found the traditional dodge of fastening mussel flesh on to the hook with wool to be very effective in stopping this problem, and I alway have a nasty feeling when I am forced to use mussel that I may be fishing with bare hooks.

A plaice bite is very sharp. If the rod is in the rest at the time do not rush to it and strike immediately; wait and let the fish have another go. It usually will. If, however, it does not come again, little will have been lost; you would almost certainly have missed the fish by striking early. If nothing happens after that first twitch, bring the bait a turn or two of the reel inshore, and wait. These remarks apply also to pier fishing. From pier or beach it is unlikely that the really big plaice will be contacted; from either type of venue a plaice of 2 lb (0·9 kg) is a good fish, and one of 3 lb (1·3 kg) or over a most notable specimen.

It is boat fishing that offers much the best chance of connecting with the really big fellows, plaice weighing 5 lb (2·2 kg) or more. The same geographical considerations of sea bed apply. In harbours, the big plaice are often found in lesser depths of water than in the open sea, and they seem to have a preference for the edges of channels, though they seldom venture into the true shallows of the flounder grounds. If shellfish are abundant and other crustaceans abound, then so much the better. If beds of pipe worms – the long slender worms which build their tubular homes of cemented sand and grit – can be found it is amost certain that plaice will be there feeding on the worms, which in themselves make excellent though rather fragile bait. Cockle beds and mussel beds should be sought. If you are preparing to fish a strange area, it often saves time to make a preliminary investigation at low tide, and to ask around for local knowledge of conditions. An abundance of mussel or cockle shells on the low tide line may give a pointer, and any angling map or chart of the area is invaluable.

A friend of mine went out fishing from Deal, which is by no means a famous area for plaice. No sooner had the boat anchored than the party began to catch plaice – good fish averaging over 2 lb (0·9 kg).

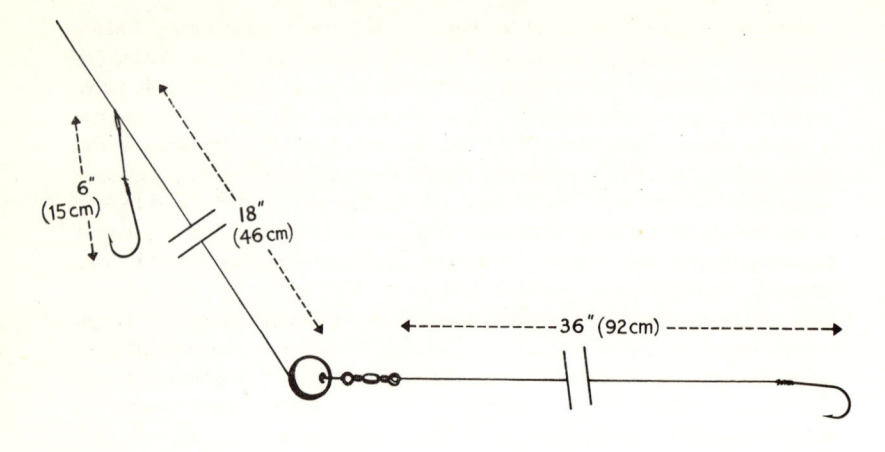

Drift tackle for plaice. The hook above the weight is optional and is not particularly favoured by the author

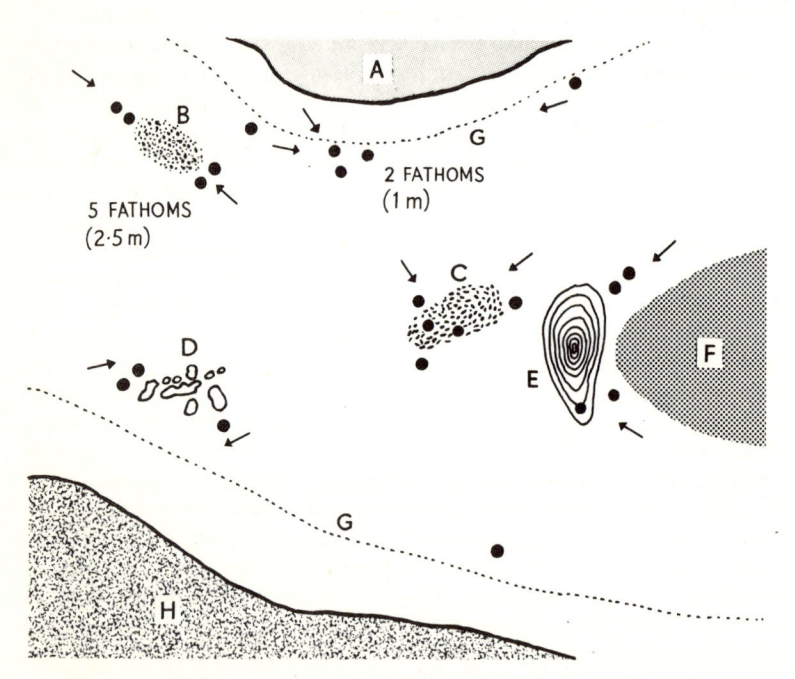

Imaginary estuary area. A, sandbank; B, shingle; C, mussel bed; D, rocks; E, hole; F, mud shoal; G, fathom line; H, flats cleared at low tide. Black dots indicate plaice zones, and arrows indicate drifts on different states of tide

'Impossible' said the skipper. 'There aren't plaice here.' But there were, dozens of them. The mystery was solved when some of the anglers began to pull up empty mussel shells. Quite by chance the skipper had anchored right over a mussel bed that was not suspected to be there.

Each member of the party caught plenty of fish, some returned home with 60 lb (27·2 kg) to 70 lb (31·7 kg) of fish. The skipper, of course, made accurate notes of the mark.

Next year my friend went back to Deal, sought out the same skipper and suggested a bit of plaice fishing. 'You'll be lucky', said the skipper. 'The trawlers found it.' Apparently the net-men had not only denuded the area of plaice, but they had also wrecked the mussel bed as well, and that was that!

This illustrates two points. One, that plaice are likely to be where mussels are. Two, that if you want to keep catching fish from a hotspot, keep the location of the mark to yourself – which, I might add, is an almost impossible task these days. As an angler who writes, of course, I usually operate on the principle that I have a duty to allow others to benefit from any knowledge I may acquire. On the other hand, I do not think any angler, writer or otherwise, wants to aid trawlers to damage the sea bed too much – and trawler men keep a keener eye on the activities of rod and line anglers than is generally appreciated.

Skin divers report that, usually, plaice feed best on a flood tide, reaching a peak of activity at the end of the tide, when the flow is steady and gentle; from that point feeding activity decreases until, on full ebb and low tide, it almost ceases. This is why I usually favour a spring tide for plaice fishing, because the end of the flood is commonly long and gentle. There is, admittedly, usually more fishing time in total on a neap tide, but conditions then are seldom as favourable. This is not the case in all areas, but I have found in my own area that it is best to start out and be in a position to fish the chosen spot about an hour before the top of the tide, packing up an hour after the start of the ebb. This is again modified in places where there are extended tidal stands, or double tides as in Poole Harbour. Here the half-ebb can be ideal for plaice fishing.

It is never safe to make categorical statements about angling – the fish too often prove them wrong! For instance, I fished the top of the tide on Middle Sands in Poole Harbour one August day on spring tide. Conditions were ideal; the plaice, I knew from previous reports, were there. But not a sniff at the bait did I get on the top of the tide or on the half tide. The ebb tide started, and as it would be a heavy one, as soon as it was well under way I let the boat drift towards its moorings. There we were, moving along at a fast clip, both rods out in the hope of a bass, when out of the blue one of the rods dipped violently, almost as if I had hit a snag. I struck. It was a fish, and as I held it the other rod banged down. By good fortune, a bit of manoeuvring, and some hearty cussing, I managed to boat both fish – each one a fine plaice of around 3 lb (1·3 kg) size. I quickly motored up again and ran down over the same spot; in half an hour on that boiling ebb I netted seven good plaice. I have never, I may add, repeated this experience.

On another occasion, while bass fishing at the harbour entrance in a 5 knot tide using live sandeel bait, a 5 lb 13 oz (2·6 kg) plaice grabbed the eel being fished by my companion.

These are exceptions, of course, but they do serve to remind the angler never to be too dogmatic.

Experience tends to indicate that the most successful method of plaice fishing, where and when conditions allow, is from a boat allowed to drift in the tide.

Obviously this cannot be done in an area dotted with rocks (unless you happen to be a tackle dealer!) but where there is an extensive area of sand or only slightly rough ground it is the best way I know. This light drift fishing cannot be done in water much over 30 ft (9·1 m) in depth. If the water is greatly deeper the more orthodox anchored fishing may be necessary, with heavier tackle, but plaice caught in this way (as on the Skerries) do not give the same pleasure as plaice caught on light tackle.

In the right area, the method is to set the boat so that the tide will take it gently across the area to be fished – allowing for wind, of course. Wind is the enemy of pleasant and successful plaice drifting, unless one is armed with a sound knowledge of local conditions and the effects of wind and tide. Here again, though, there can be exceptions. Drifting across tide, pushed by the wind, can account for fish at the right time. One should also keep a sharp look-out for surface tidal flows formed at the end of a tide, marked by lines of bubbles or debris or glassy slides. Drifting down these areas often results in fish.

Equipment to give the best control and pleasure from plaice consists of a medium-weight spinning rod of about 7 ft (2·1 m), a centrepin reel loaded with 15 lb (6·8 kg) breaking strain line (a fixed-spool reel will do the job after a fashion, but a lot of the delicate control is lost), a trace of 8 lb (3·6 kg) to 11 lb (4·9 kg) breaking strain 4 ft (1·2 m) to 5 ft (1·5 m) long – the longer it is the better, but it should never be longer than the rod for obvious 'landing fish' reasons – and a ball weight stopped with a swivel. It may be desirable to go even lighter with the trace, but then one courts disaster from snags. The weight used is dictated by local conditions, but with most drift fishing in suitable areas a lead of 1 oz (28 g) to 2 oz (56 g) will be found sufficient in the fastest tide.

To fish this tackle, let the weight run down to the bottom, then gradually adjust the amount of line until the tackle is dragging along the bottom behind the drifting boat. It may be found necessary to let out more line several times to get the right angle of line, at which the tackle stays hugging the bottom. The amount of line which has to be let out varies, of course, with the speed of the tide, and if there is a wind taking the boat across tide it will be found necessary to let out more line than if it is a straight drift.

Whether one holds the rod or not when drift fishing like this is a matter of personal preference. After considerable experience of both ways I like, whenever possible, to set the rod down over the transom so that the tip is within 1 ft (0·3 m) or so of the water, keeping a sharp eye on the movement of the tip and a hand poised to grab the rod. It may be splitting hairs, but I have the suspicion that one has a marginal advantage if the movement of the hand is not transmitted to the bait.

The first indication of interest is likely to be a small vibration of the tip, usually followed by a sharp pluck. Do not strike at this: that pluck usually means that the plaice is taking a 'sample', and as they are the fastest 'spitters' in the business one is unlikely to make contact. If a real pull does not happen right away this does not mean that the fish has lost interest. Often it will still be following the potential meal. One trick to encourage the fish is to let out a little line gradually and smoothly, so that the pace of the bait slows up or even stops. Any jerkiness in this operation usually scares the fish off. If there is no response to this ploy (more often there will be) raise the rod top slowly to take the bait off the bottom momentarily.

Plaice, by the way, do not always take a bait by sucking it on the bottom. Sometimes they will stand almost on their tails and strike with all the sinuosity and speed of the cobra. Some really fine films made in the North Sea by the Ministry of Agriculture and Fisheries show this action quite plainly. When the fish are in this mood it sometimes pays to fish the bait several feet (0.91 m approx.) off the bottom.

I well remember an occasion when, fishing for plaice off Bournemouth pier, a fish gave me the initial pluck, then followed the bait nearly a quarter of a mile (0.402 km) across the Durley Sands. I tried every trick I knew to get it to take properly, but failed. It just kept on nibble, nibble, nibble, convincing me that it was a fish of small size. At one end of the drift I reeled in slowly before restarting the motor. Halfway up there was a strong snatch which nearly tore the rod out of my hand. It was a first-class plaice of 5 lb (2.2 kg). Moral: never think a small bite comes only from a small fish.

A piece of 'modern' tackle for plaice and flounder fishing is the baited spoon. Many lures sold are more likely to catch anglers than fish, but the spoon has been well-proved as far as flatties are concerned. There are many stories about who invented the baited spoon and when, but all I know is that its use has only been widely recognized since the last war.

When on my own, I often fish for plaice with two rods – one rigged with a baited spoon, and the other with an ordinary trace. The ratio of fish taken is usually three on the baited spoon to one on the trace. On occasions, I must admit that this ratio has been reversed, but not often enough for me to doubt that the baited spoon offers an advantage. Except, perhaps, in November and December, when the larger plaice are getting a bit heavy with roe and sluggish, and therefore disinclined to waste energy on the chase.

Among plaice anglers there has been a good deal of discussion on why a wobbling or revolving piece of metal should attract flatfish. Some say it stirs up a cloud of sand and that the fish come to investigate what is going on. Others say that it resembles a small fish in trouble, and most sea fish, not least the plaice, are

Metal spoon lure

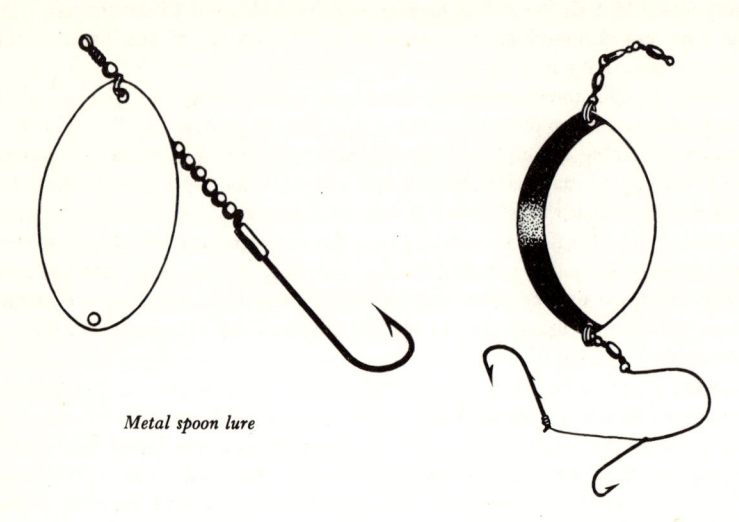

Scandinavian ice lure

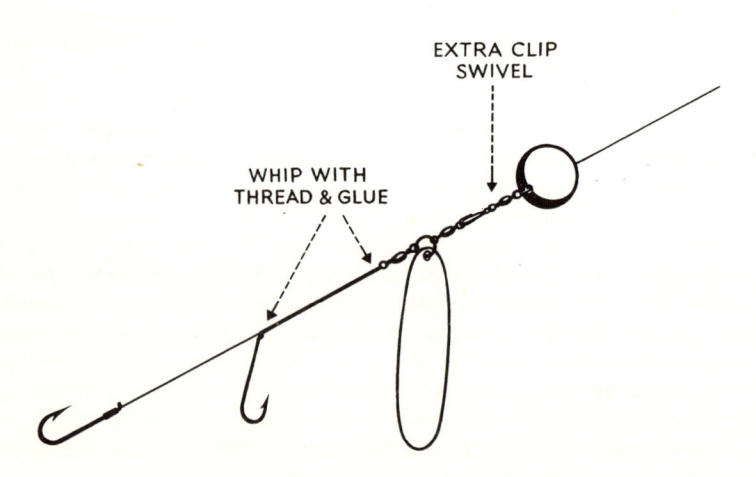

EXTRA CLIP SWIVEL

WHIP WITH THREAD & GLUE

Tandem hook arrangement on a light plastic spoon

predatory. Others maintain it is mere curiosity on the part of the fish, and plaice have plenty of this it is true. I have caught both plaice and flounders, and had a string of four or five fish following the hooked one to the surface. Yet another school of thought considers that the underwater vibrations caused by a spoon are heard by the fish as a sort of 'come and get it' signal. Whatever it is, it works.

Of the three types of spoon – those which revolve on their own axis, those which revolve on a separate axis, and those which just wobble – I have preference for the wobbler. It has a very efficient action and does not kink the line, like a spinning spoon can do despite swivels. There are light plastic wobbling spoons and heavy metal ones; both have their uses in different conditions. The light spoon needs a weight above it, the heavy one is its own weight.

Most kinds of spoons for flatties are sold with a single hook attached. I like to improve on this with a tandem hook arrangement, adding a second swivel. The tandem arrangement has several advantages: both hooks are baited and provide a good visual bulk of food for a hungry fish, if a snag tears one bait off or a crab gets it you still have the other, and the tandem hook will strike a fish which may be only mouthing the bait more efficiently than a single one.

The spoon is fished from the drifting boat just as a trace is. The light plastic type is the one to use in a fast tide or deep water, because the lead used in association with it can be changed to suit the conditions. I like to mount the bullet lead, stopped by a swivel, about 2 ft (0·61 m) above the spoon, though Dr. Blackburn, who was a most successful Pool Harbour plaice angler, with at least two 7 lb (3·1 kg) specimens to his credit, and many 6 lb (2·7 kg) plus fish, used to put the lead almost on top of the spoon. He used to be seen drifting about with two rods, raising and lowering each one alternately in the manner of an engine.

If the tide is slow and smooth, with little wind, and a depth of not much more than 14 ft (4·2 m) or so, then the heavy wobbling spoon fished without a weight, such as the ice-lure type, is my choice. I believe that the use of the ice-lure, first produced in Scandinavia for char, as a flattie lure was first proved in Poole Harbour. Indeed, Hubert Wheeler, a great angler and tackle dealer in Bournemouth, now unfortunately dead, and I, had quite a hand in this.

While the light spoon with weight works efficiently at a short distance from a drifting boat, providing the right weight is being used, the heavy spoon needs more distance, certainly not less than 30 yards (27·4 m). To achieve this, let out line until you find the rod top beginning to nod rhythmically. This nodding action indicates that the wobbler is swinging from side to side, a thing which seems to attract the attention of plaice.

If you fish the spoon in the Dr Blackburn way, raising and lowering the rod top continuously, it will be found that the fish usually takes the bait on the downwards movement. This means changing the direction smartly to strike, so one has to keep pretty alert.

Drifting, particularly with weight and spoon, makes it difficult to detect a bite. Roughish ground may give the simulation of constant bites, and those trying this approach for the first time are often fooled by these false knocks. A little experience makes a big difference, however, and one soon learns to tell the difference between the slower movements caused by the sea bed and the bite of an interested fish.

Static light-tackle fishing from a boat at anchor is advisable when (a) the bottom is too foul to drift without risk of continually getting snagged and losing tackle (spoons are not cheap) (b) fishing a sandy patch in a rocky area; (c) when there is no tide. If you find a mussel bed you must, of course, anchor over it to fish.

When fishing to anchor one can produce, in effect, one's own tide by casting the spoon as far as possible, pausing while it settles, then retrieving smoothly and slowly, with short stops on the way. Almost like spinning, in fact.

A plastic spoon with lead attached will do very well for this. When retrieving the spoon, fish it evenly right to the surface, rather than speed it up when you feel the weight leave the sea bed. A plaice may be following without having given any prior indication, and may not make up its mind to take the bait until it is well off the bottom – provided, of course, that it is not whisked out of sight! I have had plaice take the spoon within a few feet (0·91 m) approx.) of the surface. Perhaps the fish is afraid the meal will get away?

If fishing from an anchored boat in a tide, one can use roughly the same idea – casting uptide and letting the weight swing round in an arc until it is directly downtide of the boat. Keep the line as taut as possible all the time when doing this.

One can also trot the bait in a tide by letting it down from the boat until the bottom is felt, then raising the rod so that the tide takes the weight further, letting it hit the bottom again, raising the rod again, and so on until you have achieved an angle of stability: when it is no longer necessary to let out more line to hit the bottom when the rod tip is lowered. Both fishing the arc and trotting the weight can be done with a spoon, but in some conditions of tide the spoon will become twisted up the line, in which case it is useless.

Trotting the weight which, incidentally, is a good method of catching bass from a stable point such as a boat or a bridge, is excellent when the tide is beginning to pick up speed. It cannot be carried out satisfactorily with a fixed-spool reel; nor, indeed, is a fixed-spool reel ideal for retrieving smoothly, or adjusting the speed of the spoon, when drifting.

Baits of interest to the light tackle boat angler after plaice are numerous and include, though not in any order of preference, lugworm, ragworm, mussel, sandeel, slipper limpet, rock worm, fish skin (fresh mackerel) and, surprisingly perhaps, ordinary garden worms. Pipeworm and white rag (called whitecat in the Channel Islands) are further useful baits if you can get hold of them.

The most valuable bait is undoubtedly the worm; tough, attractive to plaice, and fairly plentiful in many areas. Why plaice should like the worm I do not know, because it is unlikely that they come across many worms in natural circumstances. If there is a choice between lugworm and ragworm I would always prefer lugworm for plaice.

Mussels are splendid for boat fishing for plaice, especially if there is a mussel bed in the locality, but they are too soft for casting. Attaching the mussel to the hook with wool thread is worthwhile for the boat angler if not the beach caster. A bite on mussel should be struck rather more promptly than on other baits. The odds are that if the fish is not hooked the mussel will already have been taken.

Because of their softness, mussels are not a good drift bait. Cockles, however, can be used because they are more durable than mussels, though softer than worms. Plaice living where cockles abound are often found to contain numbers of immature white-shelled cockles. I have tried fishing with small cockles still in their shells for plaice, but so far without success.

Hard-back crabs are often found in plaice, but are hardly considered a top bait. One method of using them is to remove the claws, legs and back shell, and hook the remains through the mouth orifice. I have taken both plaice and flounder like this, but I must admit to having qualms about it. It is too much like a small boy pulling the legs off flies!

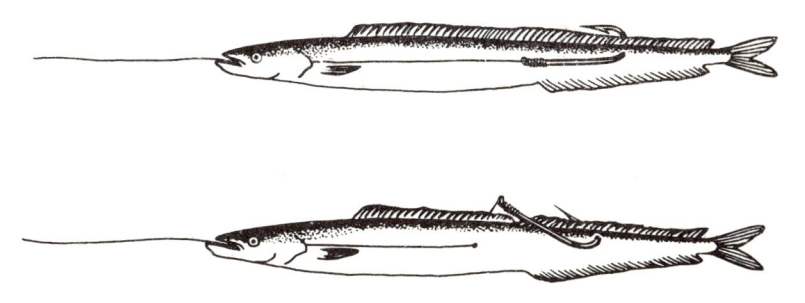

Top, *mounting for live sandeel*, Bottom, *mounting for dead sandeel*

The unconventional bait is sandeel, which is a staple diet of the larger plaice, and of the turbot. If mounted by the gills or the lip, as for bass, plaice will chew them off bit by bit, leading to the frustrated angler striking time after time without result. To counter this problem, the hook should be passed through the gills, then nicked back near the tail. If the eel is dead then it is perhaps safer to pass the hook once through the middle of the body before nicking it into the tail. Always make sure the point is exposed.

When using sandeel, a somewhat quicker strike than when baiting with worm is often necessary, but this whole question of when and how to strike using various baits is a debatable one, and I feel that personal, practical experience is the only sure way to discover the answers.

A word of warning to those using baited spoons; and also a sad tale. Always check the split ring on which a wobble spoon is mounted, or on which the hook is mounted, particularly if the spoon has not been used for sometime. A split ring can break quite easily.

One July day I was anchored over a plaice hotspot at the entrance to Poole Harbour, and as a crowded pleasure boat passed by I struck into a good fish. People on deck watched with considerable interest as I heaved at a bending rod and reached for the net. Then the plaice dived in a last ditch attempt to get away. Hampered by the net I was not quite quick enough to give line, and suddenly there was no fish and no spoon. The faces of those on the pleasure craft seemed to reflect scorn. 'Must be a beginner', I could almost hear one say to another. Investigation showed that the split ring had broken under the strain. Since then, remembering my humiliation in front of an audience, I have replaced the split rings on all my spoons every fourth time of using them at least.

Float fishing for plaice I have left until last, because to me this method has little to offer which cannot be accomplished better by other methods. The object of a float is basically to search the sea bed and to cover more water than would be possible by other means. On a stand of tide, more water can be covered by the cast and retrieve method, and in any tide the drifting boat can cover a vastly greater area more effectively. If float fishing is tried in any kind of fast tide, a lot of time can be wasted retrieving the float and recasting at frequent intervals, and if anyone is fishing with you tangles can result. However, for those who enjoy the visual satisfaction that a float offers, do not let me put you off. Many a good plaice has been caught on float tackle.

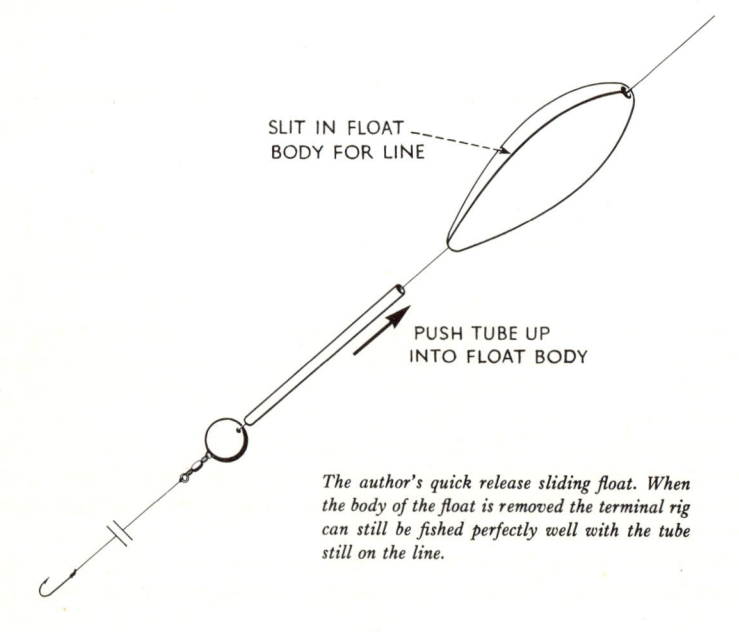

The author's quick release sliding float. When the body of the float is removed the terminal rig can still be fished perfectly well with the tube still on the line.

There are, of course, some circumstances in which a float is very useful. Crabs are often a menace in a harbour, and a float adjusted so that the bait is a little off-bottom will obviously help to avoid them. If there is a fair amount of suspended weed a float can also be useful. Fishing a sliding float is not the ideal job for a fixed-spool reel; the piece of rubber band tied on the line as a stop for the float sometimes interferes with the operation of the reel. I personally prefer a light centrepin trotting reel.

If you want to float fish for plaice, then use a rig which will enable you to put a float on quickly when the tide becomes right, and to take it off again just as quickly when the ideal period has passed. In the depth of water which plaice usually inhabit, a sliding float is, of course, essential, and I have devised a rig which, I think, does the job admirably.

Essentially, the float is one with a fairly slim cork body, capable of supporting 1 oz (28 g) of lead. A cut is made vertically down the float from the outside of the inner hole taking the centre plug, somewhat after the fashion of a Fishing Gazette float. Replacing the plug is a polythene tube – a large diameter ball-point filler tube is ideal for this purpose. When the tackle is mounted, the line is put through this tube *before* the weight and stopping swivel are attached. The slim tube above the weight makes no difference to fishing without the float, either from a drifting boat or an anchored boat. If it is desired to try the float, then the line is merely slipped through the slit in the cork body and the tube pushed up into the cork body. To reverse the process, pull the tube out of the cork body and slip the line out of the slit. Mounting and dismounting this float takes just a few seconds.

Always remember that while small plaice are eager feeders and easily caught, large ones require single-minded pursuit and much effort. Never conclude that there are no plaice in a given area simply because one method fails – *try them all.*

And I would add a word of caution, which may sound like a get-out, but really is nothing of the sort. All species have their off days, and plaice can have more off days than most. You may well fish with the right bait, the right method, and on top of a lot of plaice, and yet touch nothing. This has been demonstrated recently by sub-aqua divers, from whom anglers can learn quite a lot about plaice and their habits. In the Poole area, at least, divers have reported that anglers have been fishing right over quite large concentrations of plaice, and yet their baits have failed to interest the fish at all. Inshore trawlers have also had good catches of plaice in areas which have been unsuccessfully fished by anglers. The same thing has happened in other Channel areas, and I presume in other areas too.

Several ideas to account for this have been put forward, and perhaps the most likely is that in certain areas plaice could be finding an abundance of natural food – possibly small shrimps or something of that kind – and are disinclined to bother about an angler's offering. Trawled and speared fish have been found to contain a mass of what appears to be very small crustaceans.

There will, however, usually come a period either in spring or late autumn when plaice will take an angled bait quite avidly. The trick is to be ready to take advantage of these times.

While sub-aqua spear fishermen may help us to understand more of the habits of plaice, they may also contribute to a shortage. Being a sedentary fish, the plaice is an ideal target for the spear diver, and his continual taking of the larger fish may have an undesirable effect on inshore stocks in time.

In this chapter I have tried to give an idea of the tackle and methods I have found successful in catching plaice, but I would like to emphasize that pretty well any tackle will at times catch plaice with a final anecdote.

I was bass fishing in a favourite spot when I saw two rather forlorn-looking elderly gentlemen, complete with rods and baskets, standing on a small pier and obviously wondering what to do. They looked so lost that I felt to motor in and invite them to come aboard.

They were overjoyed, explaining that they were on holiday and thought they would like to do a bit of fishing, but had no idea where to go.

Unfortunately the tide had finished, at least for bass, and so I suggested we go for plaice in another spot not far away. To my astonishment (and secret amusement, I must confess) the two old gentlemen tackled up with hefty great reels, thick lines, monster brass paternosters, and weights of at least 1 lb (0·45 kg) class. Because they were both apparently in their eighties, and obviously this was how they always fished, I had not the heart to put them right.

Right? Not one plaice took the slightest interest in my delicately fished baits, but the two old gentlemen ended up highly delighted with a nice 3 lb (1·3 kg) plus plaice each.

They thanked me with rare old world courtesy, but my humiliation was complete when they ambled off to their hotel, one saying loudly to the other: 'I don't know. These new fangled ideas.'

MONKFISH, ANGLER FISH AND HALIBUT *Trevor Housby*

Both monkfish and angler fish are regarded as little better than vermin by most sea anglers, presumably because they offer little value as table fish, and fight weakly when hooked. At the same time, however, both species are *big* in every sense of the word, and for many sea anglers a 40 lb (18·1 kg) or 50 lb (22·6 kg) monkfish or angler fish is the largest specimen they can ever hope to catch. Because of this, I feel sure that both species should receive much more attention than they are receiving at the present time. Not only are they neglected, they are also treated badly when they are captured; why, I am not sure, but no doubt it has a great deal to do with their ugly appearance and their reputation for being somewhat dangerous.

To a certain extent, at least, this reputation is well founded, for both species carry needle-sharp teeth which can inflict a nasty wound should one become careless and fail to take proper precautions when handling and unhooking. Unfortunately, most anglers make a point of battering to death each and every monkfish and angler fish they bring in. Such action is never justified; these fish have no food value and should be returned alive and unharmed to the water, to grow bigger and provide future sport. More important still, predatory fish are essential in the sea to keep the small, rapid-breeding species under control; the indiscriminate killing of fish-eaters like monkfish and angler fish obviously does more harm than good.

Constant over-kill of big predators can soon denude big-fish grounds. In Irish waters, for example, the one time monkfish hotspots off Westpoint and in Clew

Bay are now little more than fond memories. Too many anglers killing too many big fish ruined these famous marks in the space of a few short years. Whether the packs of big monkfish will ever come back is doubtful, for as yet there are no signs of reestablishment taking place. On a recent visit to Fenit, in Tralee Bay, I was pleased to see local boatmen tagging and returning big monkfish; clearly the importance of conservation has been realized, and, hopefully, not too late to correct the errors of the past.

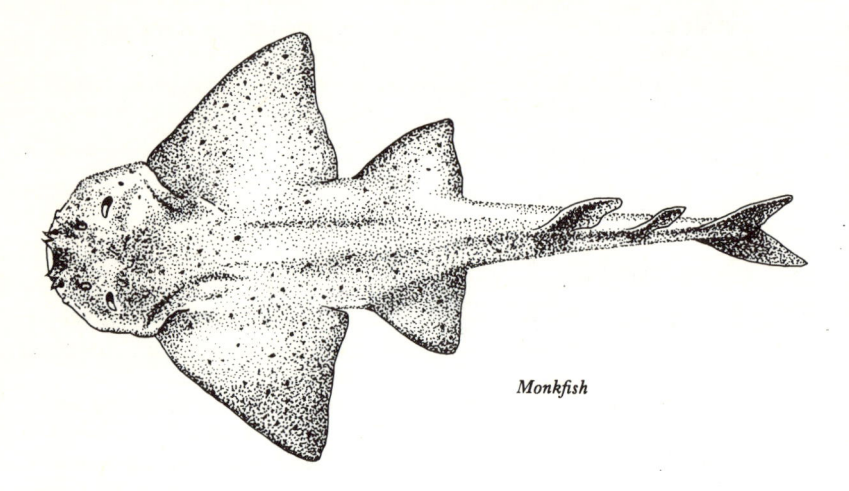

Monkfish

Monkfish

Monkfish are extremely interesting creatures; almost a direct link between sharks and skates, as their outward appearance clearly indicates. They have a high average weight and are quite capable of reaching at least 100 lb (45.3 kg). The average rod-caught specimen weighs between 30 lb (13.6 kg) and 40 lb (18.1 kg), although plenty of larger specimens are hooked and landed by both boat and shore anglers.

I was once fortunate enough to be allowed to examine a monkfish of 100 lb (45.3 kg) class, brought into a Cornish port by a commercial fishing boat, and I can remember being most impressed by the hugh mouth and the powerful appearance of the fish. It was then that I made up my mind that at the first opportunity I would try my luck at catching one of these 'odd' creatures. This, of course, was long before I had caught any monkfish on rod and line, and to be honest, when I did connect with my first one, I was most disappointed with its performance on the hook. It put up very little active resistance, and apart from the effort of pumping it up from a considerable depth it was no problem at all to boat it.

The following day I caught another weighing 40 lb (18.1 kg), from the same mark; but this one, instead of allowing itself to be led up to the gaff without protest, put up a tremendous struggle, rather in the manner of a tope. When I struck the hook home, it took off in a strong burst and made a number of longish runs before settling down to fight doggedly directly beneath the boat. Twice I had the fish to the surface, and twice it made off again in a flurry of foam, before it was finally played out and ready for the gaff.

Since that fish I have caught many more monkfish which fought with quite surprising power, and yet, normally, I would hardly class the average run-of-the-mill monkfish as a 'true' fighter; for every one that fights, several will simply give themselves up after only a token resistance.

Just the same, though, it does not pay to underestimate the power, or at least the potential power, that these fish possess and sometimes exercise; for more than a few possible record-breakers have been winched in quietly, only to go raving mad at the feel of the gaff.

A big fish has little difficulty in breaking free from a short line, so take my advice and always be prepared to give line the moment a weighty monkfish shows the slightest sign of going berserk on nearing the boat. Many anglers are caught out at this stage, and the result is often the loss of a potential record breaker.

As a commercial fisherman for a number of years, I gaffed out a good many monkfish, and came to the conclusion that the simplest and most humane method was to insert the point in the lower jaw. This way, little or no damage is caused, and after weighing, the fish can be returned to the water practically unharmed.

Despite a powerful build and the ability to produce short bursts of speed, monkfish are lazy feeders and have developed an interesting means of attracting small fish to within 'snapping' distance. Monkfish live over sand and mud areas of the sea bed, and prey for the most part on small flatfish. These it attracts by gyrating its wing-like pectoral fins against the bottom so that clouds of sediment particles are disturbed. Flatfish, being curious creatures, are attracted by the disturbance and move in after possible titbits. That is their mistake; for lurking in the midst of the darkened water is 'sudden death' in the shape of the monkfish, whose piggy little eyes are ever on the watch for food.

This fascinating species has a wide distribution, being particularly common in the southern half of the English Channel, and also off the west coast of Ireland, where large numbers appear to arrive during the summer months.

Angler Fish

The angler fish is a much more solitary character than the monkfish, and spends its life in almost complete isolation. Although I have seen several of these truly weird creatures caught, there has never been more than one taken at a time. Even in trawl nets the angler fish only crops up on very odd occasions. Local names for the species include 'fiddler fish' and 'fishing frog'. Notable specimens

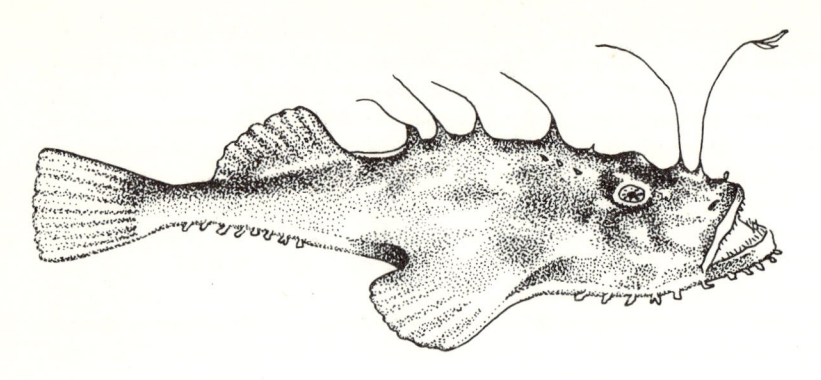

Angler Fish

include a 74 lb 8 oz (33·7 kg) fish, taken by Mr J. J. McVicar near the Eddystone in 1972; a 68 lb 2 oz (30·9 kg) fish from the shore at Canvey Island, taken by Mr H. G. T. Legerton in 1967; and a 61 lb 8 oz (27·8 kg) fish taken off the Isle of Wight in 1955 by Mr R. Bishop.

Very little is known about the movements and general habits of angler fish, although it would seem likely that they live mainly in very deep water, and those caught in shallow water are only patrollers scavenging for food. They also have a habit of turning up in the most unexpected places; bathers are often terrified by the sudden appearance of an angler fish swimming only a little way out from the beach, and boat anglers encounter the occasional specimen moving past right on the surface. Surface-swimming angler fish have been known to catch live sea birds, and on more than one occasion such an attack has been witnessed and the victim rescued from the gaping jaws of the attacker. This is not as rare or unlikely as it may sound, for sea gulls and other large water birds are frequently recovered from the stomachs of angler fish. It would seem that in shallow water they rise and engulf the birds as they float on the surface. Also, apart from birds, they swallow other unusual, non-food, items: tin cans, lead weights and even crab-pot corks have all been found in the stomachs of these fish at sometime or other.

Despite their odd shape and immense bulk, they are feeble fighters. More than once an angler has pumped an angler fish to the surface in the firm belief that his hook has become entangled in a lobster pot! Small-size angler fish tend to display a little more spirit than the larger specimens, but even then it is only a minor struggle at the very most.

Angler fish get their name from the rod-like antenna which projects from the top of the head. This rod has a fleshy flap at the extreme end which is used to attract small fish close. Once a victim has come within strike-range, the angler fish lunges forward, engulfs the quarry and settles back down on the bottom to 'angle again'. Perfectly adapted to this form of hunting, angler fish have giant, trap-like mouths which rarely miss the food-fish they hunt.

Like monkfish, angler fish have a wide distribution, and have been caught at various times right round the British Isles coastline. The most prolific areas are located along the south and south-western coasts.

General methods of catching Monkfish and Angler Fish

Both species are mainly caught by boat anglers fishing in deep water during the summer months; occasionally in the winter months, too. September is perhaps the best month of all for monkfish when, like most big fish, they will be indulging in a feeding spree prior to the arrival of the colder weather. Whether or not this applies to angler fish I cannot say; it is difficult to draw any reasonable conclusions on the feeding habits of such an infrequent capture.

Although not noted for fighting ability, sheer bulk makes the monkfish and the angler fish difficult customers, and, therefore, substantial tackle is advisable on all occasions. One of the main problems facing the angler fortunate enough to hook a big monkfish or angler fish is how to move the adversary from the sea bed – both species being in the habit of half-burying themselves in sand or mud, which imposes added strain on the tackle.

My usual outfit consists of a heavy duty, solid glass boat rod, a large capacity multiplying reel, and 45 lb (20.4 kg) breaking strain monofil line. The hook-trace is, of course, made up from wire to counteract the sharp teeth. Such tackle may seem rather heavy, but in my own fishing I have been glad of the extra strength to lift monkfish and angler fish from the bottom. Skate, incidentally, inhabit the same grounds as the two species under discussion, and gear of of this calibre will handle specimens in excess of 100 lb (45.3 kg) – it is as well to cater for this possibility.

One of my favourite monkfish marks is situated about 2 miles (3.2 km) out from the Needles lighthouse, at the southern tip of the Isle of Wight. I am sure that the attraction here is the very large pout and sole populations. While fishing this ground I have taken a number of good monkfish on live pout bait mounted on a leger or a long-link paternoster rig. I only use the paternoster during slack tides; in a fast tide it has a tendency to bunch up and become tangled.

The bite from monkfish, on both live and dead baits, is very similar to that of skate: a sharp knock, followed by two or three lighter pulls, and a final hard tug. Any attempt to set the hook before the fish has the bait fully in its mouth is likely to miss, but monkfish are rather stupid creatures which will come again at a bait a second and even a third time. I have hooked monkfish which have dropped off near the surface; yet within five minutes have brought to the boat a fish which, to judge from its size, I am convinced was the same one previously lost.

An Encounter With a Record Angler Fish

Really large angler fish are far from common in shallow water, although the odd outsize specimen does occasionally drift inshore after a gale. One of the biggest I ever saw took my bait in a rock gully off Polstreath Beach, east of Mevagissey, Cornwall. This fish, which I would estimate at over 70 lb (31·7 kg) in weight, took a limpet fished on a size 4 hook to 9 lb (4 kg) breaking strain (I was wrasse

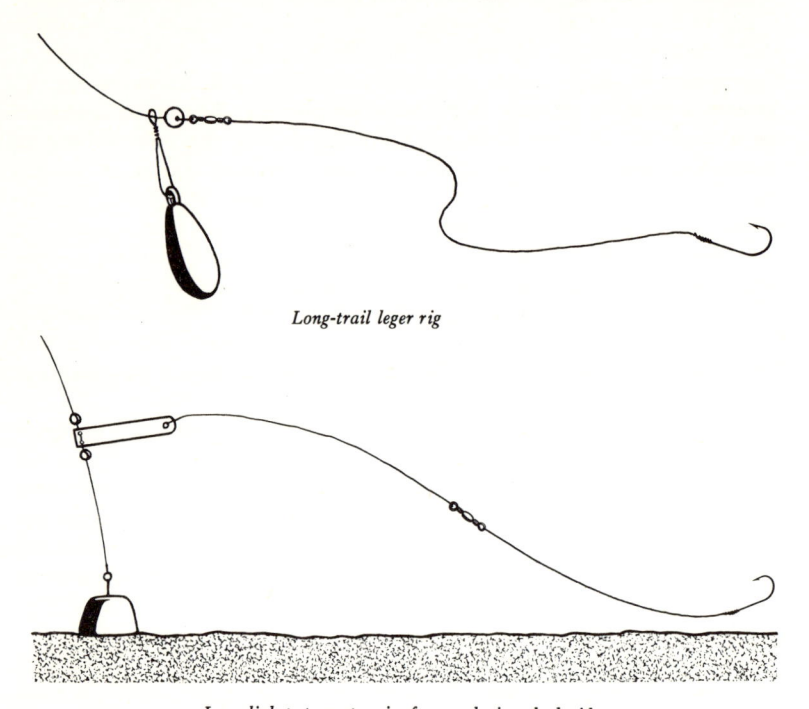

Long-trail leger rig

Long-link paternoster rig, for use during slack tides

fishing at the time). Although I felt a slight pull as the fish engulfed the bait, I did not think at first that I was anything more than snagged, for in the deep, clear water the indistinct shape of the angler fish looked like a large chunk of pale yellow seaweed.

It was not until the 'thing' surfaced and opened its huge mouth that I realised just what I had hooked. Although I was using a light spinning rod, I was determined to have a try at boating the brute. At first I thought I would succeed, for though of immense size the fish seemed incapable of any speed, and so for ten to fifteen minutes we kept up a steady slogging match on the surface. One of the things that I remember vividly about this battle was the way the fish kept opening and closing its jaws. Each time they slammed shut I expected the line to break, but it did not, and after a while I became more confident and began to pile on the pressure. At this crucial stage I made a mistake and allowed the fish to gain its head. With renewed strength it turned and swam slowly away out of the gully and into the open sea. I tried to apply enough strain to turn the fish, but it was no use, and in the end the line broke. I am confident that the size of that angler fish was enough to take the British record with ease.

Angler fish are seldom caught in quantity; they seem basically to be nomadic. The recent upsurge of interest in wreck fishing has, however, produced some huge angler fish, and it seems likely that these big, sluggish fish sometimes take up semi-permanent residence around sunken shipping. Some hefty specimens have been caught on baited pirks, but I personally believe this to be something of an angling fluke, as I am certain that such captures are the result of the pirk being dropped by sheer chance into the mouth of lurking angler fish. I cannot accept that these sluggish creatures will actually bother to chase an artificial lure, no matter how appealing it might appear to be.

Angler Fish and Monkfish From the Shore

Almost every season these species are caught by beach, jetty and pier anglers. Regarded as unusual visitors by many, I am personally convinced that they are far more common in such shallow waters than is generally suspected. This is particularly true of monkfish, which often turn up close to piers and beaches, etc., during periods of calm, settled weather. The angler fish, on the other hand, is more of a deep water species, likely to put in an appearance close to shore only after a long period of stormy weather. Angler fish are less active than monkfish, and it seems that unsettled weather is the only set of conditions that will persuade them to move from their typical, deep water habitat. Once inshore, however, an angler fish is content to stay put in a suitable area, and it is such a fish as this that occasionally falls to the shore and pier angler.

Monkfish captures are usually fish which have moved inshore with the shoals of pouting and flatfish, there (if not caught) to remain until the food supply diminishes or cold water drives them offshore.

I am fairly certain that big monkfish are responsible for many breakages which shore anglers experience. A 40 lb (18·1 kg) or 50 lb (22·6 kg) specimen hooked in shallow water is more than a match for an average beach casting outfit. Occasionally, of course, an angler is lucky enough to manage to land one of these monsters – the catches we read about in the Angling Press.

In Ireland, big catches are made at Fenit and one or two other exceptional shore fishing stations, but normally they can be regarded as rare.

Along my home stretch of the Hampshire coast, monkfish are fairly common during the summer months, and at Hurst Castle, Milford and Hordle Cliff areas, very big fish are often hooked and lost by skate anglers using fish baits. To judge from the slow, steady pace at which they move when hooked, they are almost certainly heavyweight monkfish. Although tope also frequent these beaches, their speed alone would be enough to identify them.

One of the main reasons why they are hooked so infrequently by English shore fishermen is that few anglers set out deliberately with suitable tackle and baits to catch them. If they went about the job properly monkfish would be caught, of that I am quite certain.

Monkfish are predatory, yet few sea anglers ever use livebait apart from prawn and sandeel; I have never actually met another shore angler who is prepared to try small, live fish as bait.

It is essential to use strong tackle in order to work the hooked fish through shallow water, or to hold it out from pier supports and the like. My outfit consists of a 12 foot (3·6 m) hollow glass beach caster capable of throwing a 10 oz (283 g) lead, a wide-drum multiplying reel (fixed-spool reels are little use for this fishing), 30 lb (13·6 kg) breaking strain line, and stainless steel size 4/0 or 6/0 hooks.

Obviously, shore fishing for monkfish and angler fish has only a limited potential, but in areas where they are known to visit it can be very rewarding indeed.

Halibut

Rarest and biggest of all the flatfish, the halibut is rapidly becoming a much sought-after species. Common only off the Orkney and Shetland Isles, halibut undoubtedly reach weights in excess of 250 lb (113·3 kg). Predatory by nature, halibut feed mainly on ground fish like cod, haddock, coalfish and small ling. Unlike most flatfish, the halibut is an active hunter more capable of catching its food alive. During the past decade anglers have come to realize that halibut can be taken on rod and line, and in recent seasons numerous parties have been formed to try and catch halibut from Orcadian waters. Most of the rod-caught specimens taken so far have come from the west face of Hoy Island, directly beneath the towering Old Man of Hoy rockstack.

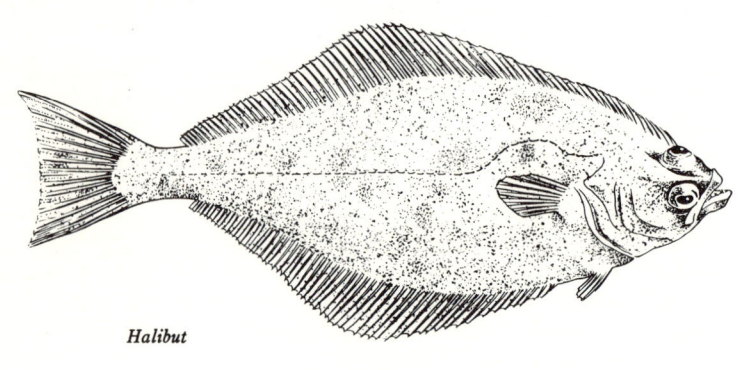

Halibut

Orcadian anglers have discovered that halibut will come readily to a baited spoon rig; the favourite spoon being an elongated, silver-plated Williams lure of Canadian origin. This is fished in conjunction with a 6/0 or 8/0 forged hook baited with fish strip. Several big halibut have also been taken on huge baited pirks, although local anglers are convinced that these lures are inferior to the baited spoon rig.

Halibut are a species surrounded by mistaken dogma. Initially, they were claimed to be fast-moving, hard-fighting fish, but recently successful halibut men have commented on the fact that they do not make more effort than one or two dives when hooked. It seems, in fact, that halibut fight more in the boat than they do in the water, using their powerful bodies and tails to smash anything that comes within their range.

I was unfortunate enough to hook and lose a halibut on the Triton Bank, Orkney, during July 1976. This fish simply shed the hook after a minute or two of rather half-hearted fighting, and I felt that had the hook held I would have boated my halibut without too much trouble.

Halibut fishing is something of a challenge, for although there appears to be a great many huge halibut in Orkney waters only a very few are actually caught by rod and line fishermen. For anyone contemplating a halibut fishing holiday, I would suggest that a 50 lb (22·6 kg) I.G.F.A class outfit is sufficiently robust to bring to the boat almost any halibut the angler is likely to encounter. For those who prefer not to take chances, however, an 80 lb (36·2 kg) class outfit would be a better choice.

Apart from the north of Scotland, halibut have also been taken in Northern Ireland waters in the vicinity of Rathlin Island. Very little serious halibut fishing has been undertaken in this area so far, and at the time of writing I believe that Orcadian waters offer the best chance of a successful expedition.

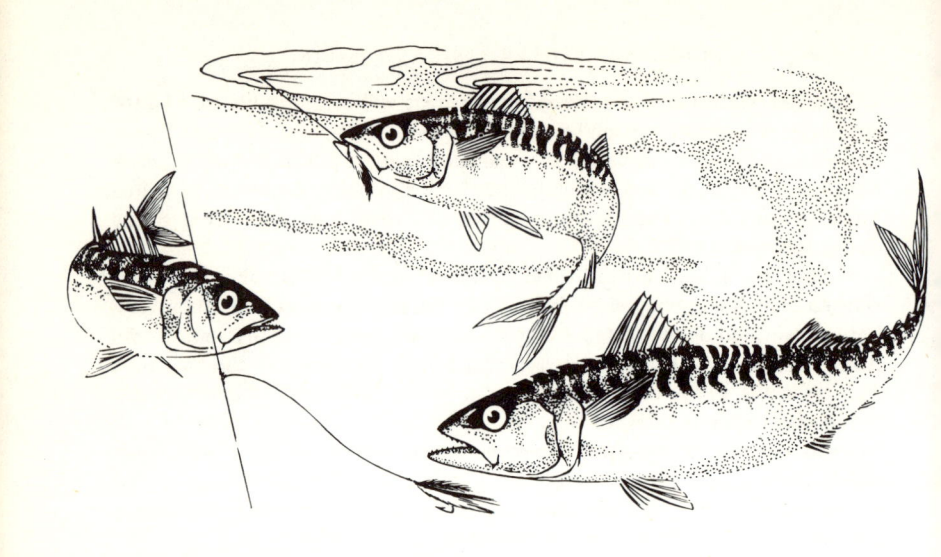

FISHING FOR MACKEREL, GARFISH, SCAD, WHITING AND GURNARD

Derek Fletcher

Mackerel

The mackerel is such a well-known species that it hardly requires descriptive detail. From May to September many thousands are taken annually by serious anglers and holiday-makers alike. The best of the sport is only to be had with light tackle, on which this fast moving, lively species is well able to display its fighting qualities.

Although a mackerel of 5 lb 6 oz 8 drm (2·4 kg) was taken north of the Eddystone Light in 1969 by Mr S. Beasley, and another of 4 lb 11 oz (2·1 kg) off Flamborough Head in 1963 by Mr L. A. Seward, it is true to say that mackerel of anywhere near this size are rare in the extreme. The typical shoal fish one is likely to encounter average between 12 oz (340 g) and 1 lb (0·45 kg). Little is understood of really large specimens, but they appear to be single fish or members of small shoals which, because they are so few, are difficult to locate with any degree of certainty.

At the start of the spring migration to British shores, the mackerel shoals remain deep; but later, as the weather warms, they move to the upper surface levels. The colder days of later summer again send them deep, and stragglers, which sometimes remain as late as December, are mainly caught while bottom fishing – particularly in harbours and estuaries.

If you enjoy light tackle fishing, I am quite sure you will discover, as I have, that mackerel are hard to beat for sheer sporting enjoyment. Easily one of the most satisfactory methods is spinning – a simple technique once the basics are mastered. The speed of lure recovery is perhaps the most important factor with this method. Many anglers fail to catch the quantity of mackerel they should, simply because they fail to vary the recovery until they find the correct speed which will attract the mackerel to chase and take the spinner. There is no set rule and it is a case of trial and error on every fishing session.

Traditional mackerel spinners are excellent lures and cost very little. It is a good idea to buy a fresh selection each year rather than continue using rusty spinners which are less attractive to a species greatly interested in flash and movement.

Many of the better-size mackerel are taken on float tackle, a very popular method, from piers in the later summer evenings. A conventional 6 in. (15 cm) cylinder float is quite suitable, weighted with swan-size split shot. The rod I prefer for this work has a length of 10 ft (3 m) and a fast tip action; combined with a centrepin reel and 6 lb (2·7 kg) breaking strain line. A trace length of 4 ft (1·2 m) is used with a number 5 hook, and joined to the main-line by a small swivel. Sandeels or thin herring strips make adequate bait.

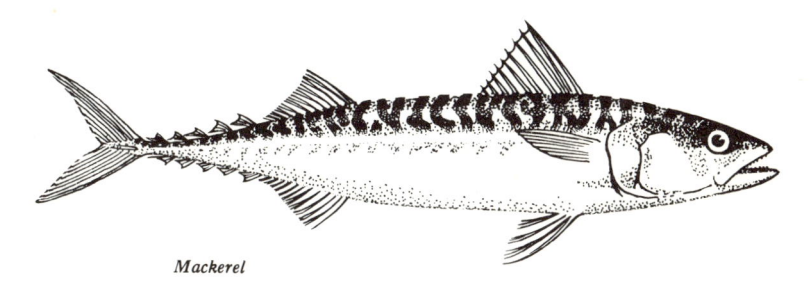

Mackerel

Drift-lining from a boat is another productive method. Use the same two baits set at a depth of 6 ft (1·8 m), and allow the tackle to drift with the current over the stern – only if tidal conditions are very strong should the addition of a spiral weight be necessary.

Early morning and late evening sessions frequently result in the best catches, although mackerel can confidently be expected at any time during the day. Best conditions occur during calm seas, especially when there is a touch of thunder in the air. During storms, the shoals tend to split up and head for deeper water.

On occasions when brit forage into bays and along beaches, they will be followed by vast shoals of mackerel which attack and eat the brit. Gulls and other sea birds also eat brit, so any disturbances caused by sea birds concen-

Mackerel fly – an alternative to spinners

Traditional mackerel spinner

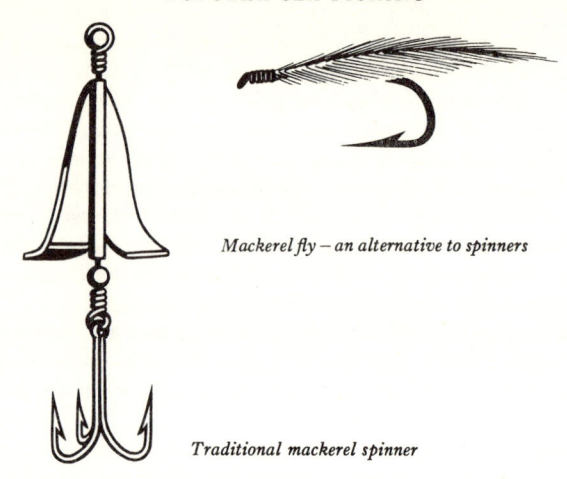

trating on one area of the sea is a good sign that mackerel might be present. At such times anglers who move in and fish through the area of activity sometimes make fantastic catches.

Apart from their obvious sporting value, mackerel can be used as bait for many other species: a whole fish for tope, dogfish, conger and skate, or cut into strips for bass, pollack, wrasse, garfish and many others. To get a good bait supply 'feathering' is the best method to employ. The rig, which can be home-made or bought at tackle shops, consists of numerous feathered hooks, multi-coloured and mounted on a long trace with a heavy lead weight at the end. In operation this is worked up and down in the vicinity of shoals, and very often several fish are taken on each cast. It could hardly be called a sporting method, and should only be used to provide a bait supply. Single hook feather rigs can be used for sport fishing as an alternative to spinning.

Garfish

Garfish

The majority of sea anglers these days are beginning to realize the potential of this strange, eel-like fish, and the opportunity for exciting as well as unusual sport. Unusual because of its fighting action – leaping out of the water, skimming the surface in bursts of speed, shaking the bait in its pointed jaw, and diving deep in frantic attempts to shed the hook. Quite an experience to play a big garfish!

Able to reach 3 ft (0·91 m) in length, the garfish has a skinny body, coloured greenish over the back and sides, with silver underparts. The angler is well advised to take extra care when handling this species and avoid contact with the razor-sharp teeth which are quite capable of inflicting a nasty wound. It is interesting to note that the lateral line is set unusually low on the small-scaled body; and in keeping with the streamlined shape, the dorsal fin is placed well back near the forked tail and in line with the anal fin.

This is a species with a large number of nicknames, including 'swordfish', 'garpike', 'pike-fish', 'eel-pike', 'sawpike', 'mackerel eel', 'mackerel guide' and 'greenbones' – the latter, because of its bright green bones which erroneously are thought to make the fish poisonous. Notable garfish include a 2 lb 13 oz 14 drm (1·2 kg) specimen taken by Mr S. Claeskens off Newton Ferrers, Devon, in 1971, and a 2 lb 9oz 2 drm (1·1 kg) specimen taken by Mr A. W. Bodfield at Dartmouth in 1963.

The species first appears in any numbers during late April, a week or two before the mackerel shoals – hence the name 'mackerel guide'. Normally they spread out into small shoals, often hunting in units of six at a time. Some of them become solitary in their habits, while occasionally a larger shoal than normal is located usually in the vicinity of rocky headlands. They do not appear to be affected by weather and I have caught them in all conditions – torrential downpours, calm seas, rough seas, bright sunlight, and so on. There movements are where the mood takes them, but piers, breakwaters, rocky coves and bays can all be expected to yield garfish during the warm months. They also move into tidal rivers at times.

Much of their time is spent chasing brit, 'joey' mackerel shoals, and sandeels. They move like lightening from below, leaping into the air as they trap the small fry in the beaky jaws. Occasionally I have found garfish washed up on the shore, apparently choked to death while trying to swallow too large a mackerel. They also enjoy leap-frogging over floating seaweed. Stopping occasionally to butt at the clumps in order to release titbits of food.

A hooked garfish is diffcult to control during its first acrobatic display of leaps and skims. While this is taking place it is wise to let the fish have its head until it tires a little and can be played in the normal manner. Some, however, have energy enough to keep up this action right to the net.

Live sandeels make an ideal bait, hooked lightly in the back which leaves them free to jerk and quiver – such movement is very attractive to the nosy garfish which will soon be round to investigate. Mackerel and herring strips cut 4 in. (10 cm) by 1 in. (2·5 cm) will also lure them. Fish sandeels and fish strips on light float tackle with the bait aranged at a depth of 2 ft (0·61 m) – deeper in estuaries. A 6 lb (2·7 kg) breaking strain line is quite heavy enough for the biggest garfish, hooked in the most snaggy conditions; remember that using tackle heavier than necessary will detract from the sport a great deal. A centrepin or fixed-spool reel completes the tackle, apart from a small float to guide the unweighted bait with the current.

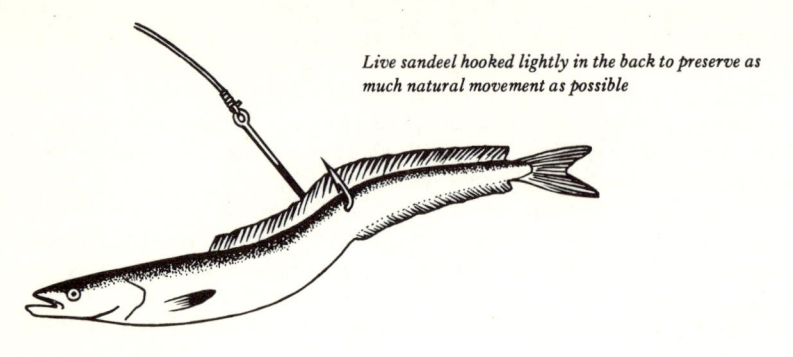

Live sandeel hooked lightly in the back to preserve as much natural movement as possible

Garfish lure made from the white gull feathers whipped to a small eyed hook

Garfish can also be taken on mackerel spinners, feathers, and even white flounder spoons. A friend of mine catches them on seaweed draped round the hook. In recent years, anglers have successfully used a lure made from a couple of white gull feathers whipped to a small eyed hook; a method which works well in rocky areas. Cast out and jerk the lure back across the surface, taking care not to do this too fast as it might cause interested garfish to turn away. This method is best used when the sea is calm and reasonably clear.

I have mentioned their appearance in tidal rivers where, although few anglers fish for them, they are often taken accidentally by anglers spinning or livebaiting. It is in the river, too, that they are observed in their most playful mood.

As a bait, garfish cut into strips can be quite satisfactory, used in much the same way as mackerel. Cutlet style, they have lured conger, dogfish and skate.

They make fine eating, too, despite all the tales about green bones!

Scad

Inform an angler that he has caught a scad and he might look rather puzzled, for, despite this being the correct name, the species is more commonly referred to as 'horse mackerel'. Other names include 'jack-fish', 'rock-herring' and 'pollack guide' – the latter because it is sometimes caught while pollack fishing. Personally, I do not think this has the slightest significance.

The species enjoys quite a wide distribution around the coasts of Britain, and anglers should expect to catch them almost anywhere during the summer

Scad

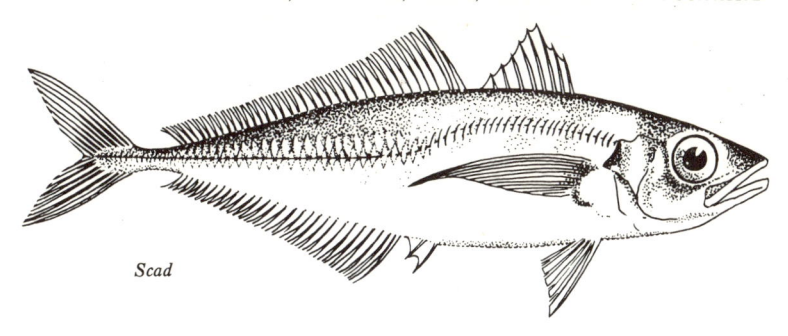

months. Piers are often very productive during the night when the scad, attracted by the lights, rise and congregate just below the surface. A quayside or pier area illuminated by a red glow seems to have a special attraction.

Although a scad weighing 3 lb 4 oz 8 drm (1·4 kg) was caught in 1971 off Mewstone, Plymouth, by Mr D. O. Cooke, very few scad even approaching this weight are reported. The average rod-caught weight is 1 lb (0·45 kg).

Coloration varies enormously, even more so with scad taken from rocky marks. This has caused problems at competitions when the exact nature of the capture has been hard to determine. However, the general colour is dark olive green, with suggestions of blue, light green and gold along the underparts. There are conspicuous dark spots on the gill covers, but scad have been taken with this distinguishing mark completely absent, which in turn only adds to the confusion. Other features are a sharp spine pointing forward before the dorsal fin, and a well-pronounced lateral line. Near the forked tail there is a ridge of keeled scales. The pectoral fins are long, and the eyes large. Handle scad carefully in a piece of thick cloth to avoid the dorsal spine.

Recommended baits are ragworm, sandeel, prawn, and strips of herring, mackerel and scad. This is a species often caught on the unusual bait, perhaps

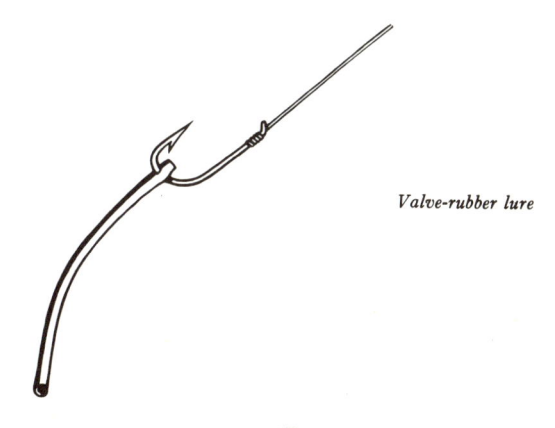

Valve-rubber lure

more so than any other fish. Several of my best catches were taken on strips of valve-rubber. The hook is nicked through one end of the rubber, and the simple technique is to keep it moving slowly through the water in an area known to contain a good concentration of scad.

The depth at which baits and lures are fished depends very much on weather conditions, but always bear in mind that they tend to rise to the upper levels after dark anyway. They will also be found near the surface in hot weather, and right on the top if conditions are thundery. Dropping temperatures will send them deeper until, in very cold water, they will be right on the bottom.

Moving baits are essential when scad fishing, either roving the offering on float tackle or jerking the rod to impart action when using a floatless rig. From the rocks one can get satisfactory action by spinning.

Although scad could not be classed as strong fighters, they will give reasonable sport in the initial stages, providing light tackle is used. A favourite scad tactic when pier fishing, is for the fresh hooked fish to thrust down towards the piles and ironwork in an attempt to snag the line on a crop of mussel or rocky crevice. For this reason use a longish rod to keep the fish and tackle well out from danger. I use a 6 lb (2·7 kg) breaking strain line, number 6 hook and 4 ft (1·2 m) trace. The sliding float should be as small and as sensitive as possible for the conditions. Scad bite in a number of ways. Sometimes the float will disappear completely; another time it may do little more than bob under and reappear immediately. Whatever the bite, strike quickly. They are greedy creatures with a knack of ripping the bait clear and leaving a bare hook.

As bait, scad are cut into strips for garfish, mackerel, bass and pollack. They are little used for other species, but an angling friend, night fishing off Old Harry Rocks, Swanage, caught a fine conger of 34 lb 8 oz (15·6 kg) on a fresh caught, whole scad. I think they would make quite reasonable big-fish bait if anglers were in the habit of using them more often.

Whiting

The whiting, one of the mainstays of winter angling, is widely caught around much of the British coastline, although the bulk of the big catches come from such spots as Deal, Folkestone, Littlehampton, Dover and the Yorkshire and Scottish coasts. A 6 lb 3 oz 3 drm (2·8 kg) whiting was caught in 1971 by Mrs R. Barrett during a trip off Rame Head, Cornwall. Average whiting weigh between 1 lb (0·45 kg) and 1 lb 8 oz (0·67 kg).

Though the major catches are made in the winter months, odd whiting can be taken nearly everywhere in the summer. For the pot these 'holiday fish' never seem as sweet-tasting as the later ones, and, because they are small in size, are more used as bait than for eating purposes. They are extremely useful as such for big species; for example conger, tope and skate, and it is as well to note that many of the national newspapers' big fish prizes fall to anglers who use whiting as hook bait.

Whiting

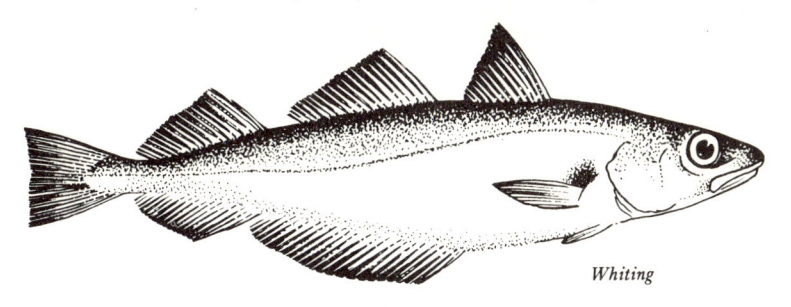

A popular name for whiting is 'silvers', an alias used a great deal. This silvery or bronze fish is a member of the cod family. Noticeable features include a pointed head, large eyes, a long first anal fin, and close-set dorsals. The tail fin is powerful and square-shaped, and there is a dark spot at the root of each pectoral fin.

Better-size whiting are usually taken following the first heavy frosts, when the cry 'The silvers are in' entices hundreds of anglers from the warmth of the fireside. Large shoals roam the inshore marks, mainly grubbing along the sea bed, and are prepared to take all manner of baits. There are times when they do become choosy, a marked change which occurs mainly when the water is very clear; so the angler, preparing for this eventuality, should carry a selection of baits with him. Among the most useful are lugworms, mussels, sprats, slipper limpet, herring strips and ragworms. When baiting up, make a generous helping such as a bunch of worms or a whole sprat, whiting are hungry fish and a large bait is most attractive to them.

The large bags – without any doubt – are made by boat anglers fishing the well-known marks, but those who suffer from sea-sickness can still have reasonable sport fishing from the shore. Excellent catches are frequently made from the ends of long piers – with the help of groundbait. This is a simple matter and only requires the distribution of chopped herring or mackerel – handfuls of slipper limpet are another useful attraction.

It is a great pity that, even in these enlightened times, so many anglers still persist in using heavy paternoster tackle when after whiting. True, when they are really on feed they indulge with complete abandon, taking as many baited hooks as one cares to lower into the depths, but this is hardly sporting in my opinion.

I much prefer to use a lightweight rig which can be used from boats, low level piers and breakwaters. This consists of a 6 foot (1·8 m) monofil trace, swivelled at one end for attachment to the main-line. Some 18 in. (45 cm) from the swivel a small plastic boom is mounted with a 6 in. (15 cm) dropper and a size 6 hook. Six inches (15 cm) from the swivel, on the trace, a small spiral weight of ½ oz (14 g) is attached, and finally, 8 in. (20 cm) above the bottom hook, a drilled bullet is held in position by a single split shot. This type of end tackle produces the best results if it is kept on the move across the sea bed.

Whiting bites are easily recognized and are best described as tugging, shaking pulls – many times the fish will hook themselves – so just keep a tight line and strike firmly.

Occasionally I hear of whiting being taken on the oddest of baits, some not normally associated with sea fishing at all. Perhaps the real question is not why the fish took it, but rather why the angler used it in the first place! There was, for instance, a report of a whiting taken on cheddar cheese; another, caught off Hastings, fell to a piece of float-fished chicken and weighed 2 lb 3 oz (0·99 kg), a fine fish indeed. A catch of whiting made by an ex-Merchant Navy man was the result of raw steak bait. The captor told me that he had often used steak for a variety of species around foreign ports, so it seems there is plenty of room for experiment with alternative baits if so desired.

Spinning with a mackerel lure will take plenty of whiting. I first realized the value of this method while boat fishing off the Dorset coast. It was during November and I was spinning in the hope of catching some late mackerel which professional fishermen had told me were around. It came as quite a surprise when, instead of the expected mackerel, I started to catch good-size whiting. Since then I have tried the mackerel lure with good results from many marks including the shore, especially the Chesil Bank near Weymouth.

Other anglers tell me of whiting caught on red and white spoons at the entrances to harbours and docks. The slow fished spoons were nearly always baited with single ragworm hooked through the head only. One bag, weighing 35 lb (15·8 kg), fell to the baited spoon method used by an angler boat fishing off Worthing. The captor, John Booth, told me that he started using spoons for whiting because of a theory he held that better catches could be made using this technique. He cast the spoon out to one side and allowed the swing of the boat to draw it back, recovering line as necessary to avoid any slack forming.

Mention has already been made regarding the value of small whiting as bait for larger species. Six inch (15 cm) strips can prove quite killing for pollack when fishing over deep-sea wreck marks. They will also lure mackerel in the summer when float fishing from piers and rocky coves. Bass are not averse to whiting strip legered in the surf, especially from beaches adjoining estuaries.

Another use for whiting flesh is mullet fishing. The boiled flesh is worked into soft macaroni paste, producing a highly flavoured hook bait. I have taken quite a number of mullet on this offering, mainly at the commencement of the ebb when they are most susceptible to a flavoured bait of this kind.

Apart from their value as a sporting quarry, and as bait, they are also delicious to eat, having a particularly fine flavour. They should be baked or fried as soon after capture as possible in order to taste their very best.

FISHING FOR MACKEREL, GARFISH, SCAD, WHITING AND GURNARD

Gurnard

Because of their average small size, gurnard are of little use to the angler. There are quite a few species but the red, yellow and grey gurnards are the three most likely to be caught while fishing. Gurnards average 1 lb 8 oz (0·67 kg); anything bigger can be considered a very fine capture indeed. The yellow species is the

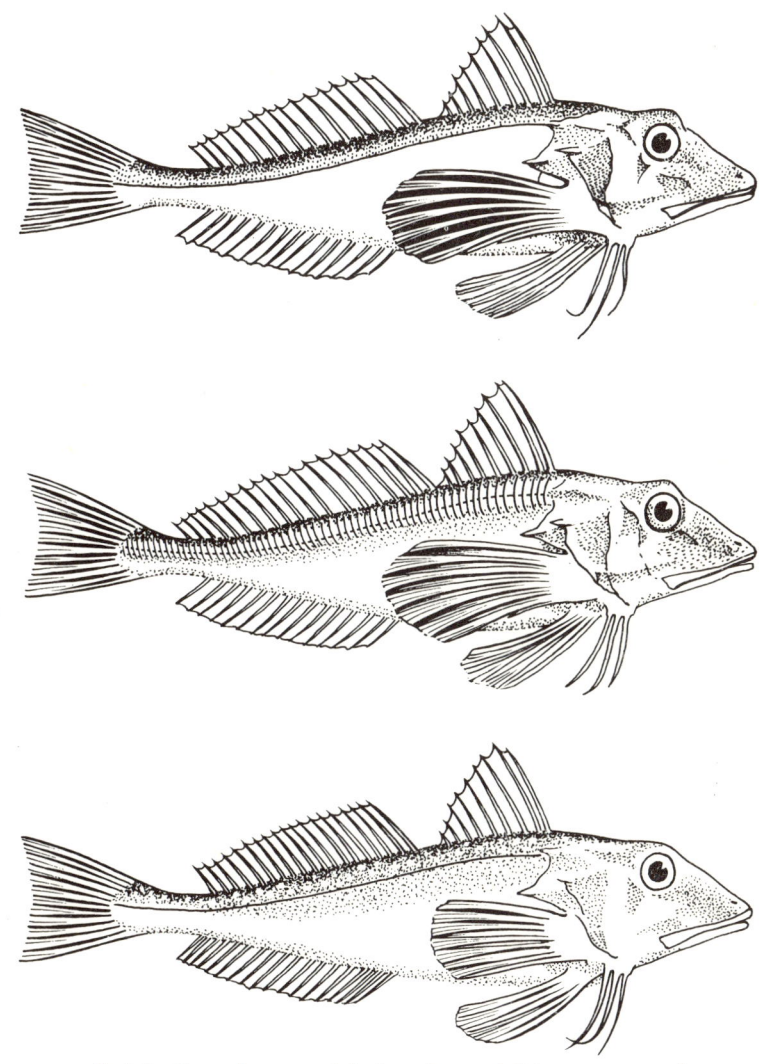

Varieties. Top, *yellow gurnard,* Centre, *red gurnard,* Bottom, *grey gurnard*

largest growing, and in 1976 Mr G. Reynolds captured a 12 lb 3 oz (5·5 kg) specimen while fishing from the shore at Langland Bay, Glamorgan. Another, weighing 11 lb 7 oz 4 drm (5·1 kg), fell to the rod of Mr C. W. King at Wallasey in 1952.

A fair number are taken each year by accident, when they are instantly recognizable by their large, square-shaped bony heads and spinous fins. The body shape is sharp and tapering; a quite ugly fish to pull out, yet excellent eating once one has recovered from the initial revulsion. The red gurnard has a deep brownish-red colouring and scales along the lateral line. Enlarged pectoral fins are a feature of the yellow gurnard which has a spineless dorsal. The angler is most likely to hook the grey gurnard, though, the commonest of the three. Coloration is grey and white with spots, though these spots are sometimes so faint that they are little more than pale marks.

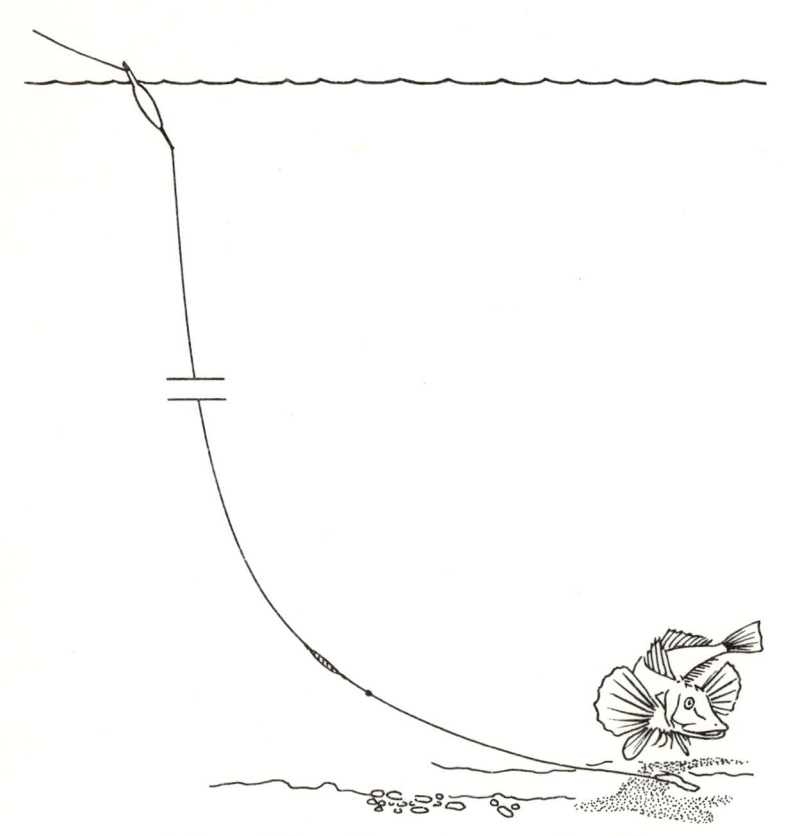

Laying-on with float tackle, a sporting way to catch gurnard

FISHING FOR MACKEREL, GARFISH, SCAD, WHITING AND GURNARD

In some parts of the country, old fishermen refer to gurnards collectively as 'crooners', for they all have the habit of producing a strong grunting noise when first taken from the water. This is caused by the air bladder deflating.

They come close inshore during summer, when they can be caught from piers, groynes, boats, rocks and estuaries. They have a very varied diet and feed heavily at intervals on shrimp and sandeel, also shellfish and immature flatties.

Although not fished for a great deal, there are occasions when large numbers are around and sport is otherwise slow. Anglers sometimes amuse themselves at such times by catching the gurnard with float tackle and baits lying on the bottom. Herring strip is a favourite lure, but they will also take ragworm, lugworm, sandeel, mussel, peeled prawns, slipper limpet and razorfish. The lightest of all tackle is required to get anything in the way of a sporting tussle, and even then it is mediocre in the extreme.

THE MULLET FAMILY *Peter Wheat*

Mullet fishing is really a very peculiar division of sea angling – in no way typical, and yet possessing a unique appeal for the sportsman who would relish a challenge without the expectation of immediate success. Methods and tackle are very much freshwater in origin, and therefore it is hardly surprising that catching mullet attracts coarse anglers as well as sea anglers. In fact, it is the angler familiar with the twitching bites of roach and dace who will be instantly at home with the quarry. Already he will understand the need for a quietly careful approach; he will also be soon aware of the shy, often finicky nature of the species, and the need to adapt to sensitive tactics.

The mullet family is common to all tropical and temperate waters – a very widespread distribution indeed. In many parts of the world I have caught species of mullet, and I still recall with great enthusiasm the fine sport I experienced in the Great Bitter Lake while on convoy through the Suez Canal – nearly thirty mullet weighing between 1 lb (0·45 kg) and 2 lb (0·9 kg), all taken on a crude hand-line rig and bread flake dunked in herring oil. So far from home it was something of a tonic to enjoy fishing for a species common to Britain and more friendly waters.

There are three principal British species: the thick-lipped or lesser grey mullet *Chelon labrosus*; the thin-lipped grey mullet *Liza ramada*; and the rare golden grey mullet *Liza aurata*. From the angler's viewpoint all three are grouped together and called simply, grey mullet. The thick-lipped species is the commonest in British waters.

Average shoal mullet weigh between 1 lb (0·45 kg) and 3 lb (1·3 kg); bigger fish of 4 lb (1·8 kg) to 6 lb (2·7 kg) class are correspondingly less frequent, and a specimen a little over the 6 lb (2·7 kg) mark is very often a local record for the place of capture.

An outstanding catch was the 10 lb 1 oz (4·5 kg) thick-lipped taken by Mr P. C. Libby at Portland, Dorset, in 1952. Outstanding, not because mullet of this size are extremely rare – in fact I remember observing several fish of this size swimming together on a number of occasions while I was stationed with the Royal Navy at Whale Island in Portsmouth Harbour – but because mullet of this size are very old, very wary beasts, difficult to tempt and, when hooked, extremely hard to beat. During the late summer of 1976 a number of superb mullet were caught from The Leys at Aberthaw in Wales. At least four of them scaled over 8 lb (3·6 kg), and the largest, taken by Mr S. Lee in September, weighed 9 lb 6 oz 8 drm (4·2 kg).

Perhaps, before going further, I should describe the major external differences between the three mullet species – it is a great deal more interesting to know exactly which type you are catching despite the general classification, bearing in mind that separate British records are recognized for the three species.

Grey-blue back and upper flanks, shading to silver lower flanks and white underparts is basic to all mullet, the sides have a slight overlay of greyish stripes running the length of the body – it is further noticeable that these fish are among the few species which do not possess a lateral line. Head shape is blunt, the back broad and thick, and the mouth surprisingly small for such a bulky creature. Scales are large, numerous, and inclined to flake off easily once the fish is landed and comes into contact with dry ground.

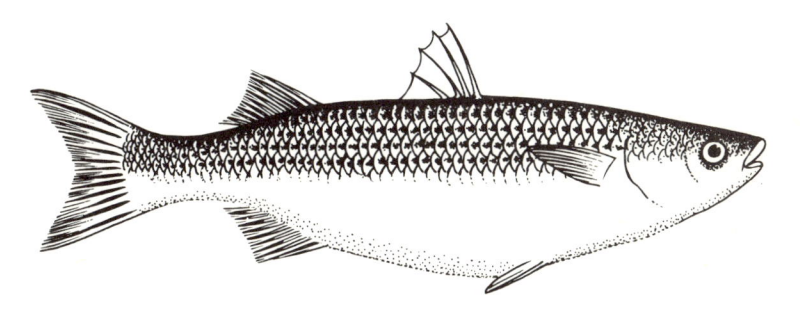

Thick-lipped grey mullet

A distinctive fin arrangement includes two dorsals. The one nearer the head has four webbed spines; the second and smaller has only two spines, followed by a number of much softer rays. It is the distance between the two dorsal fins which forms the principal means of identification. If you measure the base of the leading dorsal and then discover the dorsal distance is about twice that length, the fish is almost certainly a thin-lip. If the distance is equal it is a thick-lip.

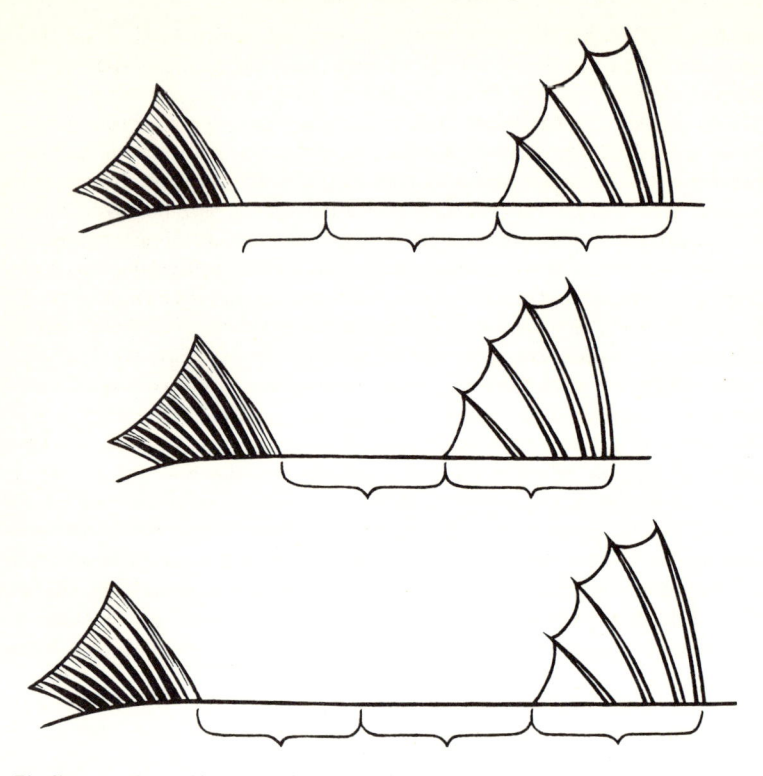

Fin distances. Top, *golden grey mullet* Centre, *thick-lipped grey mullet* bottom, *thin-lipped grey mullet*

Golden grey mullet have a distance of about 1½ times – check this even though the mullet you have caught has a golden head; the other two species develop gold patches and spots under certain environmental conditions. There can be no doubt that the golden species is rare in the extreme. Other differences, of more value to the biologist, do exist, of course, but for all practical purposes fin distance will reveal all you want to know.

Bass sometimes get mixed up with mullet; why this is I can never really understand for both species are quite distinct and major differences are soon apparent. For a quick check the bass has a lateral line which, as already mentioned, is missing from grey mullet.

Mullet make their home in shallow coastal waters rather than the open sea, but once the weather warms in the spring the shoals swarm into the brackish tidal reaches of rivers, marshland creeks, harbours, estuaries, docks, etc., taking up residence in the vicinity of pier supports, piles, permanent anchorages, warm water outlets, sewage pipes, harbour walls, and spots which receive a regular dosing of offal from cafés, canning factories and moored boats. These are the sort of places to seek and catch mullet throughout the summer and autumn months, until the weather turns cold and the fish move back to the sea. But even then, in choice areas receiving a flow of warm water, mullet will remain and feed throughout the remaining months of the annual cycle, very much as resident shoals. Under more normal conditions mullet during cold weather are torpid, and not at all easy to catch without a great deal of perseverance – even more than that required in the summertime. Unless you are set on becoming a mullet specialist, I would advise that you concentrate on the species only during summer and early autumn. Later in the year it just is not worth the effort.

Tackle-wise, freshwater gear is quite suitable for a lot of mullet fishing situations. The rod must have length and a fast action, yet also have backbone to control a strong fish. In my opinion, a hollow fibre-glass rod designed to handle tench and barbel in freshwater fishing is ideal. Length between 11 ft (3·3 m) and 12 ft (3·7 m). Fibre-glass is still often criticized as a rod material, mainly by freshwater anglers of the old 'split-cane brigade', because of its 'give' – as the rod is pulled over it takes less and less increased pressure to bend it further still. However, for mullet fishing such an action has advantages. A big mullet will fight furiously, twisting, turning, shaking – yet remember that though the lips are leathery the hook hold may be very crucial indeed. The longer the fight lasts, the greater is the risk of the hook coming free. This does not mean that one should slacken right off each time a mullet tries a little harder for freedom; indeed, this could well assist the hook to drop out. Instead, constant pressure should be maintained all the time until the captive is played out ready for netting. In my experience, the softer 'give' action of hollow fibre-glass is vastly superior for this sort of work.

For such quick-moving fish, far greater control can be exercised with a quick-retrieve, fixed-spool reel, than with a centrepin reel. A fixed-spool reel is also first choice when it comes to making accurate, long distance casts, and spinning. Just the same, though, I must admit I prefer a large diameter centrepin reel as being a more pleasant, more sensitive instrument to play a strong fish from. Personal choice and individual circumstances decides between the two types.

Modern monofil lines of reasonable reliability and low diameter in relation to breaking strain, are a welcome innovation. Mullet have highly developed senses which necessitate every effort being made to hide, as far as that is possible, the tackle from the fish. These extremely fine lines now being marketed cost a good deal more than standard monofil, but I am certain the extra cost is justified by improved chances – you can never take enough precautions with such a nervy fish as this one is. Choice of breaking strain is very much a matter of conditions. Obviously it would be very unwise to use an extra light line when fishing inside the structure supporting a pier for instance, where the strongest line will part like cotton on contact with the rusting iron pillars. Moreover, a light line would be unnecessary for hunting mullet in rough water washing back and forth through a rocky gully, where the fish are more interested in grabbing what they can as quickly as possible. I fish as light as I can in any reasonable set of conditions, for part of the fun when mulleting is to play strong fish on gossamer tackle – excitement, I can assure you, is often very intense indeed.

From time to time big mullet will be located; then it would be most stupid to sacrifice the chance of landing such a fish by using light gear. The sport then is persuading the fish to bite and getting it hooked and out of the water as quickly as possible. An increase in line breaking strain is the order of the day; after all, there is little point in hooking a mullet of say 6 lb (2·7 kg), knowing full well you do not stand a chance in a million once it gets round some barnacle-encrusted snag. If you have a fixed-spool reel with a number of spare spools you will be able to change lines in a jiffy. A range of lines from 2 lb (·9 kg) to 8 lb (3·6 kg) is none too many.

I find little use for traces of any kind. Every knot means an added weakness, so why take chances? Run the leger or float up the main line, then attach the hook direct. Eyed hooks with short shanks, in a range of sizes from 16 to 8 take care of most situations, but do make sure they are of the very best quality. It is a sound idea to carry hook selections with silver, bronze and gold finishes – to match bait colour. This is a small point, but worthy of attention.

Most float fishing requires little more than a swan quill, cleaned, painted bright red at the tip and varnished over-all. Swan pins are cheap enough to buy, but should you find a dead swan in the estuary, take advantage and remove the wings with a saw. You will have enough quills from a pair of wings to last a lifetime. Small floats can be made by cutting 2 in. (5 cm) or 3 in. (8 cm) sections from the clear ends of big quills, blocking them with balsa plugs, and waterproofing in the normal way. A sliding float comes in handy for water of great depth when mullet are feeding along, or close to, the bottom. I use the type with a dowel stem and a streamlined cork body. The line is passed through the bottom ring and stopped at the required depth with a split shot or a plastic plug stop, or a monofil stop knot.

The normal fixed float is held in position with thick rubber float caps at tip and base, then cocked so that just the tip is showing—just how much tip is

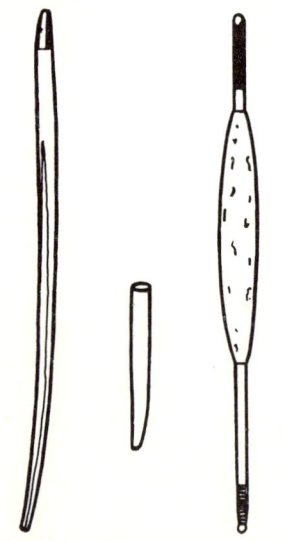

Floats, left *to* right *swan quill, half quill, and cork- on-dowel stem slider*

THE MULLET FAMILY

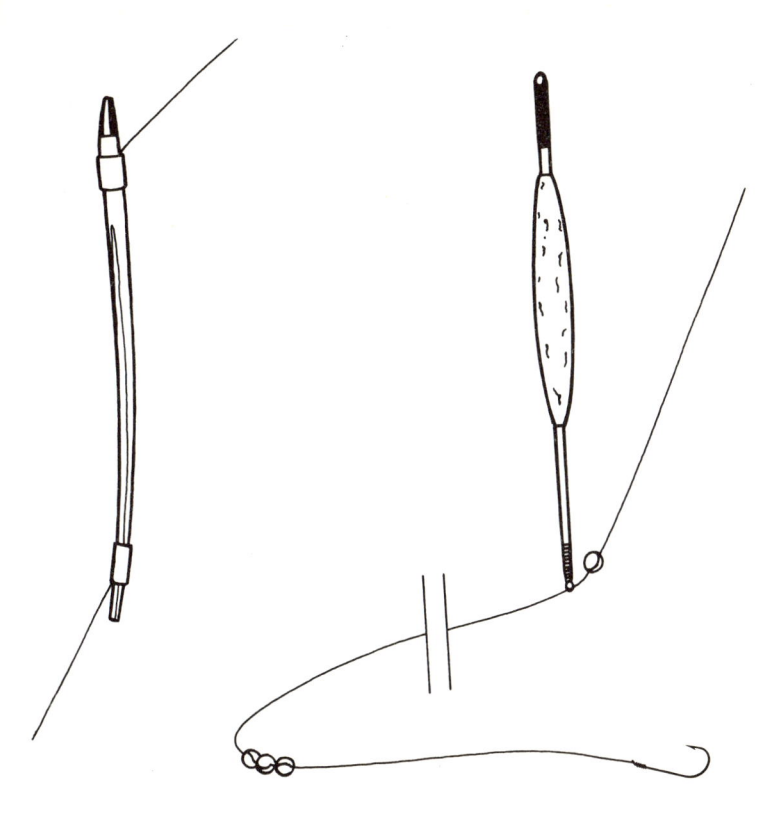

Left, *fixed float attached with thick rubber caps at tip and tail* Right, *slider float attached with a split shot as a depth stop*

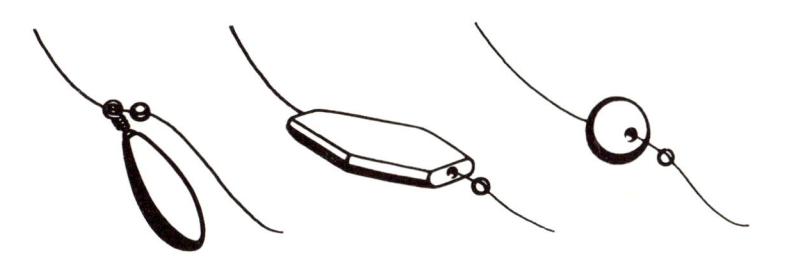

Suitable leger weights, left *to* right: *Arlesey bomb, coffin lead, and drilled bullet*

allowed above the surface depends on both conditions and tactics. Fishing at a distance or in a choppy water will require 1 in. (2·5 cm) or more; close in tactics when the water is like glass can be covered by a tip of $\frac{1}{4}$ in. (6 mm) or even less. Split shot for cocking purposes is bought by the ounce in different sizes – swan, AAA and BB, etc. The hard, shiny black sort, which so easily cuts a fine line if it is pinched on too hard, is best avoided in favour of soft shot which can be opened and closed with the fingers very easily indeed.

There are many types of leger weights. Those most useful from the mullet angler's viewpoint are Arlesey bombs, coffin leads and drilled bullets, in size $\frac{1}{4}$ oz (7 g) $\frac{1}{2}$ oz (14 g) and $\frac{3}{4}$ oz (21 g). Other small items worth having along on your trip are streamlined bubble floats for use with surface baits and for driftlining. The streamlined type, half filled with water, has little resistance to a taking fish, and for this reason is preferable to the more common ball-shaped bubble. A landing net is essential – the larger the better. I prefer one of the modern lightweight jobs with a triangular frame and a telescopic handle.

Salt water, as many anglers have found to their cost, corrodes tackle intended primarily for freshwater fishing, unless it is thoroughly cleaned after each trip. On return home all tackle used should be given a good soaking in a bath of fresh, cold water, and then wiped dry. Reels require extra attention and should be well oiled after drying with a multi-purpose spray-on lubricant.

When it comes to the actual fishing, there is far too much to learn to ever become a true mullet expert. The successful techniques and methods of one area are often next to useless in another, so one can only hope to catch mullet regularly by concentrating on a particular spot, studying the habits of a single shoal, and very often devising new methods to suit the results of your findings. Herein lies the crux of the whole sport. Mullet are not uncatchable anywhere, despite what you might be told to the contrary, but they do have highly developed senses and a good deal of effort and guile will be needed if they are to be caught. The very fact that their feeding habits differ from place to place only increases the challenge – indeed, a bag of fish after a series of blank days laced with much frustration is reward of the very sweetest kind.

I remember when I was stationed at Gibraltar. With little to do I was able to put in a lot of fishing time after the mullet which inhabit the outer and inner sides of the South Mole. I fished hard and long at every opportunity from the concrete and rocks which formed the seaward side. Dotted along the length of the Mole were troughs dropping into the sea, and down these the duty sailors, from the warships in the harbour secured alongside, emptied their messdeck gash buckets at the end of each meal. Mullet swarmed back and forth in the offal below the shoots at feeding times, and yet despite much effort I landed very few mullet indeed.

The Spanish dockyard workers did rather better with their 18 ft (5·4 m) cane rods, tight lines, and large balls of paste made from stale bread and high-smelling Spanish cheese, pressed round big, rusty hooks of unknown origin. This tackle, in their hands, is extremely sensitive, and at the first indication of a take, the successful angler would lift his rod with a swift movement, feel the fish, and with a smooth swing literally pluck it from the water to lie flapping and gasping on the rocks behind him.

Most of these mullet were small in comparison with those I had spotted on the inner side of the Mole which forms the harbour. I did not see them often, and mainly in the late evening close by the large, square, floating fenders. Some were enormous, to say the least. Towards the end of my stay, when hope had become somewhat battered with countless blank trips, I went down to the Mole rather later than usual; in fact it was dark before I arrived. Approaching one of the catamaran fenders, 'mullet-sucking' became distinctly audible along the outer edge. Little more effort was required beyond the casting out of a piece of crust in the direction of the sucking noises. Within seconds there was a great cloop which reminded me of carp; the crust had been taken and I was into my first harbour mullet. An hour later it was all over; the mullet had gone, but not before I had hooked and landed twenty members of the shoal weighing, individually, between 3 lb (1·3 kg) and 5 lb 4 oz (2·3 kg). Success was beyond all expectations, but never was it repeated.

Mullet which are subject to heavy quantities of offal are fairly easy to catch since they are conditioned to feeding on the food items thrown or expelled into the water. Providing a method is chosen which presents a similar bait in a natural manner they are not slow to suck it down. It is the mullet engaged in weed-feeding which have a reputation for not being catchable. Such fish browse on the soft weed which grows along harbour walls, the hulls of old ships, groynes and piers. It is quite likely that they do not eat the weed for its own value but rather to get at the small creatures living in the weed. Whatever the answer, anglers' baits are not given a second glance, so these fish are thought to be beyond the bounds of capture. This is not completely true; they can be caught, but it very much depends on the amount of effort you are prepared to make to be successful.

The whole idea is to get these mullet feeding on what you want them to eat — preoccupied with hook bait rather than the minute life in the weed. This means groundbaiting, perhaps the most important consideration in this sort of angling. Groundbait can be made from a number of basic ingredients: minced crab, herring and bread, mixed together to form a pulp, will do the trick; so will prawns, shrimps, mackerel guts and bread, well soaked in pilchard oil. A groundbait list would really be quite endless; enough to say that the mixture should be smelly and full of tempting titbits. In slow moving water, the pulpy mess can be thrown in by the handful, but for long term baiting up over several days, which may be required to wean a shoal from the weed, it is a better plan to suspend the mixture in net bags, refilling at intervals as necessary. On the actual day of fishing the area is liberally fed with loose mix as the final attraction to get them really feeding.

Even mullet which move right up rivers into completely fresh water can be caught. I have watched them feeding on soft weed; and also leisurely moving upstream close to the bank, occasionally stopping to scrape the surface of the silt to extract vegetable matter, minute organisms and freshwater shrimps. In the early part of the year they are noticeably shy, but later, when they have lost their natural caution, it is possible to observe them at very close quarters without their showing the slightest sign of alarm. I have had a number of good mullet while river fishing in late summer, mainly after baiting a swim for most of the day with handfuls of maggots. What fighters river mullet are! They are quite the equal of sea trout in my experience.

Mullet baits are numerous; many of them of local use only. I think it is true to say that, if the fish are subjected to a steady stream of food particles of some kind or other, they will eventually start eating them. It is a good plan to study the shoal you are after and then decide what bait is most likely to appeal. Pilchard and herring cubes have caught plenty of mullet; small harbour ragworm and immature lugworm also have excellent reputations, particularly in the vicinity of sewage outfalls. Floating crust, bread flake, and bread paste kneaded in fish oil, all work well in harbours and from piers. For really finicky feeders, small particles of cooked crab teased on to a size 14 or 16 hook may be the answer – if you have enough patience, that is! River estuaries can be fished with bread or maggots, although freshwater species such as roach and dace, which thrive in brackish conditions, may often be a menace.

Use the simplest method possible for the conditions. Many times a loose-lined bait with no float or weight, either slow sinking or floating, will catch mullet when all other methods fail. The shoals are inquisitive, constantly on patrol inspecting everything they sense around them. A surface bait amid a quantity of food particles stands an excellent chance of getting taken. The strike is made, if you can see the fish, as soon as the bait enters the mullet's mouth. If the water is murky, watch the line where it enters the water and strike as it moves off.

Without doubt, float fishing is the most popular method. The tackle is rigged up in the normal way with the shot bunched so that a long 'tail' is left. Bites vary enormously, from slow sinks to the slightest dipping nibble. Experience is the only way to a greater understanding of the many different indications – at first do not expect to catch a fish every time the float makes a movement. Obviously when the float goes under strongly you will have little difficulty in making contact, but hitting slight knocks at just the moment when the fish has the bait in its mouth is not at all easy.

Bubble float fishing is an excellent way to catch shy mullet at long distance, or when they are feeding on waste carried out on the tide. A torpedo bubble is threaded on the line through the two small holes, leaving a 'tail' of about 3 ft (0·91 m). The bubble, three quarters full of water, is weighty enough for casting purposes, yet offers little drag to a biting fish.

For surface-feeding mullet out of normal casting range I use a different technique, crude but useful. The method is to roll a crust up and fix it on the line with a couple of half-hitches 1 ft (0·3 m) above the hook which is then baited with a small piece of flake or paste. The cast is made, and very soon the whole thing is a soggy mass. Interested mullet nudging around will find the hook bait floating a little way from the main lump. As a fish takes the bait and moves away, the line comes free from the crust and the strike is made. It sounds weird but it does work.

Much the same thing is possible with a chunk of block salt in place of the bread. In this case the salt disperses in seconds, leaving you with just the baited hook among the mullet. Using this technique, a slow sinking bait of pea size can be fished at a considerable distance.

Two and three hook nylon paternosters can be an advantage when mullet are feeding in deep water under the rod tip. The rod is held the whole time and bites felt through the line. Simple legering with a small Arlesey bomb is a method for distance work along the bottom. Keep the line slack to allow for the initial mouthings at the bait. Many anglers adorn their terminal rigs with swivels to counteract the twisting action of a hooked mullet, but personally I doubt if these swivels are really necessary and I question the wisdom of adding more unnatural weight to the line than is absolutely essential.

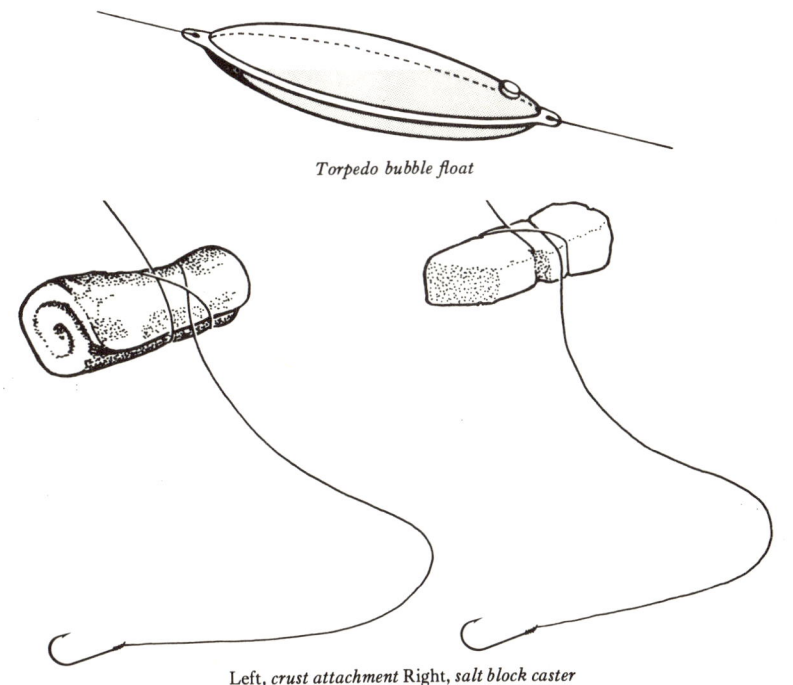

Torpedo bubble float

Left, *crust attachment* Right, *salt block caster*

Because of the often shy nature of mullet, there is an everpresent need to keep your movements as inconspicuous as possible. Dull clothing is a great help; one also needs to keep well back out of view and not stamp about making noise vibrations which will be transmitted to the fish. Although the mullet is a sea fish, it should nevertheless be realized that it does not have the bold nature of most sea species – ready to bite at anything at any time. Lack of caution and finesse of approach is very often the sole reason why mullet are not being caught.

A few years ago I was spinning a river several miles above its harbour for sea trout. The water was extra clear, so that each stone and weed clump was easily seen. Close by the arches of a road bridge about a dozen mullet were sporting in the afternoon sun and as my Mepps spinner came buzzing past them, one of the shoal would break away and chase after the lure, losing interest only as it neared the bank. I did not catch any mullet on this visit, but a return trip when the river had more colour gave me two mullet from the road bridge swim.

Mullet spinning is not popular and it is only of local importance. Nevertheless, it is effective and worth trying anywhere. The standard Mepps lure is as good as any, although the traditional pattern is a silver, willow leaf bar-spoon, about 1 in. (2·5 cm) long with a row of red beads along the bar. The method works even better if a small harbour ragworm is draped around the treble – in fact, the ragworm primer is very often the difference between catching mullet and doing little more than making them chase the lure. Why they should

Left, *mullet spinner*
Right, *Mepps spinner*

take a spinner is hard to say. They are non-predatory by nature, so it would seem that it is their curiosity more than any desire for food which motivates them to move after and snap at lures.

Angling for mullet is not everyone's idea of true sea fishing. For many it lacks the excitement of the deep water marks, the lonely atmosphere of the winter cod beaches, or the chatty friendliness of the club competitions. There are many blanks for every success and yet, to be fishing when a shoal goes mad, feeding with complete abandon, is to experience some of the finest and most exciting fishing imaginable.

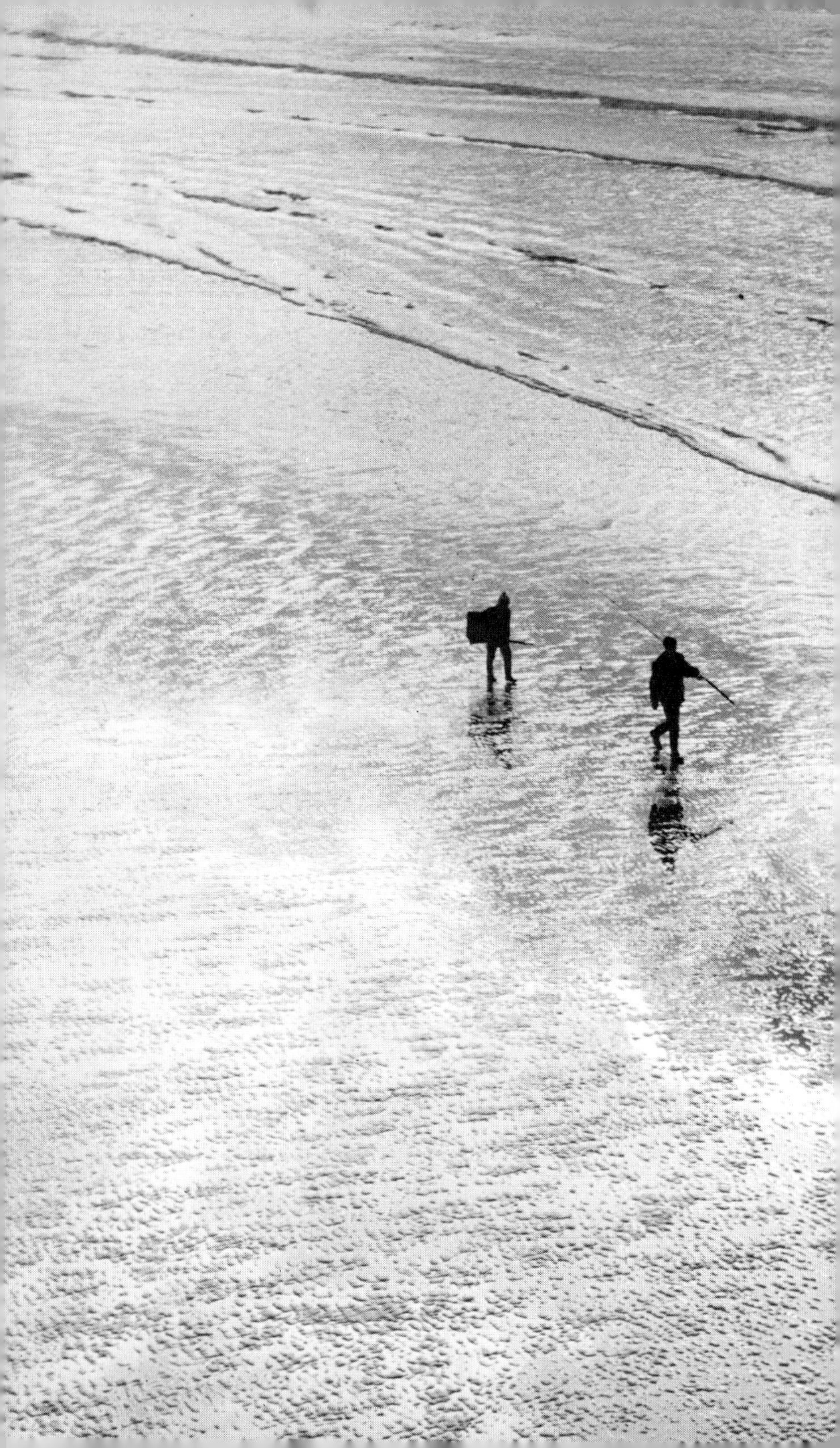